MW00786288

MIND *INTO* MATTER

MIND *INTO* MATTER

ARCH Transforms Science Into Sustainable Enterprise

STEVE LAZARUS & UDAYAN GUPTA

GONDOLIER

MIND *INTO* MATTER : *ARCH transforms science into sustainable enterprise*
Copyright © 2006 Steve Lazarus & Udayan Gupta

Published by: Gondolier, an imprint of Bayeux Arts, Inc.,
119 Stratton Crescent SW, Calgary, Canada T3H 1T7
www.bayeux.com

Edited by Arjun Gupta

Library and Archives Canada Cataloguing in Publication
Lazarus, Steve, 1931-
      Mind into matter : ARCH transforms science into sustainable
          enterprise / Steve Lazarus & Udayan Gupta.
      ISBN 1-896209-98-X
  1. ARCH Venture Partners (Firm)--History. 2. High technology
      industries--United States--Finance. 3. Venture capital--United
      States--History. I. Lazarus, Steve, 1931- II Gupta, Udayan,
      1950- III. Title.
HG4963.L39 2006   338.4'36097309045   C2006-901314-4

First Printing: April 2006
Printed in Canada

Books published by Bayeux Arts/Gondolier are available at special quantity discounts to use as premiums and sales promotions, or for use in corporate training programs. For more information, please write to Special Sales, Bayeux Arts, Inc., 119 Stratton Crescent SW, Calgary, Canada T3H 1T7.

All rights reserved. No part of this publication may be reproduced, stored in a retrieval system, or transmitted, in any form or by any means, electronic, mechanical, recording, or otherwise, without the prior written permission of the publisher, except in the case of a reviewer, who may quote brief passages in a review to print in a magazine or newspaper, or broadcast on radio or television. In the case of photocopying or other reprographic copying, users must obtain a license from the Canadian Copyright Licensing Agency.

The publishing activities of Bayeux/Gondolier are supported by the Canada Council for the Arts, the Alberta Foundation for the Arts, and by the Government of Canada through its Book Publishing Industry Development Program.

CONTENTS

PROLOGUE

SCIENCE: THE ENDLESS FRONTIER

A Report to the President by Vannevar Bush, Director of the Office of Scientific Research and Development, July, 1945

Scientific Progress is Essential

We all know how much the new drug, penicillin, has meant to our grievously wounded men on the grim battlefronts of this war - the countless lives it has saved - the incalculable suffering which its use has prevented. Science and the great practical genius of this nation made this achievement possible.

Some of us know the vital role which radar has played in bringing the United Nations to victory over Nazi Germany and in driving the Japanese steadily back from their island bastions. Again it was painstaking scientific research over many years that made radar possible.

What we often forget are the millions of pay envelopes on a peacetime Saturday night which are filled because new products and new industries have provided jobs for countless Americans. Science made that possible, too.

In 1939, millions of people were employed in industries which did not even exist at the close of the last war - radio, air conditioning, rayon and other synthetic fibers, and plastics are examples of the products of these industries. But these things do not mark the end of progress - they are but the beginning if we make full use of our scientific resources. New manufacturing industries can be started and many older industries greatly strengthened and expanded if we continue to study nature's laws and apply new knowledge to practical purposes.

Great advances in agriculture are also based upon scientific research. Plants which are more resistant to disease and are adapted to short growing season, the prevention and cure of livestock diseases, the control of our insect enemies, better fertilizers, and improved agricultural practices, all stem from painstaking scientific research.

Advances in science, when put to practical use mean more jobs, higher wages, shorter hours, more abundant crops, more leisure for recreation, for study, for learning how to live without the deadening drudgery which has been the burden of the common man for ages past. Advances in science will also bring higher standards of living, will lead to the prevention or cure of diseases, will promote conservation of our limited national resources, and will assure means of defense against aggression. But to achieve these objectives - to secure a high level of employment, to maintain a position of world leadership - the flow of new scientific knowledge must be both continuous and substantial.

Our population increased from 75 million to 130 million between 1900 and 1940. In some countries comparable increases have been accompanied by famine. In this country the increase has been accompanied by more abundant food supply, better living, more leisure, longer life, and better health. This is, largely, the product of three factors - the free play of initiative of a vigorous people under democracy, the heritage of great national wealth, and the advance of science and its application.

Science, by itself, provides no panacea for individual, social, and economic ills. It can be effective in the national welfare only as a member of a team, whether the conditions be peace or war. But without scientific progress no amount of achievement in other directions can insure our health, prosperity, and security as a nation in the modern world.

FOREWORD

Discovery creates the future. The world is filled with secrets and fortunately there has always been a small set of people who devote their lives to solving these mysteries. They are driven by a variety of motives and incentives – the pursuit of wealth or fame or power, the drive for a better life, the itch of curiosity, the goad of competition, or simply an obsession with the problem.

Through the centuries these explorers, researchers, inventors, tinkerers stood on the shoulders of their predecessors to reach the next new thing. Some observers hailed what came to be called progress, some resisted it. Change was seen as threatening or disruptive (well before this word achieved something of a positive connotation). Chinese mandarins passed rules to suppress new ideas. Dutch weavers threw wooden shoes into new machines. New concepts about the motions of the universe were condemned as heresy. Galileo was forced to recant his conclusion disputing the central unmoving position of the earth in the solar system. Nevertheless, under his breadth he muttered, "But still it moves." The world moves, and generally it moves forward and upward. The new thing will out - eventually.

But where and when a discovery is made, who will employ it, and how it will be used, can be seriously affected by legal, political, and economic systems and by education, communication, and transportation infrastructures. Intangibles such as the general freedom to question, the appetite for risk, even the level of respect for failure influence the location, timing, and consequences of discovery.

There is enormous distance between the point of discovery and the point of fully diffused take-up in the society. This diffusion requires effort and capital. In the United States, for the last half century, the first increments of this effort and capital have been supplied by a class of entrepreneurial financiers called venture capitalists.

Venture capitalists gather pools of funds from private equity investors and invest these funds, and more importantly their concentrated effort in the creation of vehicles for the distribution of new products, and the diffusion of new ideas. The riskiest segment of this investment cycle is the origination, the moment when nothing becomes something.

The money that lights the fuse on this rocket is called "seed" and "early stage" venture capital. It is the smallest slice of the venture capital pie.

In 1986 the trustees of the University of Chicago created an unusual organization. It was cumbrously titled The Argonne National Laboratory/ The University of Chicago Development Corporation. This was quickly shortened to the AR-CH Development Corporation and the organization soon became known as ARCH. This year marks the 20th anniversary of that initiative.

During the course of those twenty years ARCH evolved from a small under-funded technology transfer function on the second floor of Walker Museum in the Hyde Park campus of the University of Chicago (sometimes described as "on exhibit" at the museum) to a unique seed and early stage venture capital partnership with offices throughout the United States. ARCH is governed by the same four people who began with it in 1986, it has founded or co- founded 115 new companies, and manages over one billion dollars. It has maintained an unwavering fidelity to its original objective. ARCH finds ground breaking discoveries in university, government, and corporate laboratories and transforms this science and technology into viable entrepreneurial start-up companies. ARCH then nurtures these companies to independence. Along this twenty year span there have been some successes, some failures, and many lessons learned. This book is an attempt to share those lessons.

INTRODUCTION

When in his 2006 State of the Union speech President George Bush announced the American Competitiveness Initiative to encourage American innovation and strengthen the US ability to compete in the global economy, he was simply underscoring the fact that investments in science and technology have paid enormous dividends – improving the lives and livelihoods of generations of Americans. More research in both the public and private sectors will not only improve our quality of life, said Bush, it will also ensure that America will lead the world in opportunity and innovation for decades to come.

Surprisingly not everyone is clear on the process of transforming basic science into accessible sustainable technology and sustainable businesses. At the federal level, funding for basic research has become more and more application specific, often cutting off promising research that doesn't deliver a desired outcome within a narrow time window. At the corporate level, R&D spending is more about development - research to extend the lives of existing products, rather than to usher in new ones.

Even venture capitalists, who began by investing in ideas that were basic and undemonstrated at best – ideas that gave rise to companies such as DEC, Intel, Genentech, and Amgen - have mostly shifted their sights to investing in more developed, later stage and generally less risky ideas.

In 1994, while I was at *The Wall Street Journal*, I wrote a front page piece – they call them leders – on ARCH Venture Partners, a small venture fund based in Chicago. Although there were others attempting similar strategies, ARCH then was at the forefront of working with research labs and universities in taking very early stage technology, investing money and people, and helping these technologies grow into substantive and thriving businesses. More important, ARCH and its partners were covering ground that most others stayed away from. Nearly 12 years later, ARCH continues to practice the same strategy – with greater success and even fewer competitors.

In its two decades of existence, ARCH has had considerable financial success. Its first fund, launched in 1989, had an internal rate of return of 29% and returned nearly $26 million to its investors. In the process, it also created a half dozen or so companies that developed significant breakthrough products, opened new business horizons and created 500 new technology-related jobs. In its subsequent funds, the results are even more telling.

I have always contended that the value of venture capital is not simply in its financial potential - though that is not an insignificant part - but in its ability to nurture and grow valuable intellectual property into new businesses, new jobs and a sustainable economy. And as President Bush and the U.S. search for their competitive advantage in this vast global economy, the strategy and the practice of ARCH is an important lesson to consider.

Of the total assets that Americans – institutional investors, pension funds, individual investors – put to work in the financial marketplace, venture capital is still a relatively small portion. Indeed, when the early institutional investors funded the industry, their focus was as much on the industry's ability to use research and technology – two of this country's most prized assets – as to shaping and transforming the economy.

The success of an ARCH isn't just in the capital and profits it has returned to its investors, but in the manner in which it is helping a wide range of people carry out the process of technology transfer. The real questions about the success of technology transfer go beyond financial returns. Has it created new companies? Has it created new jobs? Has it helped instill a culture of entrepreneurship and created a pool of entrepreneurial talent? Has it helped change the regional economy? What kind of impact has the process had on science, technology, education, and on the economy? The basis of measurement should be the metrics of impact.

My hope is that *Mind into Matter* will serve another important and vital function - provide public policymakers, scientists, university administrators, venture capitalists, and others a primer on technology development. Its aim is to create an understanding of what it takes to mine the tremendous research troves of national laboratories, universities, and other research facilities and how time-consuming and people-intensive it is. The voices and narratives in *Mind into Matter* are important perspectives in the process of transforming research into development.

Marketing Ideas:
Hungry for Funds, Universities Embrace Technology Transfer But the Pitfalls Abound When Academicians Try Becoming Entrepreneurs - Passions Flare Over Propriety

Udayan Gupta, *The Wall Street Journal*, Friday, July 1, 1994

CHICAGO - Keith Crandell is a high tech Johnny Appleseed, cultivating research institutions for ideas that could grow into big money makers.

One day he is at Argonne National Laboratories, crafting a business strategy for a liquid-metal technology. Another day he is at the University of Chicago, helping commercialize water-pollution technology stemming from research to foil ship barnacles.

The scientists need Mr. Crandell's green thumb. With defense cutbacks and budget crunches, the nation's top universities and scientific institutions have watched their government funding sink, to 58.7% of research costs in 1992 from 66% in 1976. To keep research afloat, these institutions have had to pump in big sums of their own money. And they are raising it by holding technological bake sales.

Since 1980, when the government first allowed universities and laboratories to reap commercial profits from federally funded projects, top institutions have been licensing their research. Now, more and more think the big money is in commercializing the research themselves. So they're turning to technology-transfer experts like the 33-year-old Mr. Crandell to mold professors and administrators into entrepreneurs.

NOT SO EASY

The task is proving tougher than the Institutions could have imagined. Of the hundreds of such programs set up in recent years, one after another has been dragged down by political infighting, conflict-of-interest charges and waste. A few, like Mr. Crandell's, are getting results. But others have had to scale back drastically.

Nowhere has the controversy been more heated than at

the University of California system, where a plan for a $100 million technology-transfer fund generated such rancor it was abandoned.

The idea was proposed five years ago by university technology-transfer official Carl Wootten. He calculated that financing commercial development of university research and owning a stake in those ventures would pump in annual revenue of more than $200 million by the year 2000 - four times what the university now derives from licensing research.

ACCUSATIONS AND TURMOIL

But the specter of turning academicians into businessmen unnerved the university community. Many felt the idea raised prickly questions about conflict of interest and the propriety of commercializing basic research. A university task force recommended a slow start to avoid inflaming passions on the issue.

Before the program could even get started, turmoil erupted. Articles in the San Francisco Examiner and an industry newsletter, Technology Access Report, claimed that the technology-transfer office had jumped the gun and was secretly investing in inventions before it had authorization. The Examiner also accused Mr. Wootten of violating state conflict-of-interest rules by personally investing in a business run by a longtime friend and then steering some $375,000 in university contracts to that friend's firm.

The accusations stoked smoldering opposition. A group of 43 University of California scientists, including Nobel Prize winners Michael Bishop and Harold Varmus, wrote a letter asking university President Jack Peltason to abandon the venture fund. They contended the plan would compromise science by pressuring academics to pursue profit-making.

Meanwhile, Silicon Valley venture capitalists were lobbying university and state officials to kill the project. Since many made their fortunes taking inventions from universities and commercializing them, few had any interest in having a middleman there to slow the process and eat into their profits.

WASHINGTON TAKES NOTICE

The university technology office denied jumping the gun on investments, and a university audit committee cleared Mr. Wootten of all conflict-of-interest charges in January. But it was too late to save the fund. The university decided to shelve the project. In March, it went a step further and curtailed activities of its highly successful central technology licensing office, ceding to each of its nine campuses and three laboratories authority to develop technology transfer policies. The decentralization was the death knell for Mr. Wootten's grand plan.

Such controversies are making Washington lawmakers take notice. The Senate began hearings on technology-transfer issues in April. The National Institutes of Health are revising regulations governing the relationship between government funded scientists and industry. And the Department of Commerce is seeking to modify licensing requirements set out in the Bayh-Dole Act of 1980, the law that fostered the current technology-transfer system by lifting the government's ban on licensing federally funded research.

These agencies are hoping to establish new guidelines before the tensions between commerce and academia become crippling. A major roadblock has been that "there is no overarching, federally mandated conflict-of-interest policy for federally funded researchers today," says Nelson Dong, a Minneapolis attorney who specializes in technology-transfer issues. With no rules of the road to follow, most universities have proceeded timidly in exploiting their technologies.

Despite the headaches, the potential payoff for commercializing research is increasingly alluring. "Every campus is hoping it can find new sources of revenue," says John Preston, head of the licensing office at Massachusetts Institute of Technology.

But Mr. Preston warns that most programs "certainly won't make money for five or more years." And Mr. Dong notes that "only 50 or so" of the scores of university-based licensing operations that have sprung up in recent years are generating any significant income.

HITTING THE JACKPOT

The programs are kept afloat by the hope of finding that single, elusive blockbuster - for example, a gene-splicing patent developed by molecular biologists Stanley Cohen and Herb Boyer that is expected to bring $200 million to Stanford University and the University of California.

To hit such jackpots universities must risk their own capital. And in doing so, they find themselves having to set up virtual venture-capital funds - often with sorry results.

To manage and fund its technology transfer efforts, Johns Hopkins University in 1988 formed an independent corporation called Dome Corp., along with a development arm, Triad Investors Corp., capitalized by the university and outside investors. The goal was to turn inventions into prototypes and create new companies to market the resulting products.

But of the $20 million in capital that the program was expected to raise, only $5 million materialized - $3 million of it from the university itself. Many institutional investors shied away, fearful of losing money in an untested venture fund that lacked experienced management.

By the beginning of 1990, the fund's spending had put it almost $2 million in debt, and Dome was more recognized for its lavishly appointed offices overlooking the Chesapeake Bay than for any deals it had fostered. University officials decided the idea needed radical revamping. "We tried to do too much too quickly," Theodore Poehler, vice provost for research, says now.

A NEW STRATEGY

The university recruited Barbara Plantholt, a venture capitalist from Baltimore specializing in seed investing, to head Triad and restructure the technology transfer operation. Her solution was to abandon the entrepreneurial approach altogether: instead of launching entire companies. Johns Hopkins would limit its involvement to licensing technology and building prototypes.

That strategy has given the program a modicum of success. Triad is negotiating licenses worth more than $3 million on five university-developed prototypes, including a device that helps patients who have had their larynx removed to speak. "Our biggest opportunity is in licensing out these products, not in building start-tups," Ms. Plantholt says.

Given the right conditions, however, an entrepreneurial approach to technology transfer can work. Take the success of ARCH Development Corp. started in 1984 by physicist Walter Massey, vice president of research at the University of Chicago and a former administrator at nearby Argonne National Laboratories.

To bridge the gap between research and commerce, Dr. Massey first organized a task force of leading scientists and area businessmen. "Not only was it important to get their input, it also was important to sell the concept to them," says Steven Lazarus, ARCH's president.

Two years later, ARCH launched a venture-capital fund to commercialize and take equity stakes in inventions developed at the University of Chicago and Argonne. The bulk of the money - $9 million - came from four investors, including the university's endowment, State Farm Insurance Co. and two venture-capital funds.

A CYNICAL APPROACH

Through ARCH, Mr. Lazarus and six other professionals - Mr. Crandell among them - have started 17 companies and are working on several more. Yet ARCH remains highly selective.

"Our whole job is to be cynical about whether these products can ever find a marketplace," Mr. Lazarus says. When the market for a laptop-computer system for gauging patient medical histories proved too elusive, ARCH sold the technology to Nellcor Inc., a California medical company. Another project, an information-retrieval system for literature searches, was jettisoned because it seemed too arcane, he says.

Early this year, Illinois Superconductor Corp. became the first company in ARCH's portfolio to go public. The $1 million that ARCH invested now is worth more than $8 million.

"ARCH succeeded with us because they didn't try to do too much themselves," says Ora Smith, chief executive officer of Illinois Superconductor. ARCH's approach was to take superconductivity, a technology with diverse applications, and focus it on a single area: uses in wireless telecommunications. Then ARCH hired professional managers, including Mr. Smith, who came from a Silicon Valley superconductor start-up. "They never tried to micromanage," Mr. Smith says.

Mr. Lazarus says ARCH's mission is straightforward. "We are in this to make money," he says. "Most scientists we work with like the idea of making money." He adds: "Are we corrupting them? I don't think so. But this, too, remains to be seen."

THE MOVEMENT OF TECHNOLOGY

> The economy is forever going to change
> and is biological rather than mechanistic
> in nature. The innovator is the true
> subject of economics. Entrepreneurs
> that move resources from old and
> obsolescent to new and more productive
> employments are the very essence of
> economics and certainly of a modern
> economy.
>
> - Peter Drucker

THE TRANSISTOR STORY

Stanley Kubrick's film, *2001 A Space Odyssey*, begins with a brilliant image: Primitive man picks up a bone, examines it curiously, and when he is threatened, realizes it can be used as a weapon. Overjoyed at the discovery he throws it into the air and as it rises it morphs into the space ship of the future carrying passengers to a base on the moon.

A new purpose has been discovered for the bone. It has become a tool. The space taxi is a tool. We discover fire and learn it can be a tool with which to provide warmth. We encounter a need to create a furrow in the ground so that we can bury a seed. We find a pointed stick and later call it a plow. The Greeks give a name to this endlessly growing collection of tools – technology. For all the millennia new technology drives the species forward and upward.

Sometimes an artifact lies dormant waiting for the purpose that will transform it into a tool. More often a tool is summoned into existence to solve a problem. Frequently a tool is the outcome of a competition. Unfortunately, war has been a driving force for the creation of new tools, sometimes with tragic consequences. Nobel laureate physicists have asked themselves for the last half century – Was the advent of nuclear power worth the price? Tools are not always benign.

Nevertheless there is no disagreement that scientific advancement and technological progress has been of incalculable advantage to mankind and has steadily improved the human condition. But that advancement and that improvement did not occur without substantial effort. The new thing or the new idea does not get taken up through some form of human osmosis. A new enterprise with which to bring a new tool to the market, to introduce it into the economy, to enter it into commerce is often required. The creation and nurturing of such an enterprise is a high risk activity. The acceptability of risk, the itch of curiosity, the scent of opportunity, or the spur of competition led to the inventions which changed the world. In our society the taking of risk has always been an accepted part of the equation.

One of the key characteristics of 19th century America was widespread curiosity, and an urge to tinker. It was the century of Edison, Whitney, Singer, Ford, and Bell. Their inventions led to the establishment of businesses devoted to the transformation of their inventions into successful commercial enterprises. Bell's 1875 invention of the telephone led to the establishment of the American Telephone & Telegraph Company in 1885.

In 1907, AT&T recalled its former president, Theodore Vail, to deal with the expiration of Bell's original patents. Vail set as a target the creation of a transcontinental telephone system (this would be followed by the creation of a transoceanic system). In order to accomplish this an enormous breakthrough in the field of signal amplification was required. The problem was initially solved by the application of de Forest's vacuum tubes, but these proved far too unreliable. This further problem was presented to the Bell Laboratories.

The idea of the modern laboratory was relatively new. Prior to the last quarter of the 19th century, great scientists had worked alone or with a few friends in their own apartments. Academic institutions were not congenial to the "experimenters." The Cavendish Laboratory at Cambridge provided a different model. Headed by a succession of some of the world's greatest physicists including Clerk Maxwell, Thomson (discoverer of the electron), and Rutherford, it gathered in groups of students, provided physical facilities, encouraged interdisciplinary cooperation, and integrated the work into the curriculum. Its goal was the discovery of new knowledge, and the answers to difficult questions. Two of Rutherford's young associates, Walton and Cockcroft, split the atom and won the Nobel prize.

Bell Laboratories was the first of the great industrial based research centers. Founded in 1925 as a successor to the research department of Western Electric's engineering division, it emulated the model of the Cavendish, but with an expanded mission of research, systems engineering, and development. Its purpose was to drive ideas from the realm of the theoretical to the practical world of the marketplace.

Kelly, the director of Bell Labs, had theorized that an answer to the vacuum tube problem might be found in the possibility of solid state semiconductors and, in 1945, he assigned a three man team to investigate this theory. Shockley and Bardeen were theoreticians, Brattain was an experimentalist. In 1948 they developed the first solid state semiconductor – the transistor. The transistor was the crucial invention of the 20th century. Today it pervades the lives of everyone on the planet, and is the indispensable constituent of all technological progress.

Using modern jargon, the transistor would be described as a "disruptive" technology. But disruptions do not take hold suddenly or broadly. They are often initially greeted by silence or disinterest. Occasionally they are strongly resisted in defense of the status quo. In retrospect the case for a new technology may seem powerfully self evident, but new technologies must be evangelized like new religions. In the case of the transistor some military applications were initially pursued and the Japanese began to develop the first extraordinary application, the transistorized radio, but as late as 1964 the vacuum tube makers at Sylvania were still treating the transistors being manufactured down the hall as strange and difficult interlopers. Shockley was impatient to see much broader usage. He left Bell Labs, moved to Palo Alto, California, his hometown, and with financial help from Arnold Beckman of Beckman Instruments, founded Shockley Semiconductor in 1955.

Shockley hired what has been described as the greatest collection of electrical geniuses ever assembled. He, however, proved to be a difficult manager and in 1957 seven of these geniuses, including Gordon Moore, left to start a new company. They were later joined by Robert Noyce and thus became eight. Arthur Rock, then at Hayden Stone in New York flew to California to advise them and together they formed a new company. Early financing was difficult to find but they were fortunate to encounter Sherman Fairchild whose company, Fairchild Camera and Instrument, lent them $1.5 million. Shortly thereafter Fairchild exercised an option and acquired the new company. This became Fairchild Semiconductor. Here they developed a new component called the "Integrated Circuit" made up of multiple transistors and capable of performing complex functions.

It was 1959. The title, Venture Capitalist, was not in broad use at the time. Silicon Valley was not yet Silicon Valley. Arthur Rock had come out of the Harvard Business School in 1951 and had become an investment banker specializing in the financing of smaller companies. Though not a technologist he knew something about semiconductors through a prior investment, and he was a superb judge of management talent. He saw that Fred Terman, Dean of the Engineering school at Stanford, was encouraging his brightest students to start companies but that the largest pools of investment capital were in the east. In 1961 he moved to California in order to be the intermediary for these investments.

Much has been written about the departures of eight men from Fairchild in order to start Intel. They were variously called the "traitorous eight" or the "treacherous eight," but it's difficult to see who they betrayed. Led by Noyce and Moore they were making the entrepreneurial leap, creating a business of their own. Arthur Rock played a catalytic role, raising the initial funding and helping to organize the business. Noyce, Moore, and Rock incorporated Intel in 1968 and so began the evolution of the microprocessor. A primitive but fundamental technology, born in a laboratory in 1948, was now, twenty years later, ready to change the world.

Arthur Rock set the model: the venture capitalist who recognized the technology or the talent or both, and who put together the initiating funding, worked to help organize the business, and served as a partner to the scientists. He was not investing family money. He organized pools of capital and formed them into limited partnerships. Others began to emulate the approach.

The northern California peninsula composed primarily of Santa Clara and San Mateo counties became one of the great phenomena of the second half of the twentieth century. Two brand new extraordinarily important industries – semiconductor technology and biotechnology – began there. The presence of Stanford University and the inventive/entrepreneurial culture established by Dean Terman was critical. The fact that Shockley had grown up in Palo Alto was important, but Terman was the magnet that drew him back to the west coast.

Silicon Valley is sometimes described as an extension of Terman's shadow. The enormously successful venture firm of Kleiner Perkins Caulfield & Byers began in 1972 when the investment banker Sandy Robertson introduced Eugene Kleiner, one of the eight original Intel employees, to Tom Perkins, a former Hewlett Packard executive. Hewlett and Packard had been Terman's students. Several other now legendary venture firms, Mayfield founded by Tommy Davis (former partner of Arthur Rock), Sequoia founded by Don Valentine (former Fairchild Semiconductor executive), and others, appeared at about the same time, but even as late as 1980 the industry consisted of 89 firms with 4.0 billion under management. And it was predominantly concentrated in Silicon Valley.

THE ANTECEDENTS OF ARCH

Other forces were coalescing to shape the conduct of research in the United States. Prior to World War II there was little political enthusiasm for the government funding of basic research. But the fearful competition (or apparent competition) to develop an atomic weapon established a huge network of energy laboratories that were retained and expanded in the post war period. Several of them, the so-called GOCO's, were managed by contractors, usually large corporations or universities. The National Institutes of Health, which began as the Marine Hospital Service in 1798, were by 1980 a collection of 27 organizations funding biomedical research in all the major research universities in the United States at a level of $ 5.5 billion.

In the early '80s, Congress became increasingly concerned that this vast amount of government funded research was not yielding adequate economic results. Actually, Japanese companies such as Canon were taking greater advantage of the National Technology Information Service. Two pieces of legislation – The Stevenson-Wydler Act and a series of amendments to the Bayh-Dole patent protection act were passed. These had the effect of giving university managers of government labs title to any intellectual property developed by those labs. Now, at least there was an organization attached to the Lab that had an incentive to commercialize the discoveries.

One such organization was the University of Chicago. Established in 1890 by John D. Rockefeller, the University had gained a reputation for high order intellectual inquiry. It was famous for producing Nobel Laureates in economics and physics, but its legendary early president, Robert Maynard Hutchins, did not favor what he termed trade schools and so no school of engineering was established. Nevertheless when the great nationwide effort in nuclear research was launched at the outset of World War II the University of Chicago became a major participant. Faculty member and Nobel Laureate Enrico Fermi headed the team that produced the first controlled self-sustaining nuclear chain reaction in 1942 in a facility constructed under the stands of Staggs Field, the dormant football stadium.

Fermi's experiment was conducted as part of a new organization called the Metallurgical Laboratory or Met Lab, an element of the World War II Manhattan project. Met Lab evolved into the Argonne National Laboratories which has since that day been managed by the University of Chicago. Despite Hutchins' best intentions he lived to see a major engineering facility on the property.

By 1985 the research programs of the University of Chicago and the Argonne National Laboratory totaled more than half a billion dollars. The new federal legislation permitting the University to take title to the intellectual property emerging from discoveries at both represented an extremely valuable asset. Members of the faculty expressed concern about the passive and generally unproductive technology transfer function then in operation. A committee consisting of members of the University Board of Trustees and the Argonne Board of Governors was formed to design a response to these opportunities and concerns. The result of these deliberations was The Argonne National Laboratory/ The University of Chicago Development Corporation – ARCH.

The effort that created ARCH was spearheaded by Dr. Walter Massey, the Vice President of Research and Development at the University of Chicago. Massey, a nuclear physicist, had been Director of Argonne from 1979 to 1984, and subsequently head of the National Science Foundation. Consequently, the supervisory responsibility for the research programs both at the laboratory and the university rested at his desk. He created a consensus which included the President and Provost of the university, the director of the laboratory, the dean of the business school, and several major university trustees and laboratory governors. He gained the support of opinion leaders in the research faculty and on the Argonne staff. Rarely had a technology commercialization function been initiated with so strong a constituency.

Almost all university technology transfer offices at the time were patenting and licensing organizations. Massey's committee, however, added a radical new element to the design. ARCH was charged, indeed incentivized, to commercialize new technologies by building new companies around the discoveries. The work required an Arthur Rock, perhaps several Arthur Rocks.

Fortunately, at the invitation of the Dean of the Graduate School of Business of the University of Chicago, Jack Gould, ARCH was domiciled in the Business school. The student body of the school was intrigued by the new entity. Without exactly knowing what the work would be they volunteered in large numbers to be part of it. Soon there were too many to manage. It was as if the Missouri farmhands were competing to paint Tom Sawyer's fence.

Now the University of Chicago had something entirely new on its hands, but the school was famous as a place for experiment. It was said that you could try anything there as long as you didn't do it in the street and frighten the horses.

The semiconductor industry began in a great corporate laboratory, but it rested also on the seminal principles developed at the Cavendish laboratory. The biotechnology industry began with a walk on a Hawaiian beach by Cohen and Boyer, and they were standing on the shoulders of Watson and Crick at Cambridge. The economy is driven forward by the cumulative research accomplished in the universities and the great laboratories.

By the mid-80s this process was well understood in northern California and eastern Massachusetts and networks of Arthur Rock–like venture capitalists had formed in those locations to channel new ideas from mind into matter. This was not true in the Midwest. ARCH itself was very thinly funded. The abundance of new scientific and technological discoveries which had become quickly apparent required new investment. It became clear that venture capital would have to be found.

Venture capital funds on the two coasts were solicited. They found the inventions primitive but interesting. As one said at the time, "I have a gyroscope in my head that turns me around at the Nevada border." The amateurs at ARCH consequently set out to raise a dedicated venture fund. As many of the potential investors remarked at the time – sympathetically but realistically – your track record is all ahead of you.

"SO MUCH OF VENTURE CAPITAL BEGINS FROM A UNIVERSITY PERSPECTIVE"

In 1998, some two years after I left The Wall Street Journal, I started on a book for the Harvard Business School Press entitled Done Deals. The idea behind Done Deals was a simple one. Would it be possible to capture the practice of venture capital in the words of the practitioners themselves? Was it possible to portray the broader dimensions of the industry through the voices of a wide range of players?

I tried to arrange the narratives along historical lines as well as geographical lines, and it was clear that there were differences in practice historically, as well as geographically.

Among the three dozen or so narratives, one belonged to Steve Lazarus, a former pharmaceutical industry executive, who had in a relatively short period of time established a rather unique venture capital organization, one that cut across historical and geographic lines.

Lazarus' creation, ARCH, was the archetypal venture fund, designed to take very early stage ideas and develop them into real businesses. And although that had been the initial premise of the venture capital industry, too much capital and an increasing aversion to risk had propelled most venture capital funds into more mature and consequently less risky investments.

In Done Deals, Lazarus takes the reader through the various stages of the fund's formation and the issues and the strategies. In this, the first of three excerpts taken from Lazarus' narrative in Done Deals, he explores the genesis of ARCH.

Steve Lazarus in *Done Deals*

Prior to World War II there was no substantial level of organized university-based research, not in the physical sciences nor in the life sciences. In the life sciences, you only had the advent of the sulfa drugs in the '30s. World War II was a watershed of enormous proportion. After World War II came the founding of American Research and Development (ARD) headed by General Georges Doriot, based at Harvard. While Professor Fred Terman had been at Stanford for some time before that, venture investing began broadly only after World War II. When William Shockley, co-inventor of the transistor, moved from the east to Palo Alto to start Shockley Electronics, the foundation was laid for a transistor-based electronics industry in northern California.

The University of Chicago evolved during the '50s and '60s as a research university doing work in both the physical and life sciences—probably at about the twentieth research dollar position in the United States, It didn't have an engineering school, so what actually occurred there over the years were a number of covert or hidden engineering organizations.

Chicago was not a Hopkins, a Columbia, a Harvard, or an MIT, but it was respectable. However, there was no organized technology transfer. The first reason for this was that there was the usual ambivalence within the faculty about doing anything that diverted from pure research or that had the flavor of a profit motive. There were arguments about this in the senate of the faculty. But one extremely important decision had been made—that the university and the faculty took ownership of all discoveries that were made by individual faculty members. Even today in 2000 that concept is still in dispute on many campuses. But it was clearly settled at the University of Chicago. The second thing that was going on in the late '70s and early '80s was a growing concern in Congress that the nation was not getting a payoff for all the investment that went into national laboratories and research universities. There are about 700 national laboratories, with the largest concentration in defense and energy. Many of the energy laboratories for decades had been operated by management designates such as the University of Chicago. The University of Chicago managed the Argonne National Laboratory on behalf of the Department of Energy, with a $500 million annual budget in basic research. A lot of ideas were sitting in that laboratory, and nobody was looking at them for commercial purposes. In the early '80s, Congress passed the Stevenson Wydler Act and the amendments to the

Bayh Dole Patent Act and essentially the two pieces of legislation together gave the University of Chicago the opportunity to take title at no cost to discoveries at Argonne. So, you had a faculty that was doing productive research, and a potential at the Argonne Laboratory for a lot of valuable intellectual property.

The catalyst for all this, I believe, was the fact that the drug Erythropoietin, the red blood cell stimulating factor, was synthesized by Gene Goldwasser at the University of Chicago. Nobody protected it. It went into the public domain, and ultimately Amgen cloned it and it became a billion-dollar drug. Many people at the University of Chicago wondered why Stanford and UC San Francisco could participate in the revenue stream of the Cohen Boyer recombinant DNA inventions but Chicago got nothing as a consequence of Erythropoietin. All of these things came together in the mid-'80s, under the aegis of Walter Massey.

Walter was a high-energy particle physicist. He had been director of Argonne and was the VP of research at the University of Chicago. Later he went on to be head of the National Science Foundation and provost of the UC California system, and today is the president of Morehouse College. Walter was not only an excellent scientist, but he also had exquisite political skills. He pulled the basis for ARCH together, getting buy-in from some very powerful trustees, some important and influential people in the faculty, and some local businesspeople. He also designed ARCH as a not-for-profit corporation, wholly owned by the University of Chicago. Its main interest would not be in licensing technology which was the conventional way of doing technology transfer at the time, but rather in starting new companies. At that time, I was retiring from a Chicago-based company called Baxter Laboratories, and I was thinking about teaching. Walter and the fellow architects of ARCH designed a job that was simultaneously a president of a corporation, albeit a small one, and associate dean of the Business School at the University of Chicago. So I came down to Hyde Park from Deerfield, and found myself the first employee of ARCH. I had a very small budget. We had the responsibility to do all patenting for both the university and the laboratory from that budget, which was enough to sustain me and a secretary but not much else. We had a substantial amount of technology to examine.

THE ARCHITECTS OF ARCH

In 1979, Walter Massey, a high energy particle physicist, officially became director of Argonne National Laboratory. It was a period of profound change for the laboratory. Just weeks earlier, a federal audit concluded that while the laboratory's performance was "above average when compared to a broad range of federally supported laboratories," it needed more vitality and urged the University of Chicago and the AUA (the two organizations that managed Argonne) to accept responsibility for invigorating the laboratory. And in a more critical tone they observed that the prevailing environment at Argonne is "more academic than industrial."

For Massey at the laboratory and for Hannah Gray, president of the University of Chicago, the task was clear-cut. They needed to create a more dynamic and active relationship between Argonne and the University and to also bring together the University, Argonne, and the region's research & development and financial establishment in a new technology-based economy.

Around the same time, Chicago mayor Jane Byrne established a task force on high technology development with Massey as chair. The task force addressed questions such as how cities such as Boston successfully lured high-technology industries to their areas. Could Chicago, with its superb transportation network, its financial base, its skilled labor force, and its extraordinary educational, technological, and industrial assets become a leader in high-tech industry?

It would take another half-a dozen years and the work of a number of dedicated and engaged people before the University of Chicago and the Argonne National Laboratory would settle on the entity known as ARCH to help provide a solution. Twenty years later, the following sections constitute some of the recollections of the players involved in the early ARCH days.

What are some of the problems in working with mostly basic research scientists to help them identify commercial applications for their work? What kind of conflicts emerge as research laboratories and research universities explore new directions and new business paradigms? What about incentives? And, does success always bring wealth and happiness?

WALTER MASSEY

In 1942, when Enrico Fermi achieved the first controlled chain reaction with CP-1 at the University of Chicago, Walter Massey was a five-year old boy growing up in Hattiesburg, Mississippi. A graduate in Physics from Morehouse, Massey studied at Columbia and Howard University before obtaining his Ph.D. in Physics at Washington University in 1966. Massey worked on a post-doctoral fellowship at Argonne before moving to Brown to become a professor and dean of the college at Brown University. In 1979, Hannah Gray announced that Massey was being appointed the sixth director of Argonne at the age of 41. After a stint as director of the National Science Foundation and provost of the University of California system, Massey is now the president of Morehouse College in Atlanta.

In the early 1980's, everybody's dream was how do we create our own local Silicon Valley? One of the major obstacles was we didn't have the legal rights for the laboratories to help generate new businesses, and neither could the universities then, except in a complicated way. So the law changed. The second problem was that the various institutions, Fermi Lab, Argonne, University of Chicago, Northwestern, and IIT (Illinois Institute of Technology) had not really been working very closely together. We realized there was a remarkable collection of scientific and technical research institutions, and businesses in the area.

All this began during the period when the Bayh-Dole Act was being debated, first the Bayh Act, then Bayh-Dole, would allow the lab to license research, or spin-off the results of research, and would allow scientists or the lab itself to benefit. It wasn't that we were looking to try to make money, but we were involved with the City of Chicago, Northwestern, University of Chicago, the Governor of the State and a number of people in the area, to try and create or generate something akin to a Silicon Valley in the greater Chicago area. There was a lot of corporate research activity. Amoco had a research lab there, and AT&T and Motorola had laboratories.

A third obstacle was the lack of first stage venture capital. We formed some informal and formal networks with the funds that were already here. When Alan Schriesheim came on board as Director of Argonne Labs and I became Vice President of Research at the University with Alan and the Lab reporting to me, I was in a position to bring the two entities together, around the issue of venture capital. Initially, we realized that neither Argonne's nor the University of Chicago's portfolios were large enough on their own. Together, however, we'd have a reasonable size portfolio that might result in generating some valuable ideas.

We spent a lot of time talking with the Department of Energy, trying to sort through what was possible and reasonable. We got Bruce Meriwether involved and Bruce was in the Department of Commerce, he was an Assistant Secretary for something like commercialization. But Bruce was also one of these little known heroes in the government bureaucracy who pushed this notion of allowing government-funded research to be licensed. So Bruce Meriwether came out, and together we went to the University of Chicago's Board of Trustees, and presented the idea, a joint venture between Argonne and the University of Chicago, to commercialize technology from both institutions. We struck a chord there because we had on our board a number of the CEOs of local companies, like Amoco, and the big banks, such as First National who had venture capital arms. We had Art Kelly on our Board and although he didn't have a venture capital firm, he had an investment firm.

We formed the organization, but the hardest part was to find a CEO to come in, take this fledgling organization and help us shape it. We needed someone who could move easily in an academic setting, who knew the business world, and was willing to come in and take a very low salary. I said we could go up to $150,000. One of the first people we approached was John Robson who had been CEO of Searle. John succeeded Don Rumsfeld in that job, and it was Rumsfeld who suggested this might be something John would want to do. John had been Assistant Secretary of Transportation, and had fought for the deregulation of the airlines in that position. John declined our offer because he was going to be Dean of the Emory University Business School, but he suggested we speak to Steve Lazarus.

Steve Lazarus was working at Baxter and we saw no reason why he would leave as he wasn't retiring, or so we thought. We were introduced to Steve who became very excited about the ARCH position. We needed an additional ingredient - to make Steve legitimate to the academic community, he needed an academic appointment. Steve wasn't a scientist, and the only place that made sense was the Graduate School of Business. We approached the Dean and then as we thought it through, it became clear that if it would be more than a token title, that the Graduate School of Business could provide students who might be useful in developing business plans for ARCH Ventures. The pieces fell into place - Steve came on board and became Associate Dean in the Graduate School of Business.

In the beginning, we were confronted by a number of social and organizational issues in building ARCH. Unlike Stanford or MIT, the University of Chicago had not been a place where faculty were encouraged, or even given a reward, to engage in venture type activities. In that sense, the University of Chicago probably would have been the last place to start such a business project. There was no engineering school, and the University is a highly faculty driven institution. The focus was on scholarship for the sake of scholarship.

The notion of having a profit motive for scholarship and research was probably more alien to the University of Chicago than any other place. But there were younger faculty who were seeing what was happening with their colleagues, and we saw an opportunity to change that, so that's where we started. The motivation for ARCH couldn't be the idea that it would enrich individuals, as in other places. It had to be based on the notion that this was another way in which the University of Chicago could contribute to society. Our approach was to consider research that could be spun off to generate economic development and benefit the region or the nation as realizing the full benefits of that research, a goal that was consistent with the University's mission.

At Argonne, we had to convince DOE - the program officer and the managers at DOE - that the things they were funding would not detract from the research objectives of the scientists and engineers at Argonne.

Outside of the University, we had the opportunity to work with people like Mike Koldyke of Frontenac and John Canning at the First National Bank, to help us educate the financial community about the need to have local access to some venture capital, or at least to their connections to venture capital on the West Coast. These environments at the University, the DOE, and the financial community represented major disparate cultural contexts in which we had to operate.

Our model was business creation, not simply licensing. We were concerned with generating jobs because we wanted to show direct benefits to economic development. Also, Steve felt strongly, as all of us did, that licensing only sent the research to a company already in existence, turning us into the middleman. We wanted to create sustainable businesses. At that time, only MIT and Stanford had a track record in this area.

Everyday Learning made quite a bit of money and indirectly benefited the University of Chicago. However, that was a longer route, and one in which fewer scientists could see the benefits of all of the effort. If you're simply licensing, then it takes time, and we didn't then have the staff to nurture so many companies. We could only deal with so many scientists at Argonne and the University of Chicago.

The development model consisted of two components: The ARCH Fund for investing in new companies, and ARCH Development, for actually spinning off the companies. I think the model was not moving as fast as people thought it could. It required more investment than we had anticipated. Subsequently, everyone focused more on the ARCH Fund model, and when that happened (I wasn't there) the University felt that it was not as directly beneficial to the University. I think Steve and his group felt the model need not be confined to the University of Chicago. At the same time we had a change in attitude, though not a change in policy, at the Department of Energy. What we had been able to achieve at Argonne was now discouraged by the new Secretary of Energy. It may have been the growing notoriety, and I don't mean that pejoratively, but just the attention that was given to the NIH. Once NIH allowed scientists to benefit from research, they had such a huge portfolio that they attracted much more attention than we ever would have attracted at Argonne. So Congress began to pay more attention to such things, and I think people just became skittish at the DOE.

I went from Chicago to the University of California and there, as Provost, all three National Labs reported to me. Los Alamos, Livermore, and Berkeley, as well as the nine campuses, were involved in the development of a model system somewhat based on the things that I'd been involved with at the University of Chicago. It proved to be very successful. Looking at the huge University of California system, they're now right up there, top two or three in terms of income generated from licensing. The process works, but it takes a long time.

It's also important to recognize the role that team building plays in all this. Steve put together a group of people, mainly business school students, who had either worked in some scientific or technical capacity, or had some other interest in it. I think we called them ARCH Associates, and they were comfortable going into laboratories, working with scientists, and they had enough scientific curiosity and enough background that the scientists responded to them. When we were starting this up, back then there was a sense of imposition on some of the scientists. Today, scientists are probably open to venture capitalists coming into their laboratories and they go out of their way to explain things, or they don't feel they're being interrupted in their work.

I'm on the Board of Motorola. I chair the Technology Committee, which I have for a number of years, and one of the things we, like all companies have been looking at is how do you move your investments in R&D faster into pay offs in the market place? As part of that consideration we took a group up to Procter & Gamble at the invitation of John Tepper, who was also on the Motorola Board. Procter & Gamble has a very sophisticated internal process for identifying research in their laboratories, posting it on their internal networks, and connecting it with businesses looking for technologies that fit. They have algorithms that allow you to post something on it, and are then automatically able to search for what someone else is working on, and then pair them up. Still, in the end it takes human beings to interact, but it is initially important to build connections and a lot can be done online both internally and externally.

I've been on the P-CAST (Presidents Council on Science and Technology) that President George Bush ('41) established, and two years ago we did a review of the history of the Bayh-Dole Act. We looked at its accomplishments and the arguments pro and con as to whether or not it should be extended. There're some in Congress even now who argue that government funded research should not be allowed to benefit private individuals.

After 20 years new people have come along who don't remember how things were prior to Bayh-Dole. The notion is that tax dollars paid for the research and therefore should belong to the people, and you try to explain, yes, but how does it get to the people? The people don't go into the lab, so you have to re-educate each new generation. These discussions of the appropriateness of the Bayh-Dole act are taking place again, at the federal level and even in Congress.

It is likely that any major research university has a fairly sophisticated technology transfer office. I think there's been a great deal of progress. It may be that things just aren't getting the national attention that they did when we were just starting.

Still, a couple of things have happened to make the model we began with not as viable as it is now. When we started up in Chicago, we had corporations that had real research labs, and there are fewer American corporations that have research labs located close to the companies. They are dispersed around the world. The notion of local economic development, based on the cooperation of local entities, is probably a model that is not as viable now given of the onset of globalization.

A Motorola or an Amoco (now BP) wouldn't have the same interest to get involved as they did then. I don't know if the states felt they didn't get a quick enough return on their investment or, because of their own economic problems, their investment in higher education has decreased relative to the money in the university system and the private sector. Several states that had funds for technology development have either cut back their involvement or ended it all together. These two changes make it much more difficult for that model to work now.

ART KELLY

An early individual investor in venture capital and private equity, Art Kelly became involved with technology transfer in the early 1980s. He was already aware of how the major venture firms operated – he had worked with Kleiner Perkins Caufield & Byers and with specialist law firms such as Wilson-Sonsini – and he was probably one of the few who could make the connections for Chicago between technology, university policy, and venture capital.

He also was on the advisory board of an early-stage venture fund called Crosspoint Venture Partners, one of whose co-founders was John Mumford. Also on that board were Gene Kleiner, Sandy Robertson, and Larry Sonsini.

In 1982, I was a member of the visiting committee to the Division of Physical Sciences at the University of Chicago which includes all the physical sciences. At that time, the Dean of the Division of Physical Sciences was a gentleman by the name of Albert Crewe, who was generally recognized at that time as the world's leading electron microscopist, using scanning or electron beams for microscopy. Crewe knew that I was then involved with some of the venture firms on the West Coast, specifically Kleiner-Perkins and Robertson-Stephens, as part of my private equity investment management work. I had also worked with Larry Sonsini at Wilson-Sonsini. Around 1983, Crewe approached me with an idea for using electron beams to store information on a disk - magnetic storage. Read-write hadn't been fully developed at that point, and the optical storage maximum was determined by the weight of a beam of light. For Albert, the next stage beyond optical would be using electron storage, and he believed his background in electron microscopy would allow him to store information on a disk using that technology. Crewe could store more information on the same size disk than magnetically or optically, but he needed funding and asked me if the venture capital industry might be interested.

Albert Crewe's idea didn't fit what Kleiner Perkins was doing. So I talked to John Mumford and we visited with Albert Crewe. John liked the idea and was willing to get Crosspoint to put a half a million dollars into this project.

John wanted to spin-off the project from the university and have Albert go and work in a lab someplace. But Albert didn't want to leave the university where he was a tenured Professor and Dean of the division. So the challenge was how to perform a venture-based activity on the campus. John Mumford and I negotiated an agreement with the lawyers at the university whereby Albert could stay at the university, work in his lab, and Crosspoint would fund and create a joint venture company with Albert. Albert would do the research in his lab at the University of Chicago, and the University would get a royalty from that, but no equity.

It was the first time that the University had ever negotiated that kind of a transaction. Up to that point, everything they'd done was straight licensing deals, or something done by a professor with university resources, funded by the university on university time and then licensed to a third party. At that time, the University's licensing was done through UTC, an organization that provided that service to many universities at the time. The idea that a venture capital fund would fund work on a university campus was a new and original concept. Ultimately, Albert Crewe did the research and came up with a number of patents. But we had great difficulty, or he had difficulty in transferring the concept of the technology into a workable product that would be able to read-write at those very high speeds, or those very high capacities. Crosspoint put another $250,000 into it. As I recall, at the end of $750,000 over a period of about three years we ran through the venture funding, and Crosspoint concluded that it was unlikely that Albert's project, known as Electron Beam Memories, was going to be successful so they stopped the funding and the project went dormant.

With the passage of the Bayh-Dole Act, the University of Chicago began looking around and realized that they had ownership or title to their own research, and they also had the lab. They also talked to the trustees and to the legal department at the University of Chicago who made them aware of the Electron Beam Memories Transaction and that venture capital was already funding a project on the University of Chicago's campus.

Some people in the administration and a couple of trustees picked up my name as a person who was on the visiting committee to physical sciences and as the guy who made the Crewe/Crosspoint project happen. It was 1985 and they were asking what should we do in the context of Bayh-Dole to take advantage of this new law, and how do we create value? It was less an issue of how do we transfer technology, rather how do we create value for the University of Chicago out of this new law.

Walter Massey had been director of Argonne and had transferred to the University as Vice President for Research, and for Argonne. Argonne reported to him, and its director at that time was Alan Schriesheim. Alan had come from Exxon and was a chemist who'd spent his life in commercial research, working in corporate labs bringing technology into the marketplace and converting it into chemotherapy and chemicals. Alan brought a very pragmatic, real worldview to the leadership of Argonne. Alan and Walter completed the core group with Walter representing the administration. There was also a trustee at the University by the name of Kingman Douglas since deceased, and another trustee, Ned Jannotta of William Blair & Co., who subsequently became Chairman of the Board and trustee to the University.

So we came together and they brought me up to date on their intention to take advantage of Bayh-Dole, and would I be willing to participate with them in thinking through this opportunity. Although Ned Jannotta has tremendous experience and has done some banking - William Blair had a venture capital unit - he didn't have a lot of hands-on private equity or venture capital experience. And Walter came from a physics and science background. Although I had relatively limited experience in private equity, and certainly venture capital at that point, I was sort of the one-eyed man in the land of the blind.

They looked to me because of my experience working with a number of venture capital groups and because of what I'd done with John Mumford and Electron Beam Memories. There emerged an idea of creating a separate entity, wholly owned by the University, which would provide technology transfer for both Argonne and the University. My initial thought was to call this umbrella organization the Argonne Chicago Development Corporation. But that came out as ACDC, so I scratched that one before getting it on the launch pad. We then thought about Argonne Chicago with AR being for Argonne and CH being for Chicago, and that was the word ARCH, which symbolically referred to the bridge between the two. So we called it the ARCH Development Corporation, as an abbreviation for Argonne Chicago Development Corporation.

We started in '86, and that was also when we hired Steve. We came up with the concept of a separate corporation that would have its own stand-alone board of directors. I felt strongly that ARCH be a commercial venture; not just an arm of an academic institution, and that its objective would be to create value. Back then, I don't think there was any other university or national lab that was doing anything in technology transfer other than licensing and getting the royalty. I'm not aware of academic institutions that were taking equity positions. Our priority was that we'd consider the big pieces of intellectual property. We would run it through ARCH, and the first decision or test would be whether this IP was significant to justify the cost of patenting it.

If the answer was no, it would then revert back to the principle investigator, and he could do with it what he chose. If we decided to patent it, we took the lead in finding the right patent counsel and then developed the patent. Once it was patented, we then had to decide whether it was an important enough piece of intellectual property that we could or should build a company around it. If so, we would go and find a third party venture capital firm and negotiate with one or more firms, finally contributing the intellectual property for equity in the new start-up firm, as well as a royalty back to ARCH.

The role of the ARCH at that point was really as a business development entity. The first test was to determine the real value of this intellectual property and to be able to build a company around the intellectual property as opposed to licensing it. Licensing was the fallback position. If there was not enough importance for the primary objective of forming a new enterprise, then conventional licensing offered a royalty stream. There were certain financial criteria, but it was still about creating value, creating jobs, and creating a business.

The board of directors we put together consisted of some recruits, and about one-third of the representation was from either the administration or Argonne. Alan Schriesheim came on the board at that point as the director and representative of ARCH. Walter Massey was on the board. We had a couple of other University representatives including the chief legal officer, a general counsel, and outside of that about one-third were trustees. The remaining third were from industry, from outside, people who didn't necessarily have a trustee or a faculty affiliation with ARCH or, with either Argonne or Chicago. We were lucky enough to get Ted Doan, the retired chairman and CEO of Dow Chemical, who was a member of the Argonne board of governors and he would come down for board meetings from Midland, Michigan.

The limited success was in bringing in third-party venture funds. At that time, I likened the process to an hour glass with the intellectual property pouring in and ARCH, sitting in the middle of the hour glass, was the screening entity. Our job was to place that intellectual property that came through the hourglass out into either the world of private equity, or into licensing.

We had difficulty finding venture capitalists who wanted to invest equity in intellectual property that was tied to a university, to an academic institution. We concluded that if we were going to achieve this value creation, we needed our own venture fund. I give Steve Lazarus full credit for that idea, and he wanted a captive fund. A number of us were a little skeptical about whether that would result in a less than optimum decision about which technology to fund. Because it wouldn't be the marketplace deciding whether to fund it. I seem to recall the first fund that was put together was for $9 million.

I think State Farm put in $4 million and the University of Chicago endowment fund also put in some money. And there was one venture group in California that put some money in. We started funding some of those entities and, like any venture fund, we made some bad bets and had some successes.

The creation of the Everyday Learning Corporation, the Jo Anne Schiller project, was the most successful. Jo Anne understood that with every round of funding, there was dilution from management. She figured out how to get cash flow positive in about six to nine months and after the initial round of funding, Everyday Learning developed on a self-financing basis.

Still, the University seemed a little perplexed and reticent about dealing with venture capital. Individuals like Walter Massey and Allen Schriesheim saw the model as a wonderful tool that could be used to both attract and retain faculty who saw an opportunity to participate and benefit from their inventions. But ever since its founding, the University of Chicago has been devoted to basic, rather than applied research. There was a perception at the University that applied research and certainly anything that was commercialized would get your hands dirty; you were no longer a purist.

Fortunately, we had the support of the University President, Hannah Gray, and of the Provost, Norman Bradburn, and his successor, Gerhard Casper, who later went on to become the President of Stanford. Walter was the real champion within the administration of the two institutions, but without the moral support of Bradburn, Casper and Gray, it would never have gotten off the ground.

In the early 90s, when the second Fund enters, we had two entities: ARCH Development Corporation and the ARCH Venture Fund. There was a question as to whether or not it was appropriate for a university to be in the business of owning and managing a venture fund when the declared purpose of the venture fund was to make money. If the fund made a lot of money, would that jeopardize the tax exempt status of the university?

We created an endowment acting as a limited partner in ARCH One. But the bottom line was the University decided to separate the venture fund from ARCH Development Corporation. Steve and his team were given the choice of either remaining with ARCH Development or going with the fund, and they chose to go with the fund and leave the University. I recall that they raised a second fund after the fund separated from the University and that was the creation of ARCH Venture Partners which was to include Steve, Bob Nelsen, and Keith Crandell.

The split enabled Steve to then take the technology transfer model pioneered by ARCH. There was nothing like it at the national level and it created a larger pool for Steve, making it more attractive for investors to invest in ARCH Venture Partners. This meant that ARCH Development

Corporation reverted to being a licensing organization because it no longer had a venture fund. This split represented a refutation of the original concept of the creation of ARCH back in '85, '86.

When ARCH was created, we wanted a very clear division of the rewards. We set aside 25 percent of either the equity or the royalty stream off the top for the principal investigator. We did not want the principal investigators, members of the faculty at the University or Argonne, hiring accountants or auditors to get into ARCH's books and start a legal dispute that would discourage valuable, talented people who'd just invented something and make them leave.

We took the available gross data and said, whatever the value, you own 25 percent of it. The remaining 75 percent would be used to run ARCH and from that, the university and Argonne will get their share. Alan Schriesheim will tell you about the first time he had an assembly at Argonne and handed out checks to Argonne employees as part of the economic rewards for their piece of the inventions. And the belief was that by being able to say to somebody, if you invent something here and ARCH licenses it, and it generates economic value, you own 25 percent of it. And that became a powerful recruiting tool, and a way of retaining talented, creative people. ARCH Venture Partners is the enterprise creation vehicle. Somewhere between 1991-1993, there was a change in the administration and at the Department of Energy, the funding department for Argonne. Someone in Washington heard that government employees paid for by taxpayers' dollars were now getting royalty checks. It was totally transparent, and there were check award ceremonies, and it was in the Argonne newsletter so it was nothing surreptitious. The bureaucrats began questioning it. And suddenly Argonne and DOE are trying to find a way to distance themselves from this finding, and they placed essentially de facto prohibitions on any Argonne researcher receiving the benefits that we had structured into the original ARCH concept.

If you envision a four-cell matrix, with Argonne and the University of Chicago on one axis, and enterprise creation and licensing on the other axis, once you split off ARCH Venture Partners as a separate non-university owned function, you split off the enterprise creation's two cells from both the University and Argonne, and then Argonne and the DOE chose to prohibit receiving royalty checks. You're now left with only one of those four cells, which is the University of Chicago and licensing and royalty streams. By the mid-90s, it had reverted back to straight university-owned licensing.

For many of us who were there at the conception of ARCH in 1985, and who were excited about technology transfer, the initial scope that had excited us, the four cells, were back down to one. I can't speak for all the directors, but a number of us including myself had been motivated by a structure that was no longer there, and we became less engaged.

My term as chairman of the board of ARCH Development Corporation ended around 1996-1997. The board basically disbanded, because it was just a University licensing function, and was brought within the University, so there was no need for an external board. Consequently, for the last seven to eight years, I really haven't been part of this world. In hindsight, I think we were blessed with a confluence of events in the mid-80s. We shared the Bayh-Dole amendment. We had the fact that there were people like Walter Massey and Alan Schriesheim and some trustees who were enthusiastic about the idea, understood its potential, and were willing to take risks in creating ARCH. They were willing to hire someone like Steve Lazarus; someone who came from industry as opposed academia, someone who brought in business skills and discipline to the entity, and who created a whole new business by taking the financial risk and getting the funding. All of the stars were aligned for us and it all came together. We believed it would work, and in the beginning, I think it did.

The risks of keeping the venture fund in-house outweighed the rewards that would potentially come from it. I don't think we could have prevented a change in political heart at the DOE and their views on their employees getting a financial share in these activities. When Hannah retired, the moral support for ARCH at the University president level was no longer where it had once been. Walter had left and his position as vice president for research wasn't filled, so there was no organizational counterpart for Walter.

Based upon its culture, the personalities present, the needs and the opportunities, I think each university finds what's going to work at some point in time. But there's no guarantee that it's a model that's going to work, even for the same university ten years in the future. Nor is it necessarily transferable as a model to another university.

I am not sure that our federal government has really come to grips with the idea that government paid employees should be entitled to participate in the benefits of their research, and financially benefit. If we're talking about putting government taxpayers' funding toward the transfer of technology, I don't know that that this fundamental issue has been bridged. Whether it's NIH, NSF, or the National Lab System, they still would not formally condone a system whereby principle investigators on the government payroll might be financial beneficiaries.

ALAN SCHRIESHEIM

As early as the 1970s, Alan Schriesheim believed that industry in the Midwest needed a shot of scientific adrenaline and that could come from a place such as Argonne. An industry veteran well-steeped in the needs and potential of research-based development, Schriesheim recognized the untapped potential that lay in research institutions such as Argonne and the University of Chicago.

But Schriesheim, who also had the experience of negotiating public sector and private sector initiatives, understood that the process was far more complicated than generally perceived. The cultures that determined the directions that private and public sector chose to undertake were different, and often in conflict. The inability to mediate that conflict would doom any project.

I took over the laboratory from Walter Massey in 1983 and became the Lab Director at the end of the year. I came from Exxon where I had been involved in research and development, and commercialization. I was what you'd expect from someone out of industry. I had considerable experience with the Department of Energy, the National Laboratory system, and I'd been on an Advisory Committee at Argonne.

When I came to Argonne, one of the issues on my plate was the issue of transferring or commercializing the technology developed within the laboratory. It was not the number one item on my agenda, but since the government does not give money to develop projects for commercialization, (DOE does now, but it is neither DOD nor NASA) the issue was, how to get the funding to take projects that are in a very early stage in the laboratory, and put them in a position where they can be commercialized? It became clear that we needed to set up a separate entity that would potentially license technology and also form new companies.

In addition to the problem of technology transfer issue or commercialization, there was also the issue of reviving the laboratory and the laboratory system especially at Argonne. At that time, Argonne was viewed by some as having a sick lab and system. I also had an agenda of developing programs that would ensure Argonne was considered to be a legitimate part of the nation's infrastructure, that was worthy of receiving taxpayers' money.

I had the following goals: 1) Do something with the technology within the laboratory and 2) Promote the laboratory's ability to do that as a major research facility affiliated with the University.

The funding of ARCH through the University was also a large gain for Argonne. But there were cultural issues concerning the laboratory and the University system that needed to be addressed. As Laboratory Director, I felt it was fine if the University had the patent, and then we struck a deal with them. I really didn't care, just as long as we could get this into the commercialization phase. The lab had to grapple with two cultures: its own and that of the Department of Energy, both of which overlapped.

Argonne is a mixture of basic and applied research - more basic than applied and the Department of Energy was skeptical of the venture. At the Department of Energy there was an entirely different issue. If you're spending federal dollars, which are taxpayer dollars - everyone contributes to them - how can you then give a proprietary position to a single company? Moreover, a company will not develop a technology that's available to everyone. The national labs are an interesting political and technical hybrid. As administrations come and go, federal policies affect how they are run. In general, the Republicans have an industry approach. Democrats generally like the Research for National Leadership Program, which has since disappeared. The day to day problem was more cultural, dealing with bureaucracy and individuals who had real programmatic control requiring permission to work on a specific technology transmission transfer project.

As a laboratory director, whether or not ARCH made a lot of money, the laboratory is still the laboratory and when you tack on commercialization, there has to be a means by which scientists or technologists can get some recompense. I had to go to Washington and testify before Congress and say, "Look what a good job we're doing!" That was neither an insignificant nor an easy part of the rationale for technology. It wasn't so easy to do all this stuff at that time. One reason we pushed it was that it was also good public relations that would help preserve the level of funding. In those days, we earned a reputation in Washington as being in the forefront of commercialization.

The larger question is: what is the appropriate role of the Federal Government in funding R&D? And this is one of the major issues facing the country today.

There ought to be funding and technology transfer is certainly considered a mission, but it is not a mission that any money flows through. It's a mission that is ancillary to what is considered the major ones: funding Global Warming establishments. Nuclear is more effective, more efficient, safer. Out of those missions, there comes a potential project and you cannot rely on return on investment. From the book, Argonne's project costs run to about $500 million. Thus, one simply cannot justify the R&D Federal expenditure on the basis of transferring technology. It is just a derivative.

These projects aren't geared to return on investment, and there isn't a bottom line. Yes, the Federal Government does research. But you can't do research – you can't be engineering global climate change - because of the bottom line. In this sense, very few programs will ever return the amount of money that has been put into it. Does that mean we shouldn't do it? No, of course we should do it!

Having struggled with this dilemma, the taxpayers of this country have made a decision - conscious or not - that they are going to take part of our tax dollars and run long-term basic research. Why did they make this decision? There are a range of responses to this question. We blew up the Japanese with the bomb - that was our science. There is penicillin that will cure people. Ultimately, there's an intrinsic and inherent belief in the R&D and technology transfer process.

JACK GOULD

Jack Gould was on the faculty of the University of Chicago's Graduate School of Business before he became the Dean in 1983. He stayed in the post for two five-year terms until 1993. It was during that period that ARCH got started.

Like the others, Gould too was aware that the most effective mode for technology transfer was an all-inclusive process, one that could draw on various parts of the University to manage the process. He was confident that the GSB could play a vital role, not only in providing students to manage, but also in learning from the lessons of the experience.

As to the motivation behind ARCH, there had been a growing awareness among trustees at the University of Chicago that there was a lot of science that might have commercial value. This was because companies like Genentech had taken off and it was clear that while the probabilities of hitting the ball out of the park were pretty small, if you did it you could solve a lot of the financial interests of any university for a long period of time. With all the technology going on, it would be worth thinking a little bit more systematically about where it was and what could be done with it. This was enhanced by the fact that the University of Chicago was responsible for Argonne National Laboratory, where a lot of research was happening that could have practical value.

So the trustees of the University of Chicago took the initiative and they asked, "How should we be thinking about this activity?" The

University was already connected with a company called University Patents, which developed patents on possible technology, but without any sense of focus. Also, although Chicago has great physical and biological sciences, it did not have an engineering school. There were people developing physics and, with the medical center, there's a certain application.

There are other cases where universities have had a management responsibility for the department of energy. There was a change in the law governing technology developed at a national laboratory that was part of the public domain. There was no incentive to develop something you didn't own. Congress recognized this and changed the law so that one could patent material developed at a national laboratory even though it was done on taxpayer dollars.

For the trustees in this climate of change, the direction of exploration was to create the organization called ARCH Development Corporation and to provide some of the investment and endowment at the University as seed money to do that kind of thing. This is the University of Chicago. So every idea, no matter how meritorious, will be debated and examined carefully. How would it happen? Is it consistent with the mission of the University of Chicago? Is this a worthwhile place to put endowment? Is this going to really pay off? And so on. But I think nobody was aware of the full range of issues.

As I mentioned earlier, the University of Chicago has no engineering school. On the other hand, it had Argonne, and if you looked around the University, not only in the physical and biological sciences, there were places where there were business opportunities arising. There were a lot of things that had practical application and commercial possibilities, but they weren't going to emerge on their own. Somebody had to take the initiative to knock on the door and find out what these scholars and researchers were doing and let them know that an option like this might exist. And that was a fundamental part of the mission of ARCH.

We certainly knew there were other universities such as Stanford where people were coming out of engineering and sciences who were oriented to building businesses. This process involved alumni, students, and faculty. But you didn't see much of that happening in Chicago because of its orientation toward not having an engineering school but toward basic research.

I understood the trustees' motivation for ARCH and I supported it. But I had an additional agenda in that I felt we had an opportunity to work the educational side with the business school that would open some interesting opportunities for students who wanted to look at development of businesses, entrepreneurship, and venture capital. We finally addressed this issue by choosing Steve Lazarus to be CEO of

ARCH, and making him an Associate Dean at the Business School. Steve was associate dean for developing the Business School component of what ARCH was going to do. ARCH was literally physically within the Business School in a suite of offices during its earliest years. The initial interest in ARCH had nothing to do, as I understand it, with such considerations. They focused on the University's scientific fields that could have commercial value. With the legal shift, the trustees felt this was an opportunity that they were willing to make an investment of seed money into. The idea of connecting to the Business School came later.

We wanted to establish a context within the Business School where there was going to be real activity that would tap into the science around the University and create actual businesses from it. Parallel to that, there would be an opportunity to develop parts of the curriculum through learning experiences for the students. Those students who were interested would have a framework in which to work and we could give them some core training. But you needed somebody like Steve and other people that he brought in to provide the environment. So there was a real initiative, but there was also an educational laboratory.

I joined Steve and there was a space for the ARCH initiative and the ARCH program in the Business School with a relatively large number of students (30-40 per year) who became involved. These students were fanning out, talking to people in the University and then coming back and developing business plans. If it survived the business plan level of scrutiny and screening, then they would start to look for venture capital possibilities - a way to start this thing, or to license it. They were dealing with a whole range of entrepreneurial ideas and I think it was quite a successful and effective undertaking.

It was successful, in part, because we were interested in trying a lot of different things. There were no assurances that all or any of these things were going to work. But it had the appeal of bringing us together with a wholly different community than we'd been interacting with. We had this opportunity to provide more educational experiences for the students themselves and I think we also opened the door for faculty who wanted to look at these kinds of questions to have a living opportunity literally at their doorstep. It was a means to create an opportunity and also be supportive of the University initiative. My feeling has always been that the Business School should be here to help the University.

In the early stage, I was helping structure an environment within the Business School to do it. I was also a member of the ARCH board. So I was providing, along with others, some oversight of what it was all about.

The University of Chicago is a community of scholars that are really trying to think about these broader conceptual issues, but imagine a university that does not have a engineering school. It doesn't have a football team and it doesn't have an engineering school. And that tells you something about the value system of the University in that it lacked an inherent mechanism concerning technology transfer. For example, a discovery in the biological sciences with commercial application in the medical school would go unrealized unless one already had the network and knowledge of how to do something about it. There was no natural network which was part of what motivated the beginnings of ARCH.

ARCH was important and, if it were up to me, I would have been inclined to continue working with it. Even with the acknowledged changes that took place, I would have still said for us it was a very useful thing to do. ARCH has led to a much more active entrepreneurship center at the Business School. It got people thinking about other ways in which we can do these laboratory type experiments and enhance the curriculum.

We were fortunate to have people like Walter Massey and Steve and others that were excited about it and were willing to take the leadership roles to make this happen. Steve was the one who tracked the students and spent a lot of time figuring these things out and making the connections around the University.

Everyday Learning was a good example of the general philosophy of ARCH and of what it could achieve. ARCH was not limited to high-tech stuff. What they were looking for were connections between institutions that shared similar missions and goals. In Everyday Learning's case this meant shared activities and this was pretty low tech, right? I mean, here's an initiative that came out of Chicago through everyday mathematics. In order to do it, you need it to produce something that ordinary publishers, book publishers, wouldn't touch. It's a low-tech activity. It made a big difference because by doing this, they were able to quickly implement it and it had far-reaching implications and it's a good example of teaming up with then Amoco and the University of Chicago in a joint initiative. If you did an analysis of all entrepreneurial ventures and looked at the success rate, then ARCH looks pretty good relative to that benchmark.

It's all about human capital primarily – Who's going to get excited about an idea? And as I said, the University of Chicago is a community of scholars, a community of people with common interests but different - like they stand in different places and nobody can announce this is what it's going to be. It has to emerge from the community interest. That's why I think that having something like an ARCH to catalyze what happens is exactly what the University should be doing.

Are centers of development enriched by the presence of the universities there? Certainly, a place like Silicon Valley has been enriched by the surrounding universities. But I think in each case, for one reason or another, there have been other things that have created them as technological centers. One of these factors involving certain values is to see them more clearly, so when Hewlett Packard starts doing these kinds of things - you basically attract an infrastructure that makes that work. I think it's the infrastructure that drives this stuff heavily. That is to say, if you're a high tech operation, particularly in semi-conductors in Silicon Valley, and you need something, you can pick up the phone, and there's somebody out there that's doing it. And that is both people and the technology that's available. Once you get a critical mass, it continues. I think the university is part of the process, but I think it requires a much broader social and economic context to make it happen.

It is also important to recognize that it's dangerous to specify the mission of the university in terms that are too narrow. Questions concerning commercial potential are legitimate, however, I think they also narrow the scope of the impact that universities have. If one considers public policy and development, one could think about a range of factors that affect the culture within which we live, and many of those things come from what is happening at universities. This notion of an intellectual training that's continuously occurring has implications that are far broader than the transfer of technology. That's only one component. Therefore, I wouldn't just use the yardstick of technology transfers to think about what the universities are about.

BOB HALPERIN

Bob Halperin is one of the legendary figures of Silicon Valley. He spent 37 years at Raychem ultimately becoming President and then Vice-Chairman, and was a presence at the creation of many of the Valley's great companies. As a member of the Board of Trustees of the University of Chicago, he pressed to ensure that ARCH began with a primary commercial orientation, a profit motive. Indeed, it was his experience as a successful businessman and his familiarity with the entrepreneurial culture that helped persuade many that ARCH could work and have a transformational effect on its community.

ARCH got started as the result of three people having the same idea at approximately the same time: Kingman Douglas, Walter Massey, and me. My idea originally was very simple. Universities are always in need of money. Could we do a venture capital type of project to augment their revenues?

I envisioned that the people in the University would be interested enough to go forward with these things, but that wasn't the case. I envisioned some of the people such as the faculty wanting to help the institution to which they belonged.

What did ARCH achieve for the University and for Argonne? The University of Chicago has been too under-funded as a school, especially considering its assets and its resources. ARCH became a vehicle for converting the University's very considerable natural wealth and technology assets.

The ARCH board was prohibited from making investments in ARCH companies to prevent a conflict of interests, but that didn't seem right. We needed a coincidence of interests - MIT does it, Stanford did it - why should we lag behind? Universities and scientists investing side by side was the foundation of the biotech business, why not have the same here as well?

ARCH pioneered the idea of bringing venture capital into the technology transfer process in a systematic way. The idea worked well for Chicago and Argonne. Many ideas that were shelved because they seemed to offer no perceived or real value suddenly seemed to have a new life. ARCH brought in the experience of managing technology and the passion for new discovery.

THE NEED FOR SYSTEMATIC TECHNOLOGY TRANSFER

Excerpt from Steve Lazarus Presentation to the American Association for the Advancement of Science, February 1993

When I was in the McNamara Pentagon of the sixties, there was an approach to defense management which achieved the ubiquity of a theology. It was formally called Planning—Programming-Budgeting Systems or PPBS. Though the ideas originally coalesced in the headwaters of the Defense Department, the Johnson administration decreed the generalization of the concept throughout the federal government. It was then I first observed the phenomenon of bureaucratic adoption. When a concept is endorsed by authority, every activity in government is thereafter performed in the name of it. Originally Planning-Programming-Budgeting Systems served to shed great light on the problem of formulating and managing the military budget. But shortly after the concept was bureaucratically adopted, the thrust toward outcome disappeared, and what remained was what usually remains - the perpetuation of process. In the bureaucracy repetition of process, not gambling on achievement, is what safely sustains a job.

Now, 30 years later, a new excitement is animating the administration Recently the holy grail of the government, if not the entire nation, has been " to increase the international economic competitiveness of the United States." All forms of activity are urged under its banner. Most recently a strong consensus has formed around the importance of the contribution new technology can make to improved international economic competitiveness. The United States is still the preeminent research nation in the world, a veritable pantheon of Nobel laureates. Why then, it is asked, can we not take better commercial advantage of our great scientific breakthroughs and superb inventions? The usual answer is that while we are brilliant scientists and marvelous inventors, we are poor developers.

Our inability to develop is typically illustrated by the story of the VCR, invented by Ampex in California, but ultimately perfected as a consumer product through 10,000 engineering changes by Japanese manufacturers.

Within the Congress concern about development weakness has been rising for years and is now one of the emergent themes of the new (Clinton) administration. Since half the national investment in research and development is funded through the public sector- the Defense Department, the national laboratory system, and publicly funded research grants to both public and private universities - there has been an intensifying movement to make this 76 billion dollars more commercially effective. In response, new technology initiatives have erupted throughout the government, and technology transfer has become a bureaucratic mantra. Lost is the need to evolve a sound national technology transfer strategy for publicly funded research.

Recently the National Science Foundation took a searching, introspective look at its potential influence upon the objective of strengthening the international competitiveness of the United States. The resulting report included the following observations:

> [F]ailures in the marketplace have not been the result of slow transfer of academic science to industry . . . Redirecting the NSF's activities from research and education would have little or no effect on the U.S. competitive position in the near term, but would severely restrict prospects for the long term. Research and education activities offer ample opportunity to increase the potential contribution of scientists and engineers to society.

Democratic campaign white papers were not so sanguine, and promised to give emphasis to certain "critical" technologies and to "leverage the existing federal investment in technology to maximize its contribution to industrial performance." These statements and others raised the dread specter of industrial policy, the effort to pick winners at the center, which, it was warned, would consequently distort the scientific direction of the country.

Some guidance as to what might be technologically important is not a sin. I stop short of attempting to muscle basic scientists into efforts they do not individually wish to undertake, but I think initiatives such as the Department of Commerce's Advanced Technology Program are right on target.

I believe Frank Press, president of the National Academy of Sciences, has the most balanced view. He writes,

> I heard someone describe the phobia about addressing industrial policy this way: 'Like the notion of sex in the Victorian period——suppress all thought about it, never discuss it in polite society, never plan it——better do it on the spur of the moment in the dark.' Industrial policy conjures up the image of unqualified government bureaucrats 'picking winners.' Lacking experience in technology or the market and being susceptible to political pressure, the bureaucrats would make too many expensive mistakes . . . If industrial policy operated like that, this concern would be legitimate. But it need not. The fact that several advanced democracies have successfully introduced policies to improve their competitive position should soften our trepidations.

I have never liked the term technology transfer. It has always seemed such a pale and static title for an activity which, when performed correctly, is fraught with risk and filled with energy and even passion. Effective technology transfer is, at its core, an entrepreneurial activity. I have a personal and idiosyncratic definition of technology transfer. To me it is analogous to farming. It is not enough to locate seed and fertilizer. Not enough to find a farmer with arable land. Not enough to till, to scatter the seed, to water, to weed, to scare the crows away. Not even enough for the seed to take root and germinate. For it to be worthwhile, it must yield a crop, and that crop must be harvested and shipped and used. Technology transfer must be evaluated in terms of what it does, what it causes, what it contributes. Not in terms of how many representatives show up at a meeting or in terms of how many deals are signed. Product, not process. Sadly, very little publicly funded technology is transferred on this basis or evaluated in this fashion.

Life scientists speak of the "mechanism," as in what is the mechanism by which some drug causes some physiological response. Usually the mechanism involves a series of sequential events, a cascade of occurrences each one triggered by the prior event. I am interested in the "mechanism" by which federal research causes commercial activity.

There have been studies of the effect of private research. Frank Lichtenberg of Columbia University business school has done work that indicates that the rate of return on private R&D investment exceeds the return on expenditures for plant and equipment by a factor of as much as seven to one. That is, a dollar of private R&D investment appears to be seven times more potent in facilitating productivity growth and higher per capita income than a dollar of conventional capital investment. Nothing would suggest that this is the case with regard to publicly-funded R&D. In fact, the total federal licensing royalties in 1990 were $9.4 million, less than Stanford University generates itself.

The research to commerce mechanism involves several stages of development, a poorly understood activity. Development contains what scientists refer to as proof of principle, or demonstration of concept. It also contains what engineers and patent attorneys refer to as reduction to practice, frequently involving the construction of a working model. The biotechnological development of a new molecular entity almost always involves laboratory testing (in vitro), animal testing (in vivo), and human testing for safety and efficacy. This particular form of development can take five to ten years and hundreds of millions of dollars. Most importantly, development aims at a market, a customer, someone who will buy.

Neither national laboratories nor universities ordinarily progress very far down the development cycle. Consequently, it is up to industry to locate the more interesting research discoveries, negotiate to obtain title to them, and then manage them toward commercial entry.

But industry as a whole is no longer organized to accomplish this task. At one time industry employed and funded basic scientists at places such as Bell Labs and the David Sarnoff Laboratories, and these basic scientists maintained a lively dialogue with their university and laboratory counterparts. But today the industry-employed basic scientist is an endangered species. Most industrial R&D has become applied development focused on existing product lines, and, as a consequence, there is a widening gulf between university and laboratory basic research and private industrial commerce. A recent national science board report stated that (private) American spending on industrial research slowed from an average annual growth of 7.5% in constant dollars from 1980 to 1985, to only 4/10 of 1% from 1985 to 1991.

In the new industries of microelectronics, software,

telecommunications, and biotechnology this gulf has, in part, been spanned by the venture capital community. In northern California and eastern Massachusetts in particular, this community provided the risk capital and organizational impetus to bridge the development gap and bring visionary products to market. The venture capital sponsored business development accomplishments of San Mateo/ Santa Clara counties have been emulated in localities such as San Diego, Seattle, Boulder, Salt Lake City, and Houston. Almost always there has been a major research university nearby.

Rarely has this phenomenon been propelled by the presence of a national laboratory. The U.S. national laboratory system performs some of the most sophisticated research on the planet. But these laboratories are not congenial to the type of spin-off companies favored by venture capital investors. Why not?

There are over 700 national laboratories ranging from huge facilities such as the DOD Naval Research Lab, NASA's Jet Propulsion Lab, and DOE's Los Alamos Lab to tiny decentralized agricultural research stations. With few exceptions researchers in national laboratories are not personally interested in the commercial application of their work. They are researchers, often some of the best in their fields, focused on the success and the perpetuation of their programs. While university spin-offs have demonstrated repeatedly the efficacy of financial incentives and equity participation for key investigators, laboratory investigators are deterred by elaborate conflict of interest regulations and the prospect of congressional inquisitions. At national laboratories, the transaction costs associated with effective technology transfer -technology transfer that yields product sales and jobs - are high. It is far simpler to report the signing of a dozen CRADAs. The concerns over conflicts of interest are enervating. The antagonism to financial incentives is palpable. The culture, even in the face of directives from higher authority, does not place much of a value on effective technology transfer. The overriding goal is perpetuation of program, continuity of government funding, maintenance of structure, survival. And without pointed guidance and financial incentives legitimized by authority at all levels, this should come as no surprise.

Here sits the core of a major national policy issue. As a nation we wish to achieve specific economic benefit from taxpayer - funded research. The taxpayer says, with some justification, I don't want anyone getting rich on my money. But economic outcomes are galvanized by incentives, and successful technology transfer is a nationally desired economic outcome. In the Stevenson—Wydler

Act and the Bay—Dole amendments to basic patent legislation, Congress sanctioned financial incentives for federally funded researchers, investigators, and inventors.   But in practice, the system is harried, and the entrepreneurial spirit is chilled by process police seeking to punish "conflict of interest" and, much more perniciously, "the appearance of conflict of interest."

Conflict of interest is manageable.   This is accomplished by shining a bright light on the entire process of technology transfer, ventilating it, and making it as open and accessible as possible. If an individual is subject to conflict of interest, all decisions of economic consequence can be made subject to confirmation by a disinterested superior.   Detailed reports can be regularly rendered. Third-party auditors and inspectors can be invited in to examine both process and outcome.

What is not manageable is the appearance of conflict of interest.   The "appearance of conflict of interest" is measured in the eye of the beholder.   The issue of the "appearance of conflict of interest" is real, and it can have serious political consequences. National laboratory directors are unwilling to support technology transfer incentives that might land them on the front page of the Washington Post. It's hard to blame them.   I believe, however, that concern for the "appearance of conflict of interest" freezes the energy required for initiation of new enterprise.   This in turn diminishes the potential for job creation.   Job creation is the tap root of international economic competitiveness.   It is a choice. As an individual citizen, I choose to take my chances with "the appearance of conflict of interest."   But my personal choice is relatively meaningless. This choice must be made up front by those in our administration and legislature making national technology transfer policy in order to get meaningful commercial impact from the technology in national labs.

Is such a choice worth the political risk? Well, there are many ways to "create" jobs. Former governor Lamar Alexander is justly praised for winning the gubernatorial competition to bring the Saturn automobile plant to Tennessee. In my own state of Illinois, former governor Jim Thompson moved heaven and earth to bring in the Mitsubishi Diamond Star plant. Winning automobile plant location auctions creates jobs.

I suspect a far more permanent method of job creation is the combination of cutting edge science and venture capital. Twelve years ago there was no biotechnology industry.   Today that industry has a market capitalization of 50 billion and employs 80,000 throughout the United States. Amgen Corporation alone has created over 2,000 jobs in Thousand Oaks, California. This industry sprang from university-based research, research that was funded in part by grants from the National Institute of Health. Prior to 1980, it simply did not exist. The national laboratory system contains seminal technologies that could approach the achievements of biotechnology.

The 700 plus individual laboratories in the national laboratory system contain one—third of the nation's researchers. They also contain the most sophisticated one-of—a-kind testing instruments in the nation. They have the greatest potential to yield enormous new job creation. As Fortune Magazine said in 1991, "the real dollar payoff will come from relationships that ensure a process flow from the laboratories to industry."

My suspicion is that despite the urging of interested legislators and the good intentions of the new administration, the national laboratory system will prove refractory. The intermediary organization is one way of at least partially overcoming inertial resistance. It is instructive that the University of California has recently announced the creation of an intermediary organization, constructed along the lines of the ARCH model, to focus on the nine University of California campuses and the three national laboratories managed by the University of California. The National Academy of Science, after reviewing a variety of technology transfer mechanisms, recently concluded that intermediary organizations, motivated in part by financial incentives, focused primarily on new enterprise creation, have proven to be useful technology transfer catalysts. They are one of several methods which should be employed to unlock the potential of the national laboratory system.

One final thought - technology transfer is a contact sport. It has the best chance of success when it is up close and personal. Therefore, as a matter of national policy, we must empower the field. We must delegate a substantial share of decision making to field managers. If we continue to micromanage technology transfer at the center of government, it will continue to fail. We can no more create the equivalent of another biotech industry out of Washington than the old Soviet Union could set two million prices in a nine-story building in Moscow called the Gosplan.

Norman Augustine, the distinguished chairman of Martin Marietta, tells the story of Lucius Aemilius Paulus, the Roman consul who, while campaigning in Macedonia, was summoned by the senate to return to Rome and give account of his activities. Paulus addressed the following commentary to the professional critics of his age:

> (My opinion is) that commanders should be counseled chiefly by persons of known talent; by those who have made the art of war their particular study, and whose knowledge is derived from experience; from those who are present at the scene of action, who see the country, who see the enemy, who see the advantages that occasions offer, and who, like people embarked in the same ship, are sharers of the danger. If, therefore, anyone thinks himself qualified to give advice respecting the war which I am to conduct, which may prove advantageous to the public, let him not refuse his assistance to the state, but let him come with me into Macedonia.

Let him come with me into Macedonia.

One of the tragedies of Planning-Programming - Budgeting Systems in the sixties was that they led to the conceit that the distant field could be managed in detail in Washington. Consequently, the location of Vietnamese bombing targets and the type and quantity of ordinance to be dropped were decided daily in a White House war room. It didn't work. It doesn't work.

If you want to achieve a meaningful economic outcome from federally funded research, you have to do it not in Rome, but in Macedonia.

Excerpt from Steve Lazarus Presentation to the American Academy for the Advancement of Science, February 1997

Social critics describe the 19th century, not admiringly, as a material age. "Things are in the saddle," observed Emerson, "they ride mankind." The British upper classes looked down disdainfully on those who spent their time "engaged in trade," although it became increasingly apparent that the industrial revolution was, for the first time in history, creating new opportunities for masses of people whose Hobbesian lives had inevitably been brutish, nasty, and short.

Materialism, though not aesthetically pleasing nor fully equitable in its consequences, was improving the general quality of life. The galvanizing forces behind this social transformation were scientific discovery, technological development, accelerated distribution of information, and market generated capital formation.

As we approach the end of the 20th century, the coalescence of these forces continues to drive the world economy. We have painfully learned that central planning ultimately retards social improvement and that optimum freedom of individual choice is more likely to increase general opportunity. We have also learned that government can create favorable conditions for private progress. This is particularly true with respect to basic research.

The material advances of the 19th century were built upon discoveries emanating from the private and solitary work of 18th century scientists, notably the developers of the steam engine. These scientists labored to satisfy their own curiosity and to win entry to elite royal societies of their peers. There were no broad government-supported research programs. The best that a "natural philosopher" could hope for by way of subsidy was the occasional patronage of a curious aristocrat.

Not until the Manhattan Project of World War II, did the government recognize the power of publicly supported scientific programs. It took a threat of massive proportions to permit the allocation of major resources to such purposes. As was observed in a different era and a different context, there is nothing like the imminence of hanging to concentrate the mind.

With all due respect to Vannevar Bush, the reason for the continuation and indeed the popularity of government-funded research support was the persistence of international competition in the form of the cold war, and this manifested itself most concretely in the space race. The beep-beep of Sputnik orbiting the earth in 1957 was music to the ears of the funds seeking scientific community.

But the cold war is over, and while we have not yet truly reached the "end of history," the political mind is no longer concentrated on support of the research scientist. A policy focus on public sector-funded research now becomes doubly important because a research recessional has simultaneously been occurring in the private sector. For much of the second half of the 20th century, a preeminent research effort was supported by the American private sector. Great research facilities such as Bell Labs, IBM's Yorktown Heights, and RCA's Sarnoff Laboratory produced significant results, but most of these centers have been sold, dismantled, downsized, or refocused on product development. The imperative of quarterly performance results inexorably reduces support for research with multiyear result horizons. It thus becomes crucial to increase the economic productivity of publicly funded research.

The public research legacy of the last half century is a three-part structure: an infrastructure of national laboratories focused nominally on defense, space, energy, agriculture, and other avenues of inquiry; a system of research grants administered largely by the NIH and the NSF which channel tax revenues to university-based researchers; and a smaller bundle of grant-like instruments and loans aimed at companies who have petitioned for assistance in the effort to translate research into actual commercial products. The legislative appetite for these SBIRs, ATPs, TAPs, etc., waxes and wanes depending on the current attitude toward "industrial policy" or the selection of commercial winners and losers as part of the political process. At the moment many of these mechanisms appear on a legislative hit list labeled corporate welfare. But even in eclipse these facilities and programs collectively account for $70 billion of the $170 billion invested annually in the United States in research and development. This remains the largest publicly funded research and development program in the world.

The work of economists such as Paul Romer of Stanford has produced an increasing awareness of the importance of technological discovery and innovation to economic development and job expansion. Very little attention, however, has been paid to the interplay of factors and the cascade of activities necessary to produce large economic consequence from scientific and technological effort. It is crucially important as a matter of public policy that this cycle be understood.

Like the forces of wind, temperature, and pressure that coalesce beyond the horizon to ultimately produce the surfer's wave, the antecedents of invention are often invisible. They are frequently derivative, serendipitous, or by-products of efforts aimed at other purposes. They occur sometimes because finer measuring techniques have been discovered, or forming processes have been refined. Galileo was empowered to build a telescope and ultimately dispute the heavenly centrality of the earth because of Dutch advances in the grinding of lenses for spectacles.

A watershed invention is often an endpoint of research and development that has evolved over decades, even centuries, and is both cumulative and transnational in character. If you wish to understand the origins of television, you must go back to the work of Michael Faraday and James Clerk Maxwell who, in 1831, first explicated the idea of the electromagnetic wave. Between Maxwell and television were Hertz's electromagnetic waves of unusually long wavelengths, Marconi's radio transmitter, De Forest's vacuum tube, May's selenium emitter, and Zworykin's iconoscope. This short list overlooks many, but it is instructive that it contains at a minimum an Englishman, a German, an Italian, an American, an Irishman, and a Russian.

While such profoundly important discoveries cannot be commanded, the circumstances for their crystallization can be improved. More importantly, techniques for identifying key discoveries can be widely disseminated, and such activities can be replicated, encouraged, and rewarded.

If the forces that engendered the great U.S. research flowering of the last 50 years have either disappeared or are in decline, can new incentives be designed to replace them?

Many politicians and economists argue for encouragement through favorable tax policy, and reduction in the capital gains tax rates, for example, would probably be useful. But tax and fiscal policy is beyond my brief. My hypothesis is that we, as a nation, are barely scratching the surface of the economic potential of the public research investment we already make. Why is this so?

First, there is a great gulf in our society between the private and the public sector (and for the purposes of this paper I consider research at all academic institutions as part of the public sector). The two worlds attract different personalities, the inhabitants are motivated by different goals and objectives, and they often are deeply suspicious of each other. The attitude of the academic don toward the businessman often resembles the attitude of the 19th century British aristocrat toward the merchant. I have seen talented assistant professors risk unfavorable tenure decisions by spending what was considered excess time on patent applications. The attitudes of government employees have on occasion been even more disdainful. Many attempts to link public and private sector in an effort to create economic contribution from publicly funded research encounter what the University of Chicago Nobel Laureate Ronald Coase termed transaction costs - the costs of the efforts to overcome the inherent inertia and sometimes outright opposition of academic and laboratory bureaucracies.

Second, public sector institutions generally consider technology transfer functions to be mundane and low esteem activities. Only 20 research universities account for 80% of the royalties generated by all the licensing activities in the country, and even these flows are concentrated in the licenses for a few enormously lucrative discoveries. Some years ago the Department of Energy decided that success in this area could be measured in terms of CRADAs or Cooperative Research and Development Agreements between government labs and companies. A great fuss was made over the number of CRADAs signed as if process were a true surrogate for product. It would be instructive to go back and measure how much economic activity, no less job creation, these agreements actually produced.

Third, I believe there is a bias against success because success might produce wealth for a scientific entrepreneur and draw the dangerous scrutiny of congressional investigators. There is an apocryphal story about a former Secretary of Energy visiting a national laboratory and exhorting its employees to be more active in the effort to transfer technology. As he was leaving, however, he turned at the door, Colombo style, held up a finger, and said warningly, "But don't let anyone get rich."

And fourth, it has become painfully obvious that the linear model of innovation has little peristaltic force. Forward motion occurs only occasionally and erratically. Nevertheless, it has been demonstrated that these obstacles can be overcome. The ingredients require a catalyst.

Since the end of World War II, the great new technology-based industries have been catalyzed into existence largely by a small group residing in a tiny corner of the capital marketplace--the venture capital community. Venture investing traces its genesis to the individual risk-takers who funded railroad construction in the 19th century. Leaders of wealthy families--Whitney, Rockefeller, Hillman--later marshaled their wealth to support high-risk endeavors which evolved into some of the earliest venture funds such as J.H. Whitney and Venrock Associates. In the late 1940s, businessmen, political leaders, and academics agreed on the need for a research-oriented venture capital fund in the Boston area, and American Research and Development under Georges Doriot became the prototype for nonfamily-originated venture funds. Shortly afterwards, ARD nurtured Digital Equipment into existence.

Countless others had a hand in the creation of Silicon Valley, giving northern California an enormous head start in commercializing the two great technological developments of the second half of the 20th century - information technology and biotechnology. In time, other centers of technological development and venture investing emerged to complement San Francisco and later Boston. Today venture investing is conducted in several newly emergent centers of creativity that also contain great research centers: San Diego, Boulder, Austin, and the Charlotte-Raleigh-Durham research triangle of North Carolina.

Up to now venture capital has primarily focused on entrepreneurs arising from the private sector. While certain important university-based inventions were obtained through licensing, little attention has been paid to the enormous untapped potential of public sector financed research and development.

ARCH is obviously a venture-oriented model. It has five key elements:

First, strong relationships built on trust and confidence.
The partners establish strong relationships with principal investigators, assist in the codification of intellectual property, and perform detailed investigations to determine the size of potential markets and the optimal timing of introduction. When a discovery or invention appears to have the potential for sustainable and sizable return, the partners form a company, provide seed investment capacity, recruit experienced management, and organize an investment syndicate. AVP founds and leads the majority of its investments and invests in the early stage of companies in which its special skill set can add value.

Second, established access to key research centers.
The type of academic and governmental research most likely to provide a basis for successful new enterprises is highly concentrated in approximately 20 great research universities and 8 national energy laboratories. For the past ten years, AVP has established close ties with many of these organizations and has learned how to work productively within the idiosyncratic university and national laboratory culture. This experience gives AVP a unique advantage in identifying and cultivating scientific and technical developments of highest commercial potential.

Third, investments focused in core areas of expertise.
AVP invests in companies emerging from life, physical, and information sciences, and typically focuses on four major industries: specialty materials, biotechnology, medical devices, and software. Rotations of investment interest in and out of these categories make it highly desirable to maintain expertise and market awareness in each area. AVP's formation and investment strategies are specific to each business area.

Fourth, local presence in underserved investment geographies. Early stage venture investing partnerships are clustered in northern California and in the Northeast. These investors reasonably prefer to drive rather than fly to the locations of their start-up companies. This leaves many promising locations underserved by such partnerships. AVP is unique in its commitment to four locations: Albuquerque, Chicago, and Seattle, as well as New York. It maintains offices at The University of Chicago, adjacent to the Sandia National Laboratory and the University of Washington, and at Columbia University. These offices serve as hubs for exploration of research centers in a 300-mile radius. This distributed, local presence enables AVP to cultivate continuing relationships with 20 top research universities, numerous corporate research centers, and three of the largest national laboratories.

And fifth: early reduction of risk in prospective enterprises.
Seed and early stage venture investing is risky and difficult, but potentially highly rewarding. Investment is typically made at the most attractive comparative values, enabling the early investor to play a crucial role in the formation of a company. Seed and early stage investing is labor-intensive, initially requiring relatively small amounts of capital. AVP applies strategies of the most effective seed and early stage venture investors of the late 1970s and early 1980s, and painstakingly invests small amounts of capital to wash risk out of the prospective enterprise. AVP then prepares a first-round syndicate in which it remains as a participating investor.

David Birch, Paul Romer, and others have long asserted that new small business formation is the engine that drives job creation in the United States. While not all new business is research-based, it is a fact that whole new industries - microelectronics, telecommunications, biotechnology - have sprung up from the laboratory during the last fifty years. Given the ubiquity of the information network, the diffusion of research information will become increasingly more immediate, rapid, and comprehensive. As industry draws back from basic research, universities and national laboratories will play an increasingly critical role in this dynamic, and economic necessity will mandate an improved impedance match among these contending cultures.
The potential of the future will dwarf the accomplishments of the immediate past. The 20th century has been the greatest period of technological discovery in the history of the species. The 21st century, by comparison, will make it seem like the Stone

Age. If Romer and others are correct, there is a chance that this great wave of technological development will yield hundreds of thousands, if not millions, of new jobs for the citizens of the United States. But it will only happen if we are structured and organized to make it happen.

ARCH BEGINS: THE EARLY DAYS 1986-1992

"... A BLANK PAGE OR CANVAS - SO MANY POSSIBILITIES ..."

STEVE LAZARUS

I have a peculiarly adult version of attention deficit disorder. After college I spent a decade as a naval officer who sailed destroyers and learned the geopolitics of the Mediterranean. This probably accounted for my life long love affair with the sea stories of Patrick O'Brien. I then spent another decade as a naval officer based in Washington moonlighting as the assistant maritime administrator, the head of east-west trade in the Department of Commerce and other odd jobs. There was no particular pattern to my career other than a penchant for green fields and new starts.

As one of those Easterners who knew the Midwest only as fly over country, I would not have predicted that I would spend the next thirty years in Chicago, but the navy offered retirement and Bill Graham, the Chairman and CEO of Baxter Laboratories offered line responsibility so I began a career in health care. This transition was the first of my several failures at retirement.

The final line of Stephen Sondheim's musical *Sunday in the Park with George* is "... a blank page or canvas/ so many possibilities ..." Unfortunately (or perhaps fortunately), I am always intrigued by blank canvasses and their possibilities. In 1986 I had another opportunity to retire, this time from Baxter, and I had an offer from the University of Chicago to head its new self-contained company, the Argonne National Laboratory/The University of Chicago Development Corporation

(ARCH). So I retired, immediately unretired, and drove down to Hyde Park. I had failed retirement for a second time.

There was an extraordinary person at the University of Chicago named Walter Massey. Walter was a high energy particle physicist, had been Dean of Students at Brown, and most recently had been the head of The Argonne National Laboratory. As Vice President of R&D at the University of Chicago he now presided over the research programs at both institutions and he was determined to create some economic utility from these programs. He had gathered support from Hannah Grey, President of the University, Alan Schreisheim, the new head of the laboratory, several trustees and Argonne governors, Jack Gould, the dean of the University of Chicago Business School, and most importantly, several highly regarded research faculty members. This group created ARCH and started looking for a CEO.

There was some debate over the purpose of ARCH. One faction, led by Bob Halperin, Vice Chairman of Raychem and a very active trustee, was blunt. The job was to earn money with which to offset the declining research funding from NIH, NSF, and other government agencies. There was an equally strong opinion in favor of using the effort to create jobs, support the researchers and contribute to the community. At first, these goals seemed complementary, but they were not. One observer ultimately described the tension generated by the effort to simultaneously achieve these goals as a crisis of commitment.

I sought precedents to follow or at least study. There were none. Most research universities were hostile to the notion of conducting commerce on the campus and had successfully resisted earlier attempts. The Wisconsin Alumni Research Foundation (WARF) was established in 1925 to bring the vitamin-based cure for rickets to market, after faculty and trustees had banned the activity on campus. This pioneer technology transfer organization might have been a useful model for the University of Chicago except for one thing. One particular design feature in the university's blueprint, the one that had drawn me to the university and was ultimately to draw all the originating partners of ARCH Venture Partners, was the opportunity to commercialize technology by starting new companies around the discoveries. Conventional licensing could yield single digit license fees on revenue streams, but a substantial equity holding could appreciate into multiple of millions. At least that was the vision of the original designers.

The program was funded, in a meager fashion, for five years. So despite the ambiguity of somewhat conflicting goals, I had a clear idea of what it was going to take to succeed. I had to examine the research at Argonne and the University of Chicago, find one or more discoveries that might make the basis for a new company, protect the science, start the company, make it profitable, make it liquid, all within five years. How to do all this was a far different matter.

I had some help. Massey was totally committed, and Jack Gould gave me that rarest of all university commodities – office space. He also gave me a measure of academic citizenship by appointing me Associate Dean of the Graduate School of Business, the GSB. These two actions were to prove crucial.

Many universities are closed societies. They treat the intruder the way a biological system treats an antigen. The immune system marshals its antibodies; the intruding antigen is complexed and expelled. One would have expected this to be particularly true of the University of Chicago which had taken its modern form under the stewardship of Robert Maynard Hutchins. It was a temple of arts and theoretical science. Even the Graduate School of Business was considered respectable largely because it was the greatest incubator in the country of Nobel Prize winning economists.

But there is another side to the University, a maverick, unpredictable side. The University of Chicago loved experiments. Enrico Fermi produced the world's first chain reaction under football stands at Stagg field. The astrophysics department built sophisticated equipment to journey aboard spacecraft. The intruder was tolerated as long as he was doing something unusual and interesting.

The physical placement within the GSB had a totally unexpected outcome. The GSB students wanted to help. Hundreds volunteered. Ultimately about twenty committed themselves to the effort and although they were carrying a full curriculum load, devoted tens of hours a week. At first we called them the 57th street Irregulars. Later they became the ARCH Associates. They made all the difference.

The first two ARCH Associates were Bob Nelsen, class of '87, an undergraduate biologist, and Keith Crandell, class of '88, an undergraduate chemist. We formed the volunteers into two squads, one led by Bob to focus on the University and the second led by Keith to focus on the Laboratory. The plan was to comb through the research at each institution, meeting at length with investigators, reading invention discovery reports, and spending hours on telephones probing the markets where these inventions might apply. We found that almost everyone was willing to talk to the students. The Associates called this process smilin' and dialin'.

ARCH began active operations in October 1986. By the end of the first twelve months we had learned several difficult truths about our effort.

- The research programs in the two institutions were

rich with potential inventions and, with some few exceptions, the investigators were interested to see their work commercialized.

• Ownership and uniqueness of intellectual property was crucial. We had to become skilled at the patent process and at managing the cumulative cost of a growing patent estate.

• The scientist/inventor was pivotal to the process. Tenured professors were individual worlds within themselves. They were not "organization men." They sought respect, admiration, comprehension, and, above all, individualized treatment. The really good ones – the true innovators – all knew or knew of one another. They were unlikely to become promising leaders of new entrepreneurial companies. The best strategy was to find ways of working with them while enabling them to remain within their university environment.

• It was easy to fall into the trap of technological elegance. Certain inventions have enormous intrinsic appeal, but may not have a marketplace ready to buy. It takes discipline to reject them.

THE 57th STREET IRREGULARS

STEVE LAZARUS in *Done Deals*

The placement in the Business School turned out to be extremely fortunate. The student body was made up of a large number of young people who had been out in the workforce and who decided that they did not want to continue as salary men—in the Japanese sense of the phrase—but wanted to become owners. They wanted to build net worth; they wanted to control their destiny. Therefore, they wanted to go into small new enterprise, and build up from there. Several of them found me, and asked, "Is there any way we can work with you?" I said, "I can't pay you." They said, "That's okay, we'll do it voluntarily." Thus began what we first called the 57th Street Irregulars, and later—when we decided people needed to take us more seriously— the Group of ARCH Associates. I think it's coincidental, but very fortunate for me, that the two earliest members of that group, Bob Nelsen and Keith Crandell, are today my partners in ARCH Venture Partners, Clint Bybee, who came a year or two later, is the fourth general partner of ARCH Venture Partners.

What the young people started to do was go into the halls of the institution and locate the stars. I realize that's an elitist comment, but it's just like salespeople qualifying sales. Who is most likely to buy? Who is most likely to be productive? There are a lot of fairly mundane ways of finding out. Who has the most grant money? Who has the most publications? Who has the most citations? Who are members of the national institutions, the scientific elite structures who elect people? And finally, who did other scientists admire? Out of that, one could narrow it down to the 10 percent of the research faculty who were likely to yield inventions that would have intrinsic, and ultimately extrinsic, economic worth. Over time we have continued with that technique and refined it. This form of triangulation truly works.

I think the second technique we evolved was learning how

to first identify the unique invention that was not going to have much follow- on, and that was best licensed to a third party. After syndicating out the licensing candidates, we concentrated on the technologies and inventions that could be platforms for new companies. When we licensed an invention there was no certainty that a revenue stream would result. For example, all too often a molecule licensed to a Bristol Myers, or a Lilly, might engender initial interest, hut over time would be displaced by interest in other targets. It would then stay on the shelf. This was another reason to start creating companies over which you have a greater degree of control. There was, however, very little venture capital in the Chicago area. I'm talking specifically of seed and early-stage high-risk capital with which to start new companies.

We made several trips to both coasts, carrying our portfolio of technology. Everyone was interested in a number of the specific deals but nobody had any enthusiasm about getting on an airplane and flying to the middle of the continent to shepherd, nurture, and incubate an early-stage deal. This is one of the demanding characteristics of seed and early-stage investing.

So, quixotically, we set out to raise our first venture fund. That was in '87 and '88. I made something in excess of 100 visits to foundations, other venture funds, and university endowment people. Everybody thought that the idea had merit. Nobody was interested in investing. I was told over and over again that my track record was all ahead of me. There was no denying that— it was the absolute truth. There's a Catch-22 to getting started in venture capital. If you don't have experience it's hard to get started, and if you haven't gotten started, you don't have any experience. Fortunately, a friend suggested that I call on Jim Bates, then the vice chairman and chief investment officer of State Farm. So, on a Saturday I drove out to meet Jim, who had been playing tennis, at the International House of Pancakes for lunch. I talked without interruption for about an hour, at the end of which he said, "That sounds like an interesting idea, we'll put $4 million into it." Suddenly I had my first investor.

The university endowment matched that, and soon we had a $9 million fund. We invested that fund in twelve companies. We made horrendous mistakes in some of those investments. Five of them failed. But, seven of them were successful, and a couple of them were quite successful. We had a first fund that was returning a respectable return to its investors, and we were now considered legitimate venture capitalists. Not experienced, but legitimate. The university examined that set of occurrences and said, "This is no longer an experiment. We as a university are not at all comfortable with continuing as a general partner of a venture fund, so why don't we divide the entity we have created? The technology transfer and commercialization organization will remain inside the university, with the venture capital partnership going outside." At that point, in 1992, Keith Crandell, Bob Nelsen, Clint Bybee, and I stepped outside the university, created ARCH Venture Partners, and started to raise ARCH Venture Fund Two. We still had friendly relations with the university, and an opportunity to have early examination at both the University of Chicago and the Argonne National Labs. About that same time, we were invited by Columbia University in New York to take our model and open an office at the University in New York City. Some commercial interests in Albuquerque, New Mexico, helped us take the model and open an office in Albuquerque that was focused on the two huge national laboratories there, Sandia and Los Alamos. Those two labs represented $2 billion worth of basic research every year and had never seen a venture capitalist. Clint Bybee went to Albuquerque. We hired a young M.B.A. to operate in New York with Keith Crandell frequently coming into New York to supervise the operation. Bob Nelsen, who was born and raised in the Washington area, relocated to Seattle to open an office, on the assumption that the latent technology in Seattle—physical sciences, information sciences, and life sciences—was largely unexplored. There were very few venture funds in Seattle, and therefore we had an opportunity at the University of Washington to apply our same set of techniques.

ARCH Venture Fund Two proved to be an extremely successful fund. We created twenty-two companies. Six of them were follow-on investments in Fund One companies. We realized that what we were becoming was a seed and early-stage venture fund that also did later stage investing in companies of its own origin. This had two consequences. One, it reduced the overall level of risk in the portfolio. Two, it started to shorten the time to recovery of the investment.

We started to be written about. Other universities heard that we were active, realized we knew how to interact with universities, and invited us to come out and look at their technology. We started to do a lot of flying. We violated our early rule that you had to drive to the deal. What we found we could achieve was an operating relationship either with the technology transfer function in a university or with a local, small venture capital fund. For example, at the University of Michigan, we worked with the Enterprise Development Fund, which is located in Ann Arbor. In

Boulder, Colorado, we worked with Boulder Ventures. We do that today in more and more locations around the country. We found there were certain other funds who had similar characteristics to ARCH—some of whom had been around longer than we had.

"HOW DO WE ACCELERATE THE PROCESS OF TECHNOLOGY TRANSFER AND COMMERCIALIZATION THROUGH OUR TECHNOLOGY RESOURCES?"

UDAYAN GUPTA

In the mid 1980s, I had the rare opportunity of attending an unusual meeting of venture capital industry people held at the O'Hare Hilton. There were venture capitalists, investment managers and advisers, even some entrepreneurs at the conference. The discussion was about the growing attraction of venture capital and how much money it could realistically attract. The old guard emphasized that venture capital, although an alternative asset, required time and attention, not more money. After all, in terms of the total capital pool, venture capital was a relatively small amount and would continue to remain so.

Several university endowment managers noted that the first large allocations of capital into venture capital were from universities and their goals focused on the transformation of intellectual capital into business – businesses that would generate jobs, create wealth, and transform communities. In some fashion, the evidence was already visible on the two coasts – in Silicon Valley and Massachusetts' Route 128.

After the technological breakout of the early 1980s, the mid 1980s became a period of reflection for much of America, especially for governments and for many institutions. If technology can be such a powerful force in creating economic and societal change, how can we harness it? How do we accelerate the process of technology transfer and commercialization through our technology resources?

Ironically, at about the same time, one of the first such experiments in technology transfer and commercialization was taking place just miles away from the O'Hare Hilton. At the University of Chicago, which also was then in charge of managing the Argonne National Laboratory, University officials and community leaders in business and science, were forming ARCH.

There wasn't a grand design for ARCH. Its mission: To take early stage ideas and innovations, explore their potential and help the most promising ones find a market, hopefully to become business entities on their own. For research laboratories such as Argonne and educational institutions such as the University of Chicago, ARCH became the means to a new way of looking at themselves and the path to new ways of conducting themselves.

But in working with Chicago and Argonne, ARCH not only developed a strategy to support the two institutions, it also developed a unique system of its own, a system that no other venture fund has in place.

Not that other venture funds haven't had successes in taking raw technology and turning it into a successful business. But for most of them the successes have been more a matter of luck and opportunity than planning. For ARCH, the practice of taking technology out of its research settings and taking it to the marketplace has been evolving for twenty years.

"A LOT OF PEOPLE TALK ABOUT TECHNOLOGY TRANSFER, HOWEVER, VERY FEW DO IT WELL"

ROBIN PAINTER

One of venture capital's most renowned legal minds talks about ARCH

A Boston attorney specializing in venture capital, private equity, and technology transfer, Robin Painter has an extremely impressive roster of clients, institutional investors, venture capitalists and entrepreneurial start-ups. Painter has advised funds on a range of issues, including capital formations, secondary transactions, portfolio investments, internal governance and distributions and divestments. ARCH was one of her first clients when Painter began at Testa Hurwitz and Thibeault. She continues to advise ARCH on a range of issues, although she now has moved to Proskauer Rose.

A lot of people talk about technology transfer, however, very few do it well and the question is why? One reason is that you need to spend a lot of your time educating your IP base on what this business is about because seeding companies in the classic early stage venture context is a long process. For an industry that has become IRR driven, it is difficult to pull off and still maintain enthusiastic support from your investors. I think one of the reasons why ARCH has been so successful is because they've done a terrific job of educating their backers - the foundations, the endowments and all the rest – on what their mission is.

Without that understanding, people lose patience. Tech transfer isn't the kind of business where you are going to have home runs 18 months, 24 months after you make the investments. It's a long play. You have to identify the technology. You have to navigate the various pieces of that technology which often reside all over the place, in different settings - in universities and in labs – and you must get everybody to collaborate, and get some sense of the technology risk. Once that's done you have to pull together the management team. Obviously the founders - the scientific founders - are not the ones to run the company when it ultimately takes off. So you walk through the stages of identifying opportunity, identifying areas of expertise around the world, and of making some critical assessments on the technology and the market.

I remember doing deals with these guys, meeting folks in between flights in Providence. There's a lot of heavy lifting involved and that's before you even take on the management risk.

It is important you orient your investors to a cash-on-cash expectation as opposed to an IRR expectation. In some ways, ARCH has been really lucky because one result of their efforts is that the investment community has been able to shift its focus away from IRR to cash-on-cash so they are more willing to benchmark themselves on a broader basis. I think that has been a key factor. Otherwise, people will look at fund one and they ask about it when they see fund two though not expecting a lot of real movement there, but with fund three they might not be very accepting. The track method for analyzing methodology has to be adjusted.

One of the other things that ARCH has done is to roll out these whiz-bang scientists who have done an incredibly great job at technologies. They have the credibility with those scientists to focus that research toward an application that is actually going to have a commercial value in a reasonable amount of time, in real time. A lot of venture capitalists don't have that credibility and aren't able to rein in the scientists

Why don't others do it? The time to liquidity is a tough period. You must have the skill, the expertise, and the credibility to be able to forge these collaborations. You can have some terrific research going on in one lab, but the missing piece may be elsewhere. You need to know where it is and have the synergies to put it all together. The typical venture capitalist doesn't have the ability to assess the technical risk. If you look at the life cycle of risk, there's the science or technology risk, there's the market risk, there's the management risk, and the liquidity risk.

Once, when I first started doing this it was expected that for each fund you'd have two or three big winners, a lot of losers, a few write-offs and a couple of doubles and triples. The mindset of the institutional community has since changed and they'll say I am not comfortable because that was just a one-hit fund. It was okay if you had that one big hit, but investors are now looking for more consistency and a strategy.

What can screw up the transfer process? Most of the established programs have a template in place for tech transfer. This addresses the needs of the faculty, the needs of the institutions, and the revenue needs of the institutions. The bigger institutions have a plan that is institutionalized so that it's part of that institution's culture. That's not the case with more nascent programs. So where the risks involve identifying the time it will take to turn something real and the pieces that are needed to make it real, the hardest part is pulling together the right management team to make it happen. A lot of what people at ARCH do is to create a stable bunch of entrepreneurs; they pull together teams that manage the technology, teams that aren't the scientists, but the managers.

Then there is the transition problem. In the early days, the transition from the technical stage to the management stage was much bumpier than it is today. There are serial scientist-discoverers today who know what to expect. Earlier, the change was bumpy. Now it's been smoothed out.

In ARCH's early history, some of these issues existed, but the ARCH guys have learned about how to set expectations and the industry has matured and expectations are often set anyway. The folks at ARCH were the pioneers, so they set the benchmarks concerning the process.

In the early days, it was trial and error. There was a lot of diverted attention for these technologies, but ARCH has honed the model. The portfolio company's organization reflects the mission and the way through to achieve that mission.

It's clear that, over the years, ARCH has become more specialized on a domain basis. They have always had their areas of expertise, but in time, those areas have become finely honed. For the materials sciences you go to Clint, for bio you go to Bob. For IT you go to Keith. The depth of their domain expertise has strengthened considerably over the years. Even the newer members have become more specialized. Talk to the VCs around town and both Patrick and Scott are considered superstars - their reputations place them on the A-list.

Today, the firm is completely spread out geographically. The domain expertise has become increasingly tighter. While at many firms the bio guys go in one direction, the IT guys go in another direction - there's a laundry list of firms where this has happened - I was never concerned about stability at ARCH. Much of this should be considered risk factors, but ARCH has the team process down and what they are doing is remarkable.

In the U.S., a lot more can be done with technology transfer and this is a good time to do it. There is a lot of capital to engage in these sorts of activities and those sitting with pools of capital need to put that capital to work in this area.

There aren't a lot of folks offering these opportunities. Who are the real seed investors in the life sciences? There's Bob (Nelsen) and a handful of others. Who are the real seed investors in the material sciences? Clint (Bybee) and not too many others. In IT there are many seed investors, but in terms of the people who really do early stage well, there aren't too many. In IT, you aren't talking about going through the FDA.

"SPINNING OFF COMPANIES IS AN ENTREPRENEURIAL PROCESS"

KEITH CRANDELL

Keith Crandell joined ARCH at its founding and has played a significant role in the formation financing and development of more than a dozen companies, including AlfaLight, Apropos Technology Eichrom Industries, Nanophase Technologies , and Illinois Superconductor. He holds an M.B.A. from the University of Chicago, an M.S. in Chemistry from the University of Texas at Arlington, and a B.S. in Chemistry.

DOING IT RIGHT

I started working with Steve Lazarus in late 1986 at what was then called Argonne National Laboratory and The University of Chicago Development Corporation, shortly after beginning my MBA studies at the University of Chicago. I believe I was the first student to be involved in what later became known as the ARCH Associates. Prior to that time I worked for a large chemical company and as a Ranger with the National Park Service. The best part of my chemical industry experience was finding new applications for polymers and running plant trials. The fall of 1986 was a busy time as I was completing course work for my masters in chemistry while a full time student at the Graduate School of Business.

I read about the formation of this new entity set up to commercialize technology from the University and Argonne in the school newspaper and thought it looked interesting. My first meeting with Steve Lazarus was a little awkward since I did not know exactly what type of work Steve was doing but I was sure I could help. Steve had just been hired as ARCH CEO and did not then really know what he wanted done and was not too sure what role graduate students could play. The meeting lasted about 20 minutes and ended well. Steve gave me some guidance about his charter and handed me a description of an invention he pulled from his brief case, the invention was from Dr. Michael Roizen, Chairman of the Anesthesia Department. Steve suggested I meet Dr. Roizen, find out what the invention was about and meet with Steve in a week's time to tell him what I had found out. The invention was a fairly simple idea to store drugs in an operating room in a way that they would be organized but readily available. I looked at what it would take to manufacture the organizer and spoke with some anesthesiologists to determine if they would want to use it. A week later, I met with Steve for about 20 minutes and explained what I had found. Steve asked me what I thought the next step should be and suggested I speak with other industry experts he knew to get their perspective. He encouraged me to pursue that path and meet again in a week.

ARGONNE

I started to gravitate toward inventions at the Argonne National Laboratories because the technology base there fit my experience and interests in chemicals, materials and instrumentation. I think Clint worked on Argonne projects for the same reason. During that time, I also worked on an engineering software spin-off from Iowa State University that one of the other GSB graduate students who worked as an ARCH Associate, Matt Rizai, PhD, had co-founded and boot strapped. That company, EAI, later went public and ultimately became part of EDS.

My job at Argonne became focused primarily on identifying centers of excellence, developing relationships with leading researchers and organizing companies around those centers and researchers. I also became an initial operator of each new company until a real CEO could be recruited. First, I worked on Illinois Superconductor (ISCO) which went public, then on Nanophase Technologies which also went public, then on Eichrom which was sold and finally on Qmax which we ultimately shut down. Each operator tour lasted about a year.

I also became an ARCH point person trying to facilitate the development of policies and practices at Argonne for dealing with start-ups. This involved interacting with DOE program managers, legal staff, and Argonne administration, University research administration, industry and researcher interests and it was a lesson in diplomacy. Steve Lazarus' experience negotiating with the Soviet Union trading grain for dissidents in the 1970's, I imagine, was ARCH's best preparation.

ARCH had to facilitate development of policy because we could not recruit management or raise money for our start-ups until we could define the role of the researcher in the start-ups, be that board member, advisor or consultant. We also needed to be able to define the start-up's relationship with the laboratory, contract research scope of work, intellectual property licenses, division of compensation and conflict of interest procedures. Each change in the structure required a consensus to be rebuilt among the stakeholders. Each stakeholder could exercise a veto by doing nothing because to do nothing (which is a rational response to difficult issues in a bureaucracy) would degrade our start-up's momentum and credibility. If this sounds involved and complex, I agree it was. Dick Weeks, a division director at Argonne at the time, characterized our job as "shoveling smoke." If anyone cares to understand why venture capitalist and entrepreneurs haven't flocked to public research institutions in the past this is one reason.

I'd like to share some ideas that I think are important about designing an entity and a process for University and National Laboratory technology commercialization so that it is successful. I should first spend a moment on terminology. My definition for commercialization success is sustainability. The most important aspect of sustainability is economic or cash flow positive operations. This is not every academic administrator's definition, but if the effort is economically successful then the other aspects of a broader definition can be addressed at leisure. I also believe that the best chance of developing a successful commercialization effort rests on the ability of the commercialization entity to spin out successful new companies. Some evidence that supports that is the $25 million ARCH generated from its first six years of operations and the fact that the vast majority of the income came from equity in our start-ups or licenses to those start-ups.

I believe that populating the commercialization entity with "entrepreneurial managers" is the single most important predictor of success. I also believe that structuring the entity to allow "entrepreneurial managers" to receive compensation that reflects the market will make the commercialization entity sustainable. This model is particularly important for the research institutions that have great research but aren't surrounded by expert seed venture capital communities or large numbers of successful entrepreneurs.

The first challenge is what should the commercialization process and entity look like at the particular institution that's interested in succeeding in commercialization. The second challenge is how to populate it with the right people. The third challenge is to choose an outward facing strategy that will succeed. The final challenge is to make sure the commercialization entity can continue to efficiently work within the institution.

Looking back at our experience at ARCH, a critical element was the structure that attracted the right type of people, allowed them to go about their business and incentivized them to succeed. The ARCH entity by design recognized that spinning off companies out of these institutions was an entrepreneurial process as opposed to a bureaucratic one. In ARCH's case, to its credit, it was able to form and foster a set of commercialization entrepreneurs.

UNIVERSITY BUREAUCRACIES

In technology commercialization most universities generally have gone for more of a system that is set up as a department that reports to the vice president of research administration or the provost. University compensation systems are set up to address tenure and academic success and generally include salary and prerequisites.

Bureaucratic processes are more easily controlled and far safer for university administrations. But choosing a process that the university is most comfortable with from an administrative standpoint is wrong because it doesn't enable you to attract and retain the people that you really need, people who are more or less the entrepreneurs. It seems strange in a way, that universities have trouble with this concept because universities are basically a band of academic entrepreneurs and have embraced the notion of researchers receiving compensation for inventions. Perhaps university administrations think of the commercialization people as non-core and cannot find a way to place their contribution on the same level as the researcher.

Many commercialization organizations rely on a single decision point model where a committee determines if an invention exists and whether it's a spin-off or a license deal to a larger company. This model is limited because a key piece of any start-up, the entrepreneur, is missing. It's difficult to know at any one point in time where the earliest and best applications are going to be. In the physical sciences many of these innovations are broad technologies where the first relevant applications are not then known. For example, in Nanophase Technologies there were perhaps twenty different compositions of nano materials that could be produced each of which had several potential applications.

In addressing these unknowns, what are needed are technology commercialization people who are skilled at finding the answers to these types of questions. These people must be willing to learn and must be advocates. They may get ten bad answers before they get one good one. They can't take the first nine "no's" necessarily as complete. In short, they need to be entrepreneurial.

SHOULD THE UNIVERSITY BE ENTREPRENEURIAL?

One question on people's minds is: Should the university administration be the entrepreneur? Should the professors be the entrepreneurs? Should you recruit somebody from industry who is more business savvy? The answer here is that all of these folks have to be more entrepreneurial because some of the initial work has to be done by the professor. Some of the initial work in business development connecting the technology with the market has to be done by the university commercialization organization before you're going to be able to attract or identify the right type of industry Chief Executive Officer. So, it's really a shared group responsibility, however, an outstanding commercialization individual can drive many marginal projects forward to success.

Commercialization structures that have more degrees of separation from the university bureaucracy allow more entrepreneurial commercialization people to be attracted. These structures are sometimes viewed as considerably more difficult to manage from the university administration perspective. The administration is often looking for a zero complaint outcome where every professor gets equal resources, even though innovations may have very different levels of commercial merit. A big issue for university administration is a professor who doesn't feel he has received as much attention as he feels he ought to have had.

At the other end of the spectrum, the big problems occur for the administration when a professor starts making serious money because she was successful commercializing technology. Some parts of the university administration would almost prefer to fail gracefully rather then deal with the problems of success such as conflicts of interest. One example is the licensing organization at a national lab that had a start-up interested in licensing a new light source technology. The lab refused to complete the license because they felt a license needed to be reserved so it potentially could be granted to a large company if the technology proved out even though the large company had no interest in the technology in its then current form.

For a bureaucratic organization, success also creates a lot of tension because there are two or three people that are clearly outperforming the rest of the organization. The administrative problem then becomes how to compensate these contributors, how to retain them, and avoid the appearance of conflicts of interest.

One criticism of entities such as ARCH, that are separate from the university and run like entrepreneurial companies is that they're basically a bunch of cowboys that cherry pick the good technology, and don't spend their time on the middle-of-the-road innovations or the clear losers. If one believes that commercialization is a university service business where every idea is equal and believes all faculty are entitled to the same amount of services, resources inevitably become inadequate. While a valid concern, it can be dealt with by developing programs to educate the marginal performers about what it takes to succeed. These programs, however, also take resources, which are hard to come by and probably will be unlikely to make a return.

A licensing executive in a university is probably going to earn a reasonable salary and perhaps he'll do as well as most of the administration and some of the leading faculty. But he is never going to do as well as a successful entrepreneur would in a non-academic setting, not even close. You have people who work at this for two, three, four or five years. If they're reasonably successful, they're either going to join one of the start-ups or go operate as a senior exec or they're going to get recruited away by some other private sector company. Another likely outcome is that the commercialization manager will work with less energy realizing that the compensation really available to her is working fewer hours.

I think the important thing that happened with ARCH was that it set up a compensation package that gave you a piece of what you created and I think that kept the crew in ARCH for the most part together, for a good six years. And that was something that probably wouldn't have been possible if the ARCH board hadn't chosen such a far sighted structure.

What we achieved with ARCH would not happen in a traditional licensing administration university setting. I don't think you'd have people that are going to work seven days a week, trying to pull companies together, getting them organized, getting them funded, and then handing the problems that arise in the early stage setting unless they're given a significant piece of the upside deal. There are some licensing administration people that will work very hard out of loyalty to the institution regardless of the outcome or reward but that is rare. I don't think it is prudent to count on this special motivation as the primary driver for success. I think it's just counter to everything we know about capitalism to expect people to do their best and hardest work and not get the same upside opportunity that they can see people get in the private for profit sector or, for that matter, what the researchers they are working with have a chance to receive.

If you're an administrative leader at a university and you're trying to figure out how to succeed in technology commercialization, getting the right people and retaining them is critical. And once you get the right people, then I think you have a chance of doing something that might be sustainable.

University sponsored seed venture capital funds also bear comment relating to compensation. A licensing executive told me that today there are about 90 funds of various types that are set up around the U.S. to commercialize technology from universities. By this measure, groups responsible for commercialization at universities clearly believe that some source of funding must be available to bridge the gap between scientific innovation and a commercial product. Most of these funds are called venture funds or some similar title. I believe this is misleading because venture capital funds have limited partners that are interested in financial returns and a general partner that receives a portion of the profit that the fund creates.

The financial structures of these funds have been time tested in the venture capital industry and are used by just about every independent private venture capital partnership. This is the proven incentive structure that allows the most talented managers to be recruited and retained. Most university venture capital funds I'm familiar with lack these two fundamental components. The result is less talented individuals are hired to run the funds and no group is particularly interested in the financial success of the fund. In essence, it becomes one more source of "grant money" for university researchers. Pretending to have venture funds when the funds are not venture capital by most measures is a victimless crime (if you ignore any promises made to the funding sources) in that if the venture fund fails to be profitable the university community still enjoys a significant benefit since it was able to do research with the funds.

PRE-SEED FUNDS

The first venture fund raised by ARCH had financial limited partners and a profit sharing structure for the employees of the general partner.

There are "pre-seed funds" where the strategy is to take an idea for a product and get to a prototype or prove that you can build a certain commercial product and then license the innovation. They're almost product development funds, and some people view that as something that could lead to more licensing revenue. The university "venture fund" basically becomes a proxy for real product development work. The problem with product development work inside a university is that this type of work requires highly specialized knowledge of applications. Universities may be doing okay at that, but it's pretty hard for them to mimic the behavior of a top private sector company, especially when they don't specialize in any particular area in terms of product or market knowledge. What some commercialization efforts forget is that they are competing with the best private sector companies in many cases. The exception might be in the device and pharmaceutical areas where the researchers have a clinical orientation.

Several potential sources of help exist to improve the applications knowledge of the commercialization organization. They can tap into the alumni, which is really important in terms of industry contacts and scientific view point. Graduate students can be used to help with a lot of the legwork and to run down issues such as: Where does the commercial potential lie? It's great to have the experience, to be from the industry. But there's nothing that is a substitute for getting the most recent data. You can have somebody who spent 15 years in an industry and can come up with a general idea of what the application landscape is like, but they won't recognize a breakthrough because they haven't become current on the industry needs. Trust, but verify. When they're starting to architect these commercialization organizations, many universities forget that they have tremendous assets such as the alumni and the board of trustees, and it's important to get such people involved. It does make it messier for an administrator that none of these trustee and alumni helpers can be controlled exactly the way an administration employee could.

If university administrators by themselves had all the skills and vision that was needed to do venture capital, then the world of venture capital would presumably be populated with people from academic, bureaucratic backgrounds. But we don't see that at all. I think the key there is to take advantage of these latent capabilities that the academic institution has and find a way to organize them and get them working together on behalf of university to commercialize the technology. There is a need to match top academics with top commercialization talent to succeed. The incentive structures should enable that match to be made.

One other challenge of university spin-offs is the appropriate operating strategy. I believe this operating strategy needs to be at least as outward facing as it is focused on the innovations developed at the university. An advanced materials company can illustrate the importance of this capability. Suppose you have got a breakthrough platform technology. You have to move the company forward. You are going to need access to capital to begin to build a plant, and to scale up the technology. You need to understand the markets where products are supposedly going to be heading. There are gaps in knowledge and understanding at your university on these topics.

In starting Nanophase Technology Corporation, we understood that technology was developing in parallel; in tandem at multiple institutions all round the world. In that case, we worked with scientists from Germany as well as throughout the United States to capture the best intellectual property position, applications insight, and the most scalable technology. If you don't realize that you're on a much larger technology playing field, then you might tend to do sub-optimized single institution spin-offs instead. Start-ups with a myopic view, with single academic founders, small intellectual property estates, poor knowledge of potential applications, etc. tend to develop into "stovepipe" start-ups. They treat all outsiders as competitors.

BUILD A LEADER COLLABORATIVELY

What is really needed to be successful is to set out to build the leading company in the space, and to be the number one or two or three investment player in order to make money. That means you have to consolidate the intellectual property from other institutions around the world. You have to bring the other leading academics into the company and have a role and incentives for them. You need an outstanding management team with excellent visibility into the applications and great syndicates of venture funds. If all this cannot be accomplished in a lead position, then it is still possible to succeed by combining your efforts with the leaders you have identified.

I think that ARCH Venture Partner's strategy is to do what we do best even better. I think that with $100+ billion a year of government-funded research in the United States, ARCH is still only scratching the surface of the opportunity. We can do a better job of identifying the top academics and developing relationships. We can do a better job of seeing trends on the application side and where technology can influence the application. We can do a better job of using equity capital efficiently with non-equity sources of financing to close technology application gaps. We can partner more effectively with large corporations in some of the applications that are suitable for partnering. And we can do an even better job of making sure that we recruit the best managers for our companies so they can execute.

AT THE UNIVERSITY OF CALIFORNIA

In the last few years we've been working with University of California system. I think that's one of the indications of the direction that we're headed which is to work with the biggest, most well-established groups that have tremendous potential and that are interested in commercialization efficiency. I would say for the last 50 years the U.S. has, more or less, had its own way in terms of leadership scientifically with some exceptions for certain Japanese and European efforts.

One way to think of this future opportunity is once a new company is organized, up and running, syndicated, consolidating intellectual property and headed for the market, execution is absolutely the key in making money for investors. The largest pools of the best technology start up managers, which drive execution, are here in the United States. So far for ARCH Venture Partners, it has meant that our U.S. start-ups may have subsidiaries in other countries, which have dedicated managers that are able to work closely with the US parent. So far we have not been co-founding or making investments in start-ups that are beginning in China or India. Our geographic hybrid model has been working very well.

In the United States the efficiency of commercialization is hindered by the division of research into basic and applied. The notion has been that only applied research can be commercialized. We are realizing that there's plenty of good basic research that applies to commercially important problems. This means that the pool of people that are doing work of interest to ARCH Venture Partners is increasing in the United States. Where in 1988 it was that one out of 100 inventions disclosures a year at a place such as Argonne National Laboratories was a potential start up, in 2006 there might be several times that number of interesting inventions and researchers. Still too few researchers and great innovations, but still a huge increase.

The types of people that are being recruited for commercialization efforts today don't have to necessarily be pioneers such as Steve Lazarus was in 1986. There's a growing body of knowledge and experience on what it takes to succeed doing this stuff. The venture capital community is getting better at it as well. That will create more opportunity. There are fewer underserved geographic areas, but presumably you'd begin to see indications of a saturation point in the number of spinouts and amount of venture financing if we were reaching full capacity. I'm still feeling this is probably a 50-year cycle and we're 20 years into it.

INTELLECTUAL PROPERTY, RESEARCH DOLLARS, LICENSE REVENUES

The richness of the entrepreneurial community and smart seed money on the coasts has allowed commercialization arms to specialize in license transactions, and reap the benefits. Then the question is what about the $75 billion that's spent on research outside of those areas and what are we going to do for those folks? I was thinking about the Bayh-Dole Act the other day. It said that the contract operators of the government labs could take title to the intellectual property developed at the institutions. This legislation was basically saying that universities are going to get these intellectual rights. Universities may have been an obvious choice at the time since they employed the researchers making the innovations. In addition, the federal government was not making progress in commercialization so universities may have been viewed as the best available alternative in their 1980's form.

If you came in from another planet and were designing an entity to commercialize technology would you choose universities to do the most difficult commercialization work in the world? I think the answer is you might not. You might not decide to choose universities based on their administrative skills, lack of successful track record in commercialization, and inability to attract and incentivize industry entrepreneurs in their then current form. The university commercialization structure is still evolving. It has made a lot of progress. It's helped. But I think it really does require a separate structure.

It's not prescriptive that the ARCH model is the answer. What it is, is a bunch of smart people, pushed by events, who chose a structure to accommodate all these different interests, and had a reasonable level of success out of it. ARCH teaches you that if you do it right, you might do it better than what's currently the norm or if you do it right, you can probably have some success with it. It also teaches you that its structure and management is something that has to be evaluated and maintained, repeatedly, in order to continue to reap the benefit. It's not a one-time set and forget exercise.

In the United States we have the technology, the entrepreneurs, smart money and we have access to most of the markets. This process certainly works at a level even though the time to cycle through the process may be quite a bit longer then the current theoretical limit. What needs to happen next is to find a structure that allows the cycling through these processes at a much faster rate with less friction using the university umbrella.

Successful technology entrepreneurs are going back to many countries in Asia and elsewhere. The global reach of markets facilitated by the web, has made it much easier for successful entrepreneurs to access market and technology information. From a global competitiveness standpoint this means that researchers outside the United States are not going to have to take the time to learn every lesson that has been learned in the United States in commercialization in the last twenty years to perform well. Since these foreign countries are setting up commercialization entities for the first time, they are not encumbered by the organizational structures that were designed for other purposes. Another implication of this trend is that the standard for United States-based university commercialization will be even higher in the future, and it will put more pressure on the people that are being selected to do the work. This means that evolving the organizational structure and trying to recruit the best talent becomes even more important.

GLOBALIZATION

India's IIT probably produces the top engineering graduates in the world. There are also eastern European and Russia where the system's broken in a lot of ways, but excellent scientists are coming over here and learning. They may not feel the same way about intellectual property rights as we do right now, but that won't slow their learning. China? The same trend. India has an intact legal system and intellectual property law that's improving. Most of these countries really value the intellectual capital they have and do not want their economies to be only a low cost labor outsource in the long run.

I think our approach to finding opportunities is going to focus on looking closely at innovation in these remote underserved geographic areas. The trend in outsourcing or moving operations to Asia has its effects on our portfolio companies now. For example, in the life sciences area a portfolio company might well consider outsourcing animal trials, or certain medicinal, natural product or synthetic chemistry projects. This will mean more efficient use of the capital for the company. Producing libraries of molecules for less than the $250,000 a year it costs to keep a chemist in a laboratory in the United States makes business sense. I think that is an interest, but we can really take advantage of that opportunity directly from the perspective of a portfolio company. If a portfolio company in the U.S. wants to consider lowering its costs it can outsource and we can offer a network of contacts to assist. As a venture capital group, it is not obvious to me that we need to be located in remote geographies to assist portfolio companies in this activity or organizing or funding the outsourcing companies themselves to make that work. The really interesting opportunity, in my mind, is actually looking at the innovation centers. We spend our time with the top academic minds here. They teach us about the future. We build companies around that. When the conditions develop for us to work this way in other remote geographies we will. Our job now is to really look for those top academics relationships and breakthrough ideas.

What you're going to see is certain centers that come up around those big ideas: the equivalent of a Carver Mead developing VLSI or equivalent technology and spawning a cluster of these related industries. It'll come up around those big idea people, and I think we want to be a part of that.

INTERNATIONAL COMPETITION

Some of my partners made a recent trip to Asia and visited a hospital where they're doing some bone growth research. The researchers there in short order ran the control and the graft of the bone growth material on the same patient, each on a different side of the patient's skull. Then they took a bone biopsy out of his skull. Ultimately, the researchers plan to repair both sides of the patients cleft pallet. My partners related that there are a couple of things you learn from that exercise. One is that the human body has an incredible ability to resist infection. The second thing you realize is that these researchers are going to learn things about bone growth that it's going to take us tens of years to catch up on. I think right now there's a sense in the United States to perhaps discount the innovation work in China, Korea, and some other areas. While saying that this research is not as safe as in the United States is true, it doesn't change the fact that those researchers who are conducting the experiments will learn a lot. This learning will lead to advances, which could result in leadership in certain fields.

Folks in Copenhagen, the U.K, Singapore, and Taiwan are also studying the innovation/commercialization interface really carefully. They all have a slightly different emphasis, but they're serious about trying to improve. Many are just too small and they've got to choose among a half a dozen technology areas where they're really going to be trying to be the centers of excellence in the world. I think the idea of making thoughtful choices is a good one. These efforts also can suffer from the myopic view that every spin-off is going to be just from the local technology only, not somehow combined with others. They, like their economic development brothers, have to get away from the idea that every single start-up is going to have to be physically located within a few miles of their research facility in their country in order to count it as a success.

I think that's probably the biggest misconception that the economic development perspective forces on commercialization. The reasons are simple why a spin-off does not have to be located near where the idea occurred to be a success. First, the best researchers have many good ideas not just one. Second, the researchers that are associated with a commercial success learn from that experience and make better founders in later start-ups. Third, there is a pedigree that is created with the commercial success for the researcher that makes it easier for her to recruit business talent and smart money into future new companies. Business talent and smart money are two important factors that effect location selection of new companies. Finally, the researcher has more power in selecting the location of the new company once he has been successful in the past.

NEW PARADIGMS

On the entrepreneur side, which is a really critical piece of the puzzle, we just have to find a way to choose better high technology business people and get them involved more rapidly in the start-up. And, in a university setting, you can use your alumni network, and people that have special interests in your technology, to make those matches better, and make them in a shorter period of time. You can create an ecosystem of experienced advisors and people who have done start-ups before, and help in sharing their experiences as early in the process as you can. As one looks at markets and applications, the key determinant is knowledge. If there's little or imperfect knowledge of the applications or markets, the technology is going to take longer and cost more to develop, if it develops at all.

The more perfect market and application knowledge, the better off you're going to be, the better that commercialization process is going to be. Twenty years ago scientists, if they didn't like applied research, they sure as hell didn't like doing the market or doing the application research that's involved, and being even comfortable with the topic. That's improved along the way.

I think the money side is an interesting one for the universities. What's the right way to manage funds into these seed situations? Do you do it as grants, where the proposals are peer reviewed by scientists, and then based on scientific merit selection? Do you try to have business people make the choices? Executives from large companies? Do you have venture capitalists do it? Should these funds really be put in as grants or equity, without value added and ownership from people that know what they're doing? How do you really make the funding process work best?

I think those are some of the questions that the ARCH model was focusing on. I think the answer's clear. You want the smartest people you can find that are highly motivated and willing to work a lot of hours focused on that. You want them doing reality market checks monthly, weekly, daily to evolve the new company's plans as they're getting data that shows that the planned action is more attractive or pointless. The problem with grants is you use a single decision point to make an award that works for research projects where the research plans go on for a year or two. And if the premise was wrong in a research proposal, there is still research value in completing the experiments to prove conclusively that a hypothesis was incorrect. The venture capitalist involvement is more invasive, and forces the company to make mid-course corrections if the results aren't promising. So, no need to get six decimals points of certainty and complete a multi-year work plan if an approach clearly is flawed in month three. For the venture backed company a few decimal points of data will do to show that it must make a shift in a more promising direction. This translates into efficient use of capital. Some have called it putting money in with an eyedropper.

I also think that the universities should find a way to formally embed that type of activity and knowledge into the curriculum, and define it as something that they need to develop expertise in. That can be done in a business school setting or through Kaufmann Fellows participation. You see much better entrepreneurial programs developing at the universities these days. I think that's one of the a unforeseen consequences of asking universities to manage commercialization. Technology commercialization is now understood to be a field worth studying and a discipline that's respected.

THE KNOWLEDGABLE LIMITED PARTNER

In order to have a good seed and early stage venture community, you need to have a sophisticated limited partners community. ARCH had good financial limited partners early on and that helped shape the financial outlook of the general partner. These included State Farm Insurance,

The University of Chicago Endowment and two venture capital funds, US Venture Partners and Hayes and Griffith, a local group. The limited partners should be familiar with venture capital and able to recognize value in the partnership team and the portfolio companies. Some limited partners serve on the advisory boards of the funds and, for example, act as market check on the follow-on round reserve schedule and the relative strength of portfolio company syndicates. These are two areas that represent the some of the biggest challenges to new general partners managing a small venture fund. This type of best practice knowledge is difficult to capture other than from experienced venture capitalists or advisory board limited partners.

Limited partners were not easy to find in the first two ARCH funds in the late 1980's. I think in ARCH Fund I, the group pitched over one hundred limited partners over fourteen months before finding four that were interested. ARCH Fund II was not much different, although our yield of limited partner commitments from our solicitations was higher. There is a real challenge for newer venture funds, which most university-based funds are, in seeking limited partners in the $1 million to $5 million range. For the amount of effort the limited partners put into doing due diligence on new fund relationships they could almost do direct investments themselves in companies without the fee and carry. As venture funds grow their limited partner base evolves to include larger sophisticated institutional groups. We recognized that early in the process in part from our relationship with our partnership counsel, Robin Painter, then at Testa Hurwitz and Tibeau.

In Illinois, the Treasurer has set up a fund of funds addressing exactly this point of acting as a good limited partner at the $1 to $5 million level in venture and private equity funds. The Treasurer's fund uses successful private equity investment professionals to serve as advisors to capture their experience to strengthen the funds selected for investment. If there's a community of very good $1 to $5 million limited partners, then we will see very good funds develop that are in the $100 million fund size level. I think that's a piece that's missing from the university commercialization venture capital puzzle that ARCH solved. It's not the dollar sign exactly. It's the finding of good limited partners behind the dollar. The motivations and experience of that limited partner matter.

During the four years I spent working in a large chemical company I learned a bunch about the chemical business. Some of those lessons were useful, some of them weren't useful. Not many lessons applied to Illinois Superconductor Corporation, the very first company I worked on that ARCH founded out of Argonne National Laboratory. I worked on ISCO because I had faith in Steve Lazarus and it promised to be interesting work with interesting people. I had no idea what that might entail, but I knew we were serious about starting companies so we needed one to work on. I asked myself about what we had at Argonne that held promise. The superconductor portfolio looked pretty substantial. I thought in terms of comparable opportunities and what I could manage in terms of product development. Superconductors were it. I worked hard to identify applications, organized a lab, made a few hires, raised some capital, wrote some grant proposals and built a sensor that was the first commercial product for the new materials to make it to market. Fortunately for everyone, it worked out and went public. I thought that was pretty good. In hindsight, the real inflection point is to bring in the top Chief Executive Officer early, who can help take company to the next level.

With Eichrom, Qmax and Nanophase and others the same type of process was happening. We were working like a mini-entrepreneur team for 12 months at a time. If you're 27 years old, you may be a great guy, you may hold great promise, but this only works if you have an experienced set of advisors and recruit the real chief executive officer quickly. If that doesn't happen for an extended period then the mini-entrepreneur education is, in effect, costing hundreds of thousands of dollars of other peoples' money. That's not to say that younger technical MBA types can't play a role, they absolutely can, but you can't have them running things alone for long. You need to have somebody who's really done it before in that driver's seat.

When it was Clint, Bob, Keith and Steve at ARCH, we met with each other all the time and we knew how we were doing at finding interesting things to start companies around. I think for a long time we thought that just being the finders was good enough. Hey, if we knew a bunch of interesting people and they were really great, we could roll something up and we'd hand it off to other people that were syndication partners and they'd take it the next length of time. Eventually, there might be a liquidity event.

We made a deliberate attempt to continue to build our organization and hone our model since we left the University of Chicago. Today, we're not leaving as much to chance. We are still among the very best finders and organizers of new companies from university research in this country. We have long standing relationships with executives that have solid operations experience to serve as directors. We have very good co-investors to complement us in syndicates. We have great venture partners with successful entrepreneurial experience. We are working with great CEO's that we have backed previously. We think about our financial exit. We know the investment banking community and the micro cap public managers. We know the trade sale buyers. We have sophisticated limited partners and advisory board members. We have track record. We have tried to give ourselves every advantage.

"TRYING TO UNDERSTAND HOW TO BEST EXPLOIT THE GLOBAL NATURE OF TECHNOLOGY DEVELOPMENT"

CLINT BYBEE

Clint Bybee has helped organize a number of companies including MicroOptical Devices, Cambrios Technologies, InnovaLight, Aveso Displays, Xtera Communications, and Intelligent Reasoning Systems. He holds an M.B.A. from The University of Chicago and a B.S. in Engineering from Texas A&M University.

I got involved with ARCH when it was still ARCH Development Corporation and I was at the University of Chicago. I was a volunteer with the Development Corporation when I was in Business School in the fall of 1988. I wound up looking at things in chemistry and advanced materials and then I worked with ARCH that summer between the two years of business school, spending most of my time at Argonne. I worked on materials with a company there called Illinois Semiconductor.

I left the University early, before I graduated, to take a full-time job at the State of Illinois, which had a small venture capital fund focusing on early stage companies in Illinois. I worked there for about two years and invested in a number of ARCH companies. I stayed in very close contact with the ARCH group which I subsequently rejoined. With ARCH, I spent a fair amount of time working in national labs, Sandia, Albuquerque, and Los Alamos.

RUNNING IN CYCLES

Research organizations tend to go through cycles of interest in technology transfer. These are driven largely by the funding environment. Indeed, most labs and lab management don't view technology commercialization as core to their strategy.

When the funding is good, as it is now at Sandia and Los Alamos, it's really hard. They've got only minimum criteria they must provide to satisfy Congress in terms of technology licensing. Even in bad times, when they care, they don't hire the proactive people. They have smart people that are good at answering the phone. They don't have the capability in-house to do the analysis and connect the dots allowing a certain capability. If combined with another capability at another research place, it would address something very interesting in this market opportunity. They have zero ability to do that, which is where they really need outside help. In my opinion, they don't and never will have that ability, and for most universities, I think it's the same way.

SETTING UP ARCH INDEPENDENT OF THE UNIVERSITY

ARCH Development Corp. was unique in that it was set up as a separate entity, with a separate board, which enabled the company to hire Steve on a salary commensurate with his business experience - a salary that had no correlation to a university faculty salary structure. The salary issue is a problem most universities have. I think it's hard for universities to internally put together capabilities that are proactive and bring together market insights. It's hard work and they have good, honest workers, but the workers go home at five and do something else. That's not the lifestyle of the start-up company.

Before we go spend a ton of money, we think about what the risks are and how to systematically reduce and eliminate the fundamental risks to validate the idea that there is a big business in the future. Sometimes this involves jumping in, as acting CEO, to pull together technology and the initial people. Get the momentum going, and organize the financing incentive kit. Whatever the initial kind of activation energy barrier is, move beyond it and move forward to the point where you can answer the question, "Can this be a company worth a decent amount of money in the long-term?"

The transaction costs for developing these companies is high. By the time it takes to negotiate a license, pull the initial thinking together, and create the initial theme, it can translate into very high transaction costs. It's easier to wait until that piece of the process is complete and that's why not a lot of people do it.

HITTING THE ROAD TO NEW MEXICO

We got to Albuquerque because of Steve's relationship with the CEO of a company called BDM International. BDM was acquired by TRW in 1997. BDM was a beltway bandit type company, and a pretty big presence in Albuquerque. A big portion of their business was Sandia

National Labs. BDM was one of the companies that made a fair amount of progress towards bidding on the operation of Sandia after AT&T announced that it no longer would. As part of that bid for Sandia and other things BDM was engaged in, it needed a tech commercialization story of its own. In the mid '90s, any time you bid on a DOE or DOD contract, you had to have a dual use tech transfer story.

BDM had tried to roll out its own tech commercialization capability several times, and it hadn't worked. The idea was to team up with ARCH, because these guys seem to know what they're doing. That's how the Albuquerque idea came to be. There were scientists out of the University of California looking at other areas, and that seemed like an interesting idea to us, because between Sandia and Los Alamos and parts of UNM, there's $2 to $3 billion a year of federally funded research that gets metered through there. Maybe twice that if you consider black (secret) programs. The hypothesis was something of commercial value ought to come out of that funding, especially given Sandia's engineering research focus on electronics and semiconductors.

So that's how the Albuquerque piece started. As that got off the ground, my major focus was getting to know the bright thinkers and scientists at Sandia. About six months into that exercise, we found this group in the compound semiconductor research area on what I call vertical cavity surface emitting lasers (small semiconductor lasers). The group at Sandia had taken the technology to the point where it looked like it could be manufactured. We worked with two of the scientists there to start a company with an initial goal of trying to find the big market application.

We were able to leverage the infrastructure at Sandia, and we got help whenever we're able to. We try to leverage existing infrastructure, particularly capital equipment, at a university or a lab, moving down this risk pathway. We made initial devices at Sandia and got them to a number of potential customers. We needed to put some money in and we put in a small amount - a couple of hundred thousand dollars. The goal was to prove that there was a commercial opportunity. We wound up getting a partnership deal done with a company called Symbol Technologies that was working on a scanner on a ring. They needed a small, low power laser device that could modulate at high speeds, and ours was a perfect fit. As we began working on that partnership, Ethernet fell in our lap. The laser devices were the enablers for optical gig-E and 10 gig-E. By the end of the first year, we had a partnership with Symbol, and by the end of the second year, it was clear that this was really doable. Then, before the third year, we sold the company.

AUSTIN AND ALBUQUERQUE

I moved to Austin once the Albuquerque project was finished. Austin's got major research capabilities. The University of Texas alone has a research budget of probably $450 million a year. Just down the road is Texas A&M with an even larger annual research budget. In Austin, there's a good high tech entrepreneurial infrastructure in software and semiconductor. In Dallas, there's communications. So the real drive behind the move to Austin was that there's more management talent to pull into these companies and just the sort of existing infrastructure with which to build companies. As we grew as a fund, I found the availability of management talent was critically important in helping grow companies. It's hard to take a year to work on only one company, which is what I did in my laser devices.

We worked the laser devices out of a $31 million fund. We now manage a $350 million fund. One of the things we learned in spades over 18 to 20 years is that the sooner you can get professional managers into these companies, the better. Their involvement makes perfect sense because they catalyze the process. Every instinct has to be to get professional managers in these companies quickly. That was hard to do in Albuquerque, because there aren't many non-employed managers floating around looking for the next gig.

We tried an alternative approach which made better sense in Albuquerque. We had a part-time guy in Albuquerque, an entrepreneur in residence. He worked with us to evaluate opportunities, but we were also working with him on things at Sandia, Los Alamos, and in New Mexico with the idea that if we found something that was backable, we would back him as CEO. So in Albuquerque we started the process with a CEO in mind and then tried to find an opportunity to back him in.

Our entrepreneur-in-residence has now moved out to Southern California, and still works for us part-time, but he is now managing a division of a public company. We wound up not finding something to work on with him in a company while he was in Albuquerque. When you have a limited management pool, as in Albuquerque, I think that's a better way to address a market. You can solve that problem by starting with the manager you want to back and go help him find something.

New Mexico has two exceedingly well-funded DOE labs, and so there are a lot of really smart people around. And there are various entities, including the Governor, who are out there saying, "We want to help make things happen here." The governor has put a lot of money into them. On the flip side, another way to look at it is as building a technology infrastructure that's a long-term proposition. Austin clearly has more projects, and we have a little bit more bandwidth to work on this stuff, but I'm still working on things around the country.

By our second year, we were pulling together a company out of the University of Texas. We formed the company with a professor and licensed the technology from UT. We began by addressing a specific set of milestones with the core initial team, and expanding the team. At the time, he was actually still the acting CEO of the company, he's planning to rotate off by the fall of this year. It's another example where, given the technical risks and a key set of milestones, the idea is to reduce or eliminate risk to the point where we know what type of CEO to get from which industry, and also we have accomplished enough within the company so we can go find the right one.

We founded another company out of UT in mid-stride called Cambrios. The professor was a woman named Angela Belcher, who got recruited by MIT and went to Cambridge. So we started a company in Cambridge, and I was the initial CEO of that company which included Angela and her collaborator, Evelyn Hu, who is a professor at U.C. Santa Barbara, where Angie did her post-doc. I became the de facto person to pull things together. So I worked with the company, helped get it organized, get licensed, get a lease, and a place for some lab space in Cambridge with initial hires onboard. After consolidation of intellectual property, we hired a permanent CEO. Subsequently, we made the decision to move the company out to California which is where it is now. It took all of eight months.

Cambrios is physically in Mountain View now. It has just completed a $12 million financing round that included ARCH, Allied, Oxford, and a few others. It has a pretty good syndicate in place. It has a team in place that's now executing on key technical and product development milestones. It's not selling a product, and it won't be for some time. The 10 -year development goal is to put together more significant corporate partnership deals that can really help it.

In terms of the future, we're seeing more corporations try to extend technologies out. That's a good trend. I think there's interest at various levels in the corporation to figure out how they can capitalize on this development. There's also an international aspect to all of this research. It's not just one researcher at one university that's got all the pieces for a start-up company, it's that plus that person's peers and competitors at other great universities all around the globe.

If you can figure out a way to get these scientists to work together as co-founders and license technology from more than one institution, you often have a bigger base upon which to maneuver and to figure out the set of applications that are going to matter in the marketplace. It's hard going into these raw technologies to establish a priority - what the right application is - and have that sit with what the technology's really going to be able to do. Sometimes a lot of the physics rubs against you. It may mean you don't have an application and can't do what you were thinking about (consumer application), but maybe you have something that's an industrial application. So what does that mean and how does that company work? I think the broader the technology platform you've got, the more maneuverability the company needs to probe the application and exploration piece of the product. That constitutes product validation, but it's also market probing, asking "Where is this really going to have the big hit?"

GLOBALISM AND GLOBAL TECHNOLOGY

There's an international component to that validation and probing aspect. There are researchers in Europe and in Asia who may have an application. In this sense, I think the world is getting smaller. One of the trends we're seeing is where they conduct the technology research in Israel, while recognizing that half of the market is initially through the U.S. Then the Israelis form teams in the U.S. that do the management, the marketing, and the product distribution. Meanwhile, a lot of the research still continues over in Israel.

You'll also see that happening in Europe, particularly in Germany and other places where there's no strong culture of entrepreneurship, but still some very important research going on at some of their academic institutions. Part of the future is that we can't just look at the U.S. and assume it's where the best kind of globally positioned company can win in a particular area. We have to consider working in other places, and that includes China and India and probably other places as well.

At ARCH we're trying to understand how to best exploit the global nature of technology development. We've got a guy that works with us part-time, who's helping us to systematically understand as best we can what's going on in China, and at the Chinese National Academy of Sciences. We're trying to get plugged into relationships with the set of contacts that we think are going to be important over there. It doesn't mean that we have any interest in doing a start-up in China. We believe we've got to get started now, to understand those researchers and build those relationships because that's the future. But I wouldn't say we have all the answers. I don't think we're prepared at this point, to do what some of the funds have done, which is to do an ARCH India Fund or an ARCH China Fund, or an ARCH Europe Fund. The major reason for that is because technology transfer is hard to do even when it's close by.

"AT ARCH WE USE A SYSTEMATIC APPROACH THAT LOOKS FOR TRULY FUNDAMENTAL INNOVATION"

BOB NELSEN

Robert Nelsen joined ARCH at its founding and has played a significant role in the early sourcing, financing and development of more than thirty companies, including, Ikaria, Adolor, Aviron, Caliper Life Sciences, Illumina, Trubion Pharmaceuticals, Array Biopharma, NetBot, deCode Genetics, Nanosys, Alnylam Pharmaceuticals, Xenoport, GenVec, R2 Technology, IDUN Pharmaceuticals, Genomica, Surface Logix, NeurogesX, Classmates.com, Optobionics, Elixir Pharmaceuticals, and Everyday Learning Corporation, among others. He holds an M.B.A. from the University of Chicago, and a B.S. in Biology and Economics from The University of Puget Sound.

I started my first business when I was seven selling gerbils. My second business was selling blackberries in a fruit stand when I was nine. I started trading stocks when I was eleven and started several other businesses in college. So I had the entrepreneurial urge from an early stage.

I found out about ARCH from an article in *The Wall Street Journal* when Steve Lazarus joined and the *Journal* reporter described Steve's job as the ultimate job: starting companies. So I wandered into the ARCH office and, in my first year of business school, volunteered to help start companies, whatever that meant. I started working, got a desk, and essentially got a hunting license to go talk to university professors to see if they had cool technologies which could be turned into companies. I did that for a while and Keith Crandell showed up and we began doing some parallel work at Argonne and University of Chicago, although Keith's first company was out of the University of Chicago. In a what seemed at the time to be a moronic economic move I turned down all offers of high paying jobs on Wall Street and decided to work for $1200 a month for ARCH (I even set my own salary). I was 23, and turning down $80,000 a year. Basically everyone except one person told me that what I was doing was a bad idea. Everyone except a physician and friend named David LaGasse who had made a lot of money in his own account said, "Do what you like and it will pay off." It was good advice and it did pay off and in my fourth or fifth year I made more money from Everyday Learning than the president of the University of Chicago made in a year.

Our hunting license was useful because we got entree to some of the best scientists in the world, guys like Graeme Bell. Out of that candy store that had never been mined we started a lot of companies and a lot with free labor - using business school students with a technical background , many of whom are now running companies. They volunteered their effort and that volunteer spirit still happens at ARCH. We rarely have paid consultants. We think if the technology is cool enough people should work on it for free and get their rewards later - even if they already have a Nobel Prize. That's a philosophy we adopted early to test how innovative things are. If the ideas are not innovative enough to attract smart people to them then maybe we shouldn't be working on them or spending time on them.

But we did find folks like Sheila Sconiers, Paul Sally, and Max Bell, who created Everyday Learning. Brilliant and prolific scientists like Bernard Roizman who I worked with for months to try to assemble the elements of a molecular virology company, well before we helped pull together some of the same core technology to enable Leighton Read to put the technology foundation underneath what became Aviron. True geniuses like Graeme Bell helped to create Adolor. Kunio Doi's wild (at the time) vision to use "computer aided diagnosis" created R2 Technology which was the first spellchecker for mammograms, and is now the standard of care for breast imaging. We also built companies like Nioptics (Roland Winston), and GenVec (Ralph Weichselbaum, Don Kufe, and Vikas Sukhatme). And that allowed ARCH to found or be an early investor in IDUN, Caliper, Illumina, Array, deCode, Nanosys, Xenoport, Alnylam, Trubion and many others later.

Meanwhile Keith was starting some of the first high value advanced materials companies including one of the first superconductor companies, Illinois Superconductor, and the first nanotech company - Nanophase Technolgies. It was really an exciting time when we had free rein to do what we wanted and we basically had no experience and made lots of mistakes. But the Steve Lazarus philosophy was pretty much to give us as much rope as we needed so we basically ran with it. Out of that came a methodology for finding the leaders in science, in various disciplines, developing some methodologies for finding the good stuff and testing those hypotheses.

We do the Tom Sawyer thing a lot. We find something interesting, show it to a few people, have them work on it for free because it's really cool and then show it to a few more people to gather momentum. Once we have the sense that it's something real, we do the real technology push. We establish the milestones, reduce the technology risks - eyedropper the money and then go about reducing the other risks and really focusing on the commercial goals of the company.

What we do at ARCH is use a systematic approach that looks for what I would call truly fundamental innovation. To me, that means discoveries or even conglomerations of inventions that are disruptive to markets and industrial segments.

A lot of people invent things that the average scientist or businessperson cannot even contemplate happening in their lifetime. That's the one kind of deal that we like to do. Someone invents something that people thought was impossible, but you always knew was valuable - a cure for cancer, a new arthritis drug, viruses that make semiconductors, or suspended animation. Once you tell them what the new technology can do, at first they do not believe you, then they may think about it for a week and are still skeptical because they never even imagined you could do that. Eventually they are converted and want to help you paint the fence, or invest money, or whatever you want.

EARLY BIRDS

How do you find such projects? In the early days, I found them by hanging out in Chicago and then following the key technologies - like NiOptics, Aviron, or Everyday Learning. Or we found them by dealing with professors at the university, often through other professors elsewhere, at Penn or UCLA. We began to kind of wrap up a series of technologies. With Caliper, I had a relationship with the co-founder, Larry Bock, because he had come by the University of Chicago looking for technology and we assisted him and Mike Knapp in really pulling together technology from numerous universities. We were the early believers and saw other applications of the industry creating potential. One of the things that ARCH is better at, that distinguishes us from other folks, is the ability to fuse disparate technologies and to identify the disruptive ones earlier.

Institutions now know that ARCH is different and more interested in early stage technologies. We used to hear about things earlier, but usually we were hearing about science, not necessarily about companies. Often it was just "Here's an interesting guy you should meet." And most people would say, "Wow, that's too wacky." We spent three years looking at that technology like suspended animation and then turned it into something really special which will change healthcare as we know it.

If it's something like Impinj , it's because I knew Ed Lazowska, the head of computer science at the University of Washington, I asked him who is the smartest guy in the department and he said, "There's this cool guy Chris Diorio you guys should meet." And Sung-Wei Chen followed up and we had lunch with him almost a year before the company was created and he was an amazing guy with some wild ideas about semiconductors. He was doing something completely different and revolutionary and I had no deep understanding of it, but I knew enough to be excited and to know he was different. But for most VCs it would have ended there and his ideas were just too early and wild for anybody to follow up. But at ARCH we have always learned over and over again to keep an open mind and to go with our gut if we think we smell a revolutionary idea or find an innovative person. This is one of those times where I had a gut feeling so I hit it over to Clint Bybee and Patrick Ennis and they chased it down and eventually Patrick ran with it and helped to build Impinj.

One of the things we have learned is that there really are two ways to approach innovation. One approach was to take 80 people and do it, and another approach is to take two or three or five creative individuals. Many times the two or three or five or ten approach wins. In biotech we've tended to back innovations with smaller creative groups and they've tended to produce bigger impact and be more profitable than conventional biotech investments. We have companies like Caliper, Trubion, Ensemble, Ikaria, Illumina, and Cambrios that are just fundamental new approaches to working on genomics or chemistry or critical care and they're doing things people didn't think they'd be doing for a hundred years. Some of them seem like science fiction when they start and almost everybody thinks we are crazy when we start these things. Eighteen months or two years later they are calling us and begging to get into the deal.

PLATFORMS

The other thing that differentiates us is that we are making money on platforms. We're not betting on single verticals usually, it's mostly platforms. That means there's a core of technology or a fundamental technology base somewhere that, in almost every case, has multiple applications. Many times the answer is not a given regarding what the winner will be, or what the killer application is. We need to believe that there's enough fundamental promise in the technology that we will find the killer application with the management team, or look for a series of applications that describe the company without a single home-run.

You have to be a little bit weird to do what we do. You can't be a conventional thinker and think about things that are unconventional. If you behave like everybody else, then none of these things will ever get done. You have to be patient with the innovators and you have to be able to speak the language of the scientist. But to some extent, the worst thing you can do in these early technology fields is think too much, or perform too much due diligence. One of the reasons other people can't replicate what we do is because they can't see the forest through the trees. I can't tell you how many good funds turned down Caliper, Illumina, Trubion, Ikaria, and Adolor - some of which have some of the highest cash on cash returns from the seed investment to distribution in biotech history.

Most venture capitalists absolutely cannot see it that way, and they get involved in trying to avoid risk - focusing too much on the killer applications and not enough on how revolutionary the platform is. Eventually you might have to have a killer app but it might take one or two years. All of these things, even a perfect start-up, is just a set of difficult possibilities that, if one or two things go wrong, you're dead. If you have a single product company - we call them "Sand Hill Road" deals - with one single killer app, if one thing goes wrong, you're dead. In a broad-based technology, there's uncertainty in all directions but you have a portfolio of applications to balance the risks. Almost certainly the ultimate company-making killer app will not be the one you thought it would be when you started the company, but you can survive because you have had the ability within the multiple applications inside the company to have the killer app. The interesting result of all this is that if you asked the average venture capitalist if ARCH's deals are risky they'd say they're way more risky than "Sand Hill Road" deals - than the single application killer app focused deals. But they are wrong- our platforms, core technology companies, have a single digit write-off rate. We have the lowest write off rate and the highest cash on cash results in the same companies. Companies like Nanosys, Trubion or Caliper rarely fail financially.

When I was looking at Ikaria, the suspended animation project, a fundamentally different way of looking at biology, there was no single target and no pharmaceutical paradigm. Nobody from traditional pharma will get it easily. The best way to think about it is to go back and look at *The Scientific American* of 50 years ago, and you realize that many of the things we think now are completely wrong - the dogma of how things work today, will look extremely silly 50 years from today.

You have to be able to understand that our current societal knowledge is small. We don't know much - and that the state of knowledge is always progressing at some exponential rate. Things that people never think will ever happen probably can happen. Then you have to figure out how to actually get those crazy ideas into a realistic form and how to put together the team that takes the crazy stuff and makes it real. To some degree, it is more art than science.

"BOB NELSEN WOULD CALL ME EVERY NIGHT"

JO ANNE SCHILLER

Talks About EVERYDAY LEARNING and ARCH

University of Chicago professor Max Bell had a contrarian belief in how students, especially the younger ones, learned mathematics. He created a complete K-6 curriculum around that belief. Bell believed that children came to school knowing much more than we gave them credit for, and so instead of really expanding their learning, we "dumbed them down." And he was working one grade at a time and testing each grade in schools for a full year after it was written and revised to see how far kids could go; in addition to this being a whole new kind of math, that made it more relevant to children. So each year as he finished the field test, he would push the teachers to go as far as they could with the kids, and then that would determine where they started the next year.

The concept, highly effective in a research environment, simply did not seem to have commercial appeal. Core programs for the elementary classroom are not usually developed with such a philosophy. Multiple-grade programs are all designed and published simultaneously in order to meet intensive and lengthy adoption procedures before they can be purchased by a school system. Bell's program stayed within a research environment, highly lauded and embraced by a handful of forward-thinking school districts until ARCH brought it into the classrooms nationally through Everyday Learning.

Jo Anne Schiller, founder of Everyday Learning, the start-up that helped commercialize and market Max Bell's mathematics program, talks about Everyday Learning and ARCH.

Schiller's narrative points out the significance of the technology transfer process. It's not the capital alone. In fact, the capital infused by ARCH into Everyday Learning was nominal by today's standards. However, it was the ability of Bob Nelsen to identify the project and ARCH's success in recruiting just the right person for the job – a veteran publishing executive who also was entrepreneurial – and shepherding the company through various stages of development including the sale to the Tribune Co. that made the project financially viable. Make the connections, ARCH says ... but its strength is in making the right connections, not in taking over the running of a company. Although, in a number of circumstances that too needs to be done.

I had lost my job through a merger in 1988, so I was out looking for work. It was really a question of whether I become an entrepreneur or do I take another job? The University of Chicago School Math Project (UCSMP) was one of many things that came across my desk. ARCH hired a head hunter to find a CEO for the company, and they contacted me through a colleague. I was interested.

I always wanted to be my own boss, and run my own company. So I went out and looked at some of the field test sites, talked with some of the teachers. In Evanston (Illinois) the math director had been a student of Max Bell and she was field testing the product in three different schools. I talked to the math coordinator at Glenview school district, and these are all forward-thinking school districts up here on the north shore. I also talked to a couple of other teachers that were testing the program and sat through their classes, and I was pretty impressed. They all felt very strongly that someone should publish the curriculum, because it was really very good material.

I'm not an educator, I'm a business person who happens to be in education. So I relied on teachers and other educators I knew to look at the material. I got samples and sent them out to people to look at. At the same time, I recognized that it was a risky venture. Not only would we have to sell a new teaching concept, we would also have to change school district buying habits. And funding-wise, Arch didn't offer a lot of money to get started with, but I was also in a situation where I didn't have a lot to lose. ARCH guaranteed me one year's salary, and how much I got depended upon how much equity I wanted. I could take a lower salary and more equity. I went for the equity and we got started.

April is when the big math convention happens and that year it was in Florida. I went down there and the University of Chicago School Math Project had a little booth on a side aisle with all the elementary material. We were in a very unique environment at that time. A lot of things came together that also made everything more possible. First, Scott Foresman had already agreed to publish the secondary portion of the program, but they wanted nothing to do with the elementary portion, because it was coming out one grade at a time, and they also knew it would be very hard to sell. High school material could come out a book at a time. You buy an algebra book, you buy a geometry book, and you don't necessarily buy them from the same publisher.

What did we have going for us? We had the University of Chicago, and we had the math program. We also had Scott Foresman getting ready to launch the UCSMP secondary program. At that convention in Orlando, Scott had a big booth with a baby grand piano, and they had all their sales reps in tuxedos. And they were promoting the heck out of the UCSMP acronym. We were a couple of aisles away, but we also had a University of Chicago School Math Project banner hung up. People were looking for "Chicago Math" so they would come looking and some would find us and we would talk to them. The existence of Everyday Learning hadn't been announced yet, but the UCSMP acronym had become very well known. We had the right to it just as well as Scott Foresman did, and we started to use it in everything we did. It gave us an identity.

We were also in an environment in the United States in the 1980's when everybody was worrying about how poorly our kids did in math and science. Amoco had given the University a grant to start the UCSMP project because they couldn't find scientists they needed, because kids weren't taking math and going into sciences in high school and college. The entire country worried about this. There was a plethora of publications and white papers: "A Nation at Risk" (Dept of Education 1983), "The Mathematics Report Card: Are We Measuring Up?" (Educational Testing Service 1988), "Everybody Counts: A Report Card to the Nation on the Future of Mathematics" (National Research Council 1989). It was a national crisis. U.S. students weren't measuring up to foreign students in our colleges.

At the same time, the National Council of Teachers of Mathematics (NCTM) had been working for several years on a set of mathematics standards. NCTM had pulled together leading educators, mathematicians and teachers to put together a set of standards on what kids should learn in mathematics in elementary school and in high school.

Those standards were about to be published that April when I was at the NCTM convention. Max Bell had contributed a lot to those standards. So his math program and his thinking were right on, which helped us an awful lot. A lot of stars were lining up at that time – Amoco & the UCSMP project, NCTM math standards, ARCH was just getting started, and the educational environment all contributed to making it the right time to publish a different kind of mathematics program.

ARCH gave us $250,000 with an option for an additional $150,000 without dilution. I can laugh now because I told them I needed $1 million to get started. But, we never went back for that $150,000 because I was very protective of the cash we had. Out of the $250,000, they immediately took $80,000 away from us because they had incurred some expenses with a false start trying to do something jointly with the Chicago public school system that didn't work out. I was left with $170,000. I got $50,000 from the Evanston Business Investment Corporation - if I put my office in Evanston. So I had $220,000, which wasn't very much, especially when you considered that most publishers put upward of $50 million into the development of their math program.

We negotiated a contract – ARCH, the University of Chicago, the authors (Max and Jean Bell), and Everyday Learning. I mention this because Max was skeptical that we would be able to accomplish commercialization of the curriculum. At the signing, he quipped, "It's not too late to change your mind." I asked for his commitment to at least complete the curriculum through third grade.

We started off very poor, but we had a few customers and we had a product, and we did start to get revenue right away. There were ten field test sites, and they were testing the first grade program. The kindergarten program was already published and we had a teacher development package. So the first year, we had $100,000 in revenue, and in the second year, with 1st grade out, we brought in $500,000, and then we started to double every year. We broke even in the second year. After that, we supported ourselves totally on our revenue. ARCH did one other important thing for us. Since we didn't go back for the other $150,000, they provided me with a guarantee on my bank note when it exceeded our assets. Because we were so seasonal - 80 percent of school orders come in during May through August - we had a real cash flow crunch as we built up inventory in the spring until we were paid late fall. The fact that we were doubling revenue every year only made the problem more severe. The guarantee was more important than the second round funding.

More than anything else, ARCH provided us with a start-up structure. When you work for a large corporation, you don't worry about cash flow. You learn about managing P&L's because every division and every product has its P&L, but you don't worry about cash flow, and you don't develop banking relationships, that's the treasurer's job. ARCH also provided legal support with a lawyer who worked with all of their companies, and he was very reasonable and available. He would guide us through the incorporation, patents and copyrights and all the different things that start-ups worry about. Steve Lazarus joined me on our first visit to the bank. ARCH had been working with what was then NBD, which I guess is now part of J. P. Morgan, and had established credibility in their mission. I would present what Everyday Learning was all about and they knew ARCH was behind us, so we were more than just a little company that was hanging out.

I would sit down with the bank once a month and go through all of my financials in excruciating detail, which was actually an interesting experience for me. We usually met our goals. We always had a good story to tell and developed a lot of credibility with the bank. I handled most of the financials myself and brought in a retired accountant a day or two each month to check everything out.

Bob Nelsen would call me almost every night and sometimes we'd talk 'till midnight. He was always low key and chatty. He kept track and he asked a lot of questions and was there for me. I knew my business and ARCH didn't interfere. We had board meetings every other month. I was the third company in ARCH's initial fund. So the whole experience was almost as new to them as it was to me. And we were all having fun. The first couple of times I hired people, I would invite them to interview too, and they wanted to, which was fine with me.

As an investor ARCH was willing to look at a ten-year time frame if need be. I guess that's a long time for a VC group. They were always looking at exit opportunities, a buyer, or in some cases, a publisher that would distribute the product as it became available. So every time they followed a lead, I would make presentations. I guess this bothered me a little bit because I really wanted to put my arms around this company and make it mine, which I did. Our early materials were pretty basic – one color, no frills. I think they looked at this simple little Kindergarten program and saw the rest of the curriculum being published a half-grade at a time and wondered, but I'd go along with the flow, and who knew where it would go? It all worked out fine.

My biggest concern was sales. This product had to be sold with personal sales calls. How do I put together a sales organization with this kind of money? I'm at the Orlando convention musing over this question when I run into an old friend from SRA, which is where I'd spent most of my career, and Al said to me, "You need Tom Wise." And he was right! Tom Wise was just the right person. Tom, along with several other sales and marketing employees, had taken advantage of an early retirement program at SRA/IBM two years earlier. He was living out in Bozeman Montana, and was doing some freelance work for SRA, and they would send him up to Alaska with his bedroll a couple of times a year to make sales calls. But basically, Tom was bored.

I asked him to take a look at the material - he had a good curriculum background. He'd been a salesman and a regional manager for SRA. He looked at what I sent and he said, "This is good stuff. I want to be part of this." I said, "Well, I'd like you to." Because he was way out there in Montana, I thought "Western Sales Manager?" He said, "No, I want to be part of this in Chicago." I didn't have money to move him to Chicago. He said, "No problem. I'll get there." His wife had never been to Chicago. He was 62 at the time and he comes by himself, looks around, and finds temporary board in an old monastery where all he has is a bed. So Tom joins me to do sales and marketing. A couple of months later, his wife comes, and he and his son-in-law drive a U-haul to Chicago with all his stuff.

After retiring, Tom had started a newsletter and kept track of all the retired SRAers, and he knew where every one of the sales people were and what they were doing. Many were working as independent sales reps in the same territories they had covered for 20-30 years. So our first sales organization was made up of retired sales reps. They knew the territory. They knew the customers. They started on a run. It was a win/win situation. They had pensions and benefits and they carried other lines, which took them into the same buildings and to the educators we had to call on. It was risk-free for them. They worked on a straight commission and could handle the seasonal cash flow; and it solved our cash-flow problem. Nothing was paid out until someone sold something. It was a first in the industry - independent reps selling a core curriculum. It was so successful that most of those original reps are still selling the curriculum today for McGraw-Hill.

Recently, I had dinner with one of the sales reps. He and his partner worked New York City and Connecticut together and they had $27 million in sales during 2004, and they get roughly ten percent of that. This year (2005) they did another $21 million in sales. He said, "Never in my greatest dreams could I have imagined something like this happening." And I asked him, "Ray, what was it? We gave you a kindergarten program. We made you buy your own samples. We brought you in for a sales meeting to train you, but beyond that, you had to pay all your own expenses. You already were a successful rep. Why did you stick it out through those early, hard years? Why did you even accept this as one of your product lines?"

He said, "Well, I worried about it." But he talked to a friend of his who was the Superintendent of Education for Connecticut and a math author for one of the big publishing houses, and he said, "I've been watching what they're doing there at the University of Chicago. It's good stuff. Take the risk. It'll be worthwhile." And he did and he became one of our top salesmen.

Everything was going well. Max and Jean completed 2nd & 3rd grade over the next three years. They had added another writer to the author team. We were becoming a force to be dealt with in the market place. We had expanded our field test sites and had a great customer following. And we decided to go after an NSF grant to complete grades 4-6. NSF was now requiring all grantees to have commitments from publishers to be sure funded material would be distributed to the educational community. We were pretty confident our grant proposal would be funded.

But we had had a rough summer getting material to schools on time out of the make-shift warehouse we had. One of the panelists was from a school district where we delivered late and we almost lost the grant. We had already signed a contract with a professional warehousing group downstate. So we flew into Washington and presented our plans to the National Science Foundation. They approved the grant and the authors received $5 million to complete grades 4-6.

We were just getting started on 5th grade when Steve Lazarus and Charlie Brumbach, then CEO of Tribune, found themselves on the same corporate board and Steve learned of Tribune's interest in educational publishing. They had already made a couple of acquisitions and were in a buying mode. We talked to them several times over the next few months. It looked like it would be a pretty good deal for everyone. First of all, they wanted the whole company intact. Tribune didn't know the educational publishing business and were acquiring our management expertise as much as the product line. They had recently acquired The Wright Group, a reading company in Seattle, where they'd done the same thing. So it looked very attractive to me, and we continued to grow the company under Tribune. It was never the negative experience that acquisitions often turn out to be. We completed the curriculum, and Tribune invested in a second edition. During the five years we were part of Tribune we expanded our math line through high school and we added a K-12 health curriculum.

In 2000, Tribune sold all their educational companies, including Everyday Learning to McGraw Hill. They combined the Wright Group and Everyday Learning elementary materials under The Wright Group name, which is where it is today. But they retained the independent reps and the key operations management. They are now working on a third edition. And, in an interesting turn of events, they have acquired the UCSMP secondary component from Prentice Hall, who is now the Scott Foresman parent company.

According to industry reports, Everyday Mathematics was the top selling elementary mathematics curriculum in 2005 and is estimated to have 19% of the market.

FIFTEEN ELEMENTS OF THE ARCH MODEL

I. RECOGNIZE CULTURAL DIFFERENCES

While any institution is an aggregate of diverse parts, academic institutions have a number of common characteristics. They are populated with students, administrators, governing trustees, but most importantly with faculty. The faculty operates as a guild made up of apprentices (assistant professors), journeymen (associate professors), and masters (tenured professors). Once a professor achieves tenure he or she becomes a largely independent operative. The purpose of a university is to prepare students for the next stage of their lives. The faculty organizes information, teaches, and often seeks new knowledge through research. These activities are funded by tuition, donations, and grants. Performance is measured by quantity and quality of authored publications, but, more importantly, by the opinion of peers.

The hierarchically managed, profit seeking operations of commercial enterprises are very poorly understood by members of universities and often seen as alien or lower status activities. Similarly, business executives demonstrate impatience with academics and complain about their perceived inability to work within the strictures of budgets, schedules, and performance targets. In order to successfully transfer technology from the academy into the economy an impedance match must be achieved between these two dissimilar cultures.

II. CREATE INCENTIVES

Academic investigators are motivated by the possibility of achieving recognition, e.g. tenure, publication in a prestigious refereed journal, Nobel prizes. Financial gain has not been the chief driver, although the increasing limitations on grant funding since the end of the cold war have made academic institutions more receptive to the potential of gain from commercialization of technology. Individual academicians have become increasingly sophisticated regarding their shares of any potential returns from the commercialization of their inventions. Since most research is funded by grants from outside agencies coupled with infrastructures owned by the institution any product of that research is considered to be owned by the university. This rule is usually ratified by the senate of the faculty or a similar body.

III. ALLY WITH THE TECHNOLOGY TRANSFER OFFICE

Most research universities operate a technology transfer office charged with the responsibilities associated with commercialization of university derived intellectual property. Each office is different. They have different reporting relationships, staffing, patenting responsibilities, funding, and operating protocols. Most of them operate licensing programs which provide rights to certain inventions in return for a stream of royalties. In 1986 ARCH was chartered as the ARCH Development Corporation to serve as the technology transfer organization for the University of Chicago and the Argonne National Laboratory. Up until that time the university had contracted out the licensing function.

IV. UNDERSTAND LICENSING VS. COMPANY CREATION

Research discoveries fall into three types. First there is the single invention for which there is not likely to be follow-on technology. It is usually best to license these to an entity that has a familiarity (and usually manufacturing and marketing expertise) with a similar technology. Second there is a major discovery which might be the basis for a start-up company but has broad application for a number of companies. The Cohen-Boyer recombinant DNA invention would be an example. These may be profitably licensed on a non-exclusive basis to multiple users. Third there is the platform technology which may have a variety of applications and is likely to be followed by further advances. These may be the bases for start-up companies. ARCH was the first technology transfer organization to be given the option of following any one of the three paths and was financially incentivized to choose company creation wherever possible.

V. INTERACT DIRECTLY WITH INVESTIGATORS

ARCH was organizationally and geographically placed in the Graduate School of Business of the University of Chicago. The Dean of the GSB had hoped that the presence of ARCH would trigger an interest in entrepreneurial activity on the part of the students and that is exactly what happened. Over 20 students devoted extremely long hours to the revue of invention disclosures and because most of them had undergraduate technology degrees or relevant technical business experience began to interview investigators in their laboratories. Thus the organization moved from a passive to an active posture. Ordinarily academic researchers would not have made themselves accessible but they were pleased that the students had the backgrounds to understand what they were doing.

VI. FIND EARLY STAGE AND SEED CAPITAL

While licensing was recognized as a necessary function, ARCH was established and incentivized to create companies. Early on, it was confirmed that the university and the laboratory contained interesting and valuable intellectual property, in fact, more than ARCH's small and inexperienced staff could handle. But the most significant concern was the lack of start-up capital. The creation of a company requires pump priming money, and no amount of sweat equity can substitute for this. In truth, few universities have reasonable access to that form of investment called seed and early stage venture capital. In 1986 when ARCH began it was highly concentrated in the San Francisco/Silicon Valley and greater Boston areas but there was virtually none of it in the region around Chicago. Substantial efforts were made to attract early stage venture capitalists to Chicago but they bore little fruit. Therefore the directors of the ARCH Development Corp approved an effort to raise a dedicated venture fund within ARCH.

VII. LOOK FOR SCIENTIFIC ROLL-UPS (MOSAIC COMPANIES)

Company creation is an intrinsically difficult activity, but it becomes nearly impossible when there exists a requirement to work solely with the technology of a single institution. Almost immediately, ARCH recognized the advantage of combining University of Chicago or Argonne inventions with complimentary inventions from other institutions. For example, Aviron (AVIR) began as a vaccine company focused on the herpes virus work being conducted at the University. It became quickly evident that this was not enough to make an entirely new company. Vaccine research occurring at the University of Alabama and Mt. Sinai in New York were combined into the company. Ultimately, the flagship product of this company, the cold adapted flu vaccine marketed as Flumist, came from the University of Michigan. This approach evolved into the strategy of scientific roll-ups. Wherever possible an effort was made to combine as much of the relevant research in an area into a single company, thus providing a highly defensible patent estate. Adolor (ADLR), a pain control company, gathered science from eight separate institutions. The parts fit together like interlocking pieces of a jigsaw puzzle. We called these mosaic companies.

VIII. RECOGNIZE HYBRID TECHNOLOGIES/CONVERGENCE DEALS

For years the conventional wisdom with regard to venture investing was that deep specialized domain investing was more likely to lead to success than a broad eclectic "generalist" approach. But ARCH was focused on universities and national laboratories and these institutions had begun performing important research in multidiscipline centers which combined elements of life science, material science, and frequently information technology. Genomica, later acquired by Exelisis, for example, developed a sophisticated information system for the conduct of research in the life sciences. Optobionics relied on advanced microchip technology to develop a miniature eye prosthesis for the treatment of macular degeneration and retinitis pigmentosa. ARCH classified many of the new investment opportunities as hybrids and referred to them as convergence deals because they seemed to occur at the margins where two or more fundamental disciplines overlapped.

IX. DIFFERENTIATE AMONG SCREENING OPPORTUNITIES

During the 80's there were a number of venture capital partnerships and research management companies who believed in entering into an exclusive contractual arrangement to commercialize university inventions. As a consequence of its early experiences with the University of Chicago and the Argonne National Laboratory, ARCH avoided such contracts. What ARCH observed was that research evaluation was not a democratic process in which each investigator could expect an equal share of time. Eventually some faculty members were bound to be disappointed and the contract would come under a rising tide of criticism. It turned out that at each institution there existed an elite corps of discoverers and they were not hard to find. They were the members of the Academies, the most frequently published, the most frequently cited. Most importantly, they all knew one another. Furthermore, many of them were repeat inventors so that each relationship with a member of these groups had a far higher than average potential to produce additional investment opportunities. ARCH designed its screening process to first find and contact members of these groups. Along the way ARCH maintained cordial relationships with the relevant technology transfer offices.

X. FORM CONSISTENT APPROACH TO INVESTIGATOR CONFLICTS OF INTEREST

The performance of research in the academic setting carries with it a certain code of conduct. The purpose of the research is to find new knowledge, not to answer a particular question from a funding source. The results are to be published and thus shared with other researchers. The investigator is not to perform work outside the institution (usually there is some leeway granted for consulting). There are numerous examples of faculty members creating the perception of conflict of interest, actually experiencing a conflict of interest, or taking part in activities that could be called a conflict of commitment. Sometimes these activities create severe division within a faculty. Each institution is different and each one has adopted policies regarding investigator participation in a new enterprise, investigator stock ownership and general compensation, and treatment of intellectual property. Usually these policies have been confirmed by the governing body of the faculty. ARCH has always endeavored to comply with university policy in these matters and has never attempted to restrict a publication.

XI. FORM DETAILED CONSISTENT POLICY ON INTELLECTUAL PROPERTY

Most university originating early stage technology based companies are initially built around a patent or patents. The first patent applications are usually paid for by the investigator's home institution. But the action of patenting inexorably sets up a chain of increasingly expensive decisions: in which countries in addition to the United States to get protection, which continuations (expanse of coverage) to pay for, what is the annual cost of maintaining each patent. A substantial portion of the decision to invest relates to the strength, breadth, and uniqueness of the "patent estate", the complete body of exclusively held intellectual property. The action that triggers the beginning of a university based start-up company is the licensing from the institution to the company of this intellectual property. At this point the company assumes continuing patent costs. ARCH had the advantage of beginning as, in part, a licensing agency (ARCH Development Corp) and consequently spent several years on the university side of the transaction. This experience helped gain an understanding of relative patent values and appropriate royalty flows.

XII. CREATE STRATEGIES FOR DISTRIBUTED VS. CENTRALIZED GEOGRAPHY

Conventional wisdom said the seed and early stage investing could only be done successfully on a regional basis. The rule of thumb was that except for a few very special exceptions you had to be able to drive to the start-up company. But ARCH learned quite early that start-up companies could emerge from any geography and sometimes from multiple geographies. Furthermore, it was recognized that certain areas were far better served with the availability of seed capital than others. The experience encountered at Chicago was relevant for a number of places. Potential investors were skeptical that an early stage partnership could function effectively on a geographically separated basis. Nelsen had roots in Washington and Bybee in Texas. Columbia University extended an invitation to set up in New York and BDM Corporation to set up in New Mexico. Very quickly ARCH had national coverage created not by hiring new employees but by a relocation of general partners. The advent of new and powerful communications technologies – the internet, e-mail, blackberries, cell phones, teleconferencing, overnight delivery – helped enormously. But even more important was the willingness of the partners to travel incessantly and have the discipline to religiously maintain weekly telephonic and monthly face-to-face partner meetings.

XIII. TAKE LEAD RESPONSIBILITY

It has been characteristic of ARCH to take lead responsibility in any syndicate which it participated. Therefore it has taken major responsibility for the formation of first round syndicates and has usually covered each new investment with two members of the firm, one as board member and one as observer. Its board posture has been highly proactive in that it has taken a major role in the selection of CEOs, development of strategy, and the raising of subsequent financial rounds. Much of this is a legacy of ARCH's origins. The university investigator is rarely a candidate to be a start-up CEO (which is a good thing both the point of view of the company and the investigator's parent institution) so the ARCH investor has often had to fill this position until a professional manager could be hired. Early syndication has facilitated the development of well established co-investment relationships which are useful when later financing rounds must be raised, and additional investment opportunities often have come through friendly syndicate partners.

XIV. FOCUS ON CORE TECHNOLOGIES

Over time, ARCH began to distinguish among technologies. There were those inventions which produced marginal improvements and there were those which were truly transformational in nature. More and more ARCH has narrowed its investment portfolio to concentrate on these core technologies with investments in such companies as Ikaria (induced hibernation), Alnylam (RNAI science), and Impinj (RFID technology).

XV. ACHIEVE STABILITY WITHIN PARTNERSHIP

The ARCH partners have been together for 20 years, something of a stability record for venture partnerships. All came from outside the venture industry, but all had substantial scientific training and/ or experience prior to founding ARCH. From the outset the internal dynamic of the partnership has been collaborative. All decisions to invest are made by unanimous vote. No individual partner "owns" any particular investment. No individual IRR's are maintained.

EARLY OPERATIONS

HealthQual – ARCH'S FIRST INVESTMENT

ARCH's first investment, HealthQual Systems Inc., was incorporated on September 9, 1987. The inventor was Dr. Mike Roizen who was then Chief of Anesthesiology at the University of Chicago Hospitals and who has since gone on to become a celebrity as the author of Real Age. Mike now practices at the Cleveland Clinic.

Mike had studied the battery of diagnostic tests given to each pre-surgical patient and was convinced that most of them were either superfluous or unnecessary. He developed a simple four button computer ("yes," "no," "don't know," "next question") on which a pre-surgical patient could load in his/her medical history which would then be compared with an expert system in the computer memory to produce a recommended set of diagnostic procedures to be performed before the scheduled surgery. The thesis of the business plan was that the prospective savings on diagnostic tests would motivate the purchase of the equipment.

We built several machines and even sold a few. The price point was about $1000 per machine. This was at a moment when the price of laptops was falling like a stone. A key market fact was that the healthcare reimbursement system did not incentivize physicians toward saving on the costs of diagnostic tests and in fact, more tests were being added all the time in hopes of gaining some insulation from an aggressive plaintiff's bar.

The company employed one salesman who did surprisingly well, and eventually the company was acquired by a diagnostic equipment company. Some money was lost and some lessons were learned.

Mike Roizen was a good example of a serial scientist/entrepreneur, but we realized we had done far too little due diligence and had only a superficial and naïve understanding of the marketplace we were addressing. We set out to manufacture a fairly complex piece of equipment using talented but inexperienced contractors. As would be expected we had quality problems.

But we had started a company and although we had been clumsy and amateurish we demonstrated to ourselves and to our university colleagues that it could be done.

Illinois Superconductor – ARCH'S FIRST IPO

There is sometimes a scientific breakthrough which seizes the collective imagination and draws an usual amount of research focus. For the last few years it has been nanotechnology. In 1987, it was superconductivity. Superconductivity is the movement of electrons under extremely low temperatures with virtually no loss, and experiments began to show that the phenomenon could be achieved under liquid hydrogen which opened the possibility of a variety of very profitable applications.

The Argonne National Laboratory had been a major center of superconductivity research for years (superconducting magnets were used in the construction of high energy partial accelerators). The team of ARCH associates working at Argonne under the leadership of Keith Crandell prepared a business plan around the application of superconductive materials to low temperature measurement and later around increases in the quality and reliability of cell phone communications. ARCH personnel managed the company and Argonne staff helped set up the manufacturing capability. Most importantly, a professional Chief Executive officer was recruited. The company successfully made parts and interested the telecom industry in them. On the basis of that interest, the company had a successful public offering on October 25, 1993.

Illinois Superconductor remains in existence today and although it was not a home-run, it was a profitable investment. It was a profoundly important demonstration proof to the Argonne staff. It also taught us the importance of recruiting professional management as quickly as possible.

Aviron – CONGLOMERATE SCIENCE

The general partner of ARCH Venture Fund I was the University of Chicago and Lazarus, Nelsen, Crandell, and Bybee served as employees of the general partner. The Fund was tethered to the university and the laboratory in that the fund could invest only in scientific and technological inventions that originated in the two institutions. It became readily apparent that few sustainable enterprises could be developed from total reliance on such a narrow base. The answer presented itself in the form of a company called Aviron. Aviron was conceived as a viral vaccine company and, in its initial form, put together vaccine discoveries not only from the University of Chicago but also from the University of Alabama and the Mount Sinai Hospital in New York. It was what we came to call a scientific roll-up. Ultimately, Aviron licensed a cold adapted spray administered flu virus vaccine from the University of Michigan. This became a product now known as Flumist. Aviron went public and was eventually acquired by Medimmune which markets Flumist today.

As ARCH Venture Partners spun out of the University of Chicago in 1992/1993 it recognized that a local perspective, or even a small regional perspective would not work for the sustained development of successful technology based enterprises. This judgment contradicted the conventional wisdom that said seed and early stage venture funds had to be small because they were so labor intensive and had to restrict themselves to investments that were in driving distance because such investments frequently required daily attention. The general partners decided upon a strategy that came to be called the ARCH emigration. Nelsen, a native Washingtonian, moved back to Seattle and opened ARCH – North West. Bybee, a native Texan, opened an office in Albuquerque, and subsequently in Austin leaving the New Mexican office as a branch of ARCH – South West. Crandell remained in Chicago, but at the invitation of Columbia University opened an ARCH office in New York and staffed it with a new hire (the utilization of a non founder ultimately proved unsuccessful).

These moves drew questions from investment gatekeepers. Could a seed and early stage venture partnership be operated successfully on a geographically distributed basis?

The answer turned out to be yes. The great advances in communications technology were simultaneously occurring. The partnership made extensive use of lap tops, cell phones, blackberries, and teleconferencing. We learned that orderly weekly partner meetings could be held by phone. But most importantly, the decision of the founding partners to execute the dispersal themselves rather than pick up agents in the new territories was crucial.

CASES: ADOLOR, MODE, AND NEON

My editors at the Wall Street Journal always stressed, "Show, don't tell." That was 20 years ago ... But even now that advice is just as true. And the showing by Bob Nelsen, Keith Crandell and Clint Bybee of their deals respond to the question: How do you turn mind into matter? Is it simply a matter of guessing right? Is it intuition? Or is it a process that combines knowledge and experience with intuition and guesswork? How do you tackle technologies that are so far out that conventional analysis just doesn't provide many clues?

In helping start Adolor, Bob Nelsen adopted a contrarian philosophy. Why did the big pharmaceuticals decide against opioids? And if the big pharmaceuticals are perpetually wrong, maybe there is value in the pioneering works on opioids, especially when that pioneer is a world-famous scientist. Clint Bybee took a somewhat different road in helping develop MicroOptical Devices out of Sandia. The technology was not in question. Could it be streamlined and made more efficient to respond to the needs and demands of the marketplace? Could reaching out for an early customer help define and shape the product?

Indeed, finding customers early has been a key to finding validation for new ideas and technologies. In creating Neon Software with the help of industry veteran Rick Adam, Keith Crandell focused on an idea that already existed but needed to be shaped into a product for the commercial marketplace. And who could help shape and define it better than a real customer?

Nelsen, Bybee and Crandell each have different approaches to transforming mind into matter, but underlying it all is a process that has come through trial and error – and success.

"ALL THE CLASSIC INGREDIENTS OF THE ARCH START-UP"

BOB NELSEN

Explains his modus operandi in helping start Adolor

ADOLOR

Adolor began when I was skiing at Vail and I got a message from Graeme Bell at the Two Elks Lodge which, ironically, has since been burned down by eco terrorists. Graeme said he had an exciting discovery and that I needed to call him. He told me that he had discovered two, maybe three, of the opioid receptors that people had been looking for over the past 30 or 40 years and that was the beginning of what became Adolor .

Graeme was clearly a unique, smart and winning scientist. I had been introduced to him because his research which continues today involved looking for the genes for Type 2 Diabetes. He is one of the pioneers in that space, the fourth employee and co-founder of Chiron. He clearly didn't want to be bothered and he suffered no fools and didn't particularly like to talk about commercialization. But he was intrigued by the commercial aspects of science, having done it several times. He was a good stock trader, especially in biotech stocks. We had previously developed a relationship based on his discoveries in somatostatin.

Cindy Bayley, a bright Ph.D. scientist with a MBA who was working with us at the time, began to explore this research and Graeme's discoveries -- and what we did was to follow a sleuth-like trail to his collaborators and competitors. We recognized a couple of things. The world of pharmaceutical companies hated opioids. Nothing had happened to the world of opioids for 30 years since the derivatives of morphine. We had the radical idea that if you could understand how opioids worked, then you might be able to crack the code and build a really big company. So we began to try to piece and pull together and roll up all of the technology in opioids. Even though the University of Chicago's invention was one of six or seven, we began to roll in other university technologies into a University of Chicago start-up company, which was a unique approach. We weren't just looking at our own fishing pond, we were looking everywhere else. We asked Graeme who the smartest people were and started chasing them down - essentially competitors and collaborators, some of the best people, especially young names, in the opioid field. We built a nest of intellectual property with the best advisors that we could find.

In Adolor, we had all the classic ingredients of the ARCH start-up. An area where everyone was convinced nothing revolutionary had happened and a hard market. The good part of that was we had no competition and most people thought we were crazy, including the venture capitalists to whom we shopped the deal.

There were two significant aspects to what we were doing. We were looking for the Holy Grail in opioids. In researching the area, Cindy Bayley found a company in Germany called E Merck, and a scientist at Harvard who had developed the concept of peripheral analgesia. The fact that the effect of opioids wasn't only on the brain was a key insight. And the business plan of the company today is very similar to the business plan we eventually created. So we rolled up the technology. It took us only $50,000 to do it including option fees, expenses for five or six different option licenses. The lesson we learned over and over again was, don't listen to conventional wisdom. If you believe it, keep doing it. So we kept doing it and decided we had something.

We incorporated and began looking for money. But no one was biting because the conventional wisdom again was that nothing was happening in this area. The people at the major pharmas who killed the opioids programs were the same guys who were now running the big pharmas. But then we found a visionary guy, Jim Rathmann, the son of George Rathmann, the founder of Amgen. He was excited about it and loved the fact that it was contrarian. We were introduced to Jim who was investing his own money and George's money in biotech deals. Jim was willing to go in without conventional venture capital but decided that we needed at least one other investor, each putting in at least half a million. We began looking around until we ran into Annette Bianchi at Weiss, Peck and Greer, one of the founders of Cellpro and several other companies, and a protégé of Jean Deleage at Burr Egan Deleage - also a legendary biotech investor. Annette was a bit of a contrarian and liked the idea. She introduced us to Michael Lewis, one of the co-founders of Cephalon. Again this is all part of Tom Sawyer's fence - all working for free. Michael liked the idea and immediately was excited about it. Annette introduced the deal to one of her partners, Ellen Feeney, one of the original investors in Cephalon, who eventually became the investor on behalf of Weiss, Peck and Greer.

The syndicate was formed around the idea of finding the Holy Grail in opioids and peripheral analgesia and the catalytic vision of Michael Lewis. Then we were told that Weiss Peck wouldn't fund it unless we had a CEO. I began to do the smile and dial routine looking for a CEO, ultimately I ran across John Farrar and talked him into the idea that he should run this company. We ended up situating Adolor in Malvern, Pennsylvania because that's where Michael Lewis and John Farrar are from. John decided to take a risk and he almost didn't get the job because Ellen didn't think he was entrepreneurial enough and wouldn't take risks. He had a little bit of a big pharma profile. But I asked her, "Have you looked into his office, at the wall?" And she said she hadn't. He races Indy sports cars on the weekends, I told her his walls are plastered with pictures of him going 200 miles per hour. I think he has the ability to take these risks. Ultimately, she made the decision to take the risk and back him.

Adolor has one of the great return multiples in biotech. Again, one of the big lessons we learned was that syndication matters. It brings in long-term investors who will stick with it. Indeed, all of the initial investors have stayed with the company, through and past its IPO.

The company went public - almost twice. The first time it tried to go public was in March of 2000. It didn't price, but was the last remaining IPO that was almost there. We missed the window by a day. Adolor regrouped and went public the next year. It was basically the same business plan as it had at its very early stage. Adolor has a market-cap of over a billion dollars and has gone through one more CEO and has a few hundred million in the bank. It has turned out to be a commercial concern with real products. The biggest failure so far has been that we still haven't teased out the tricks of opioid biology and the dream is still there. But we have some interesting things in the pipeline that we are working on.

"THE MOST SUCCESSFUL COMPANY TO COME OUT OF SANDIA"

CLINT BYBEE

Describes MODE, Sandia's most successful spin-out

In late 1993, ARCH was invited to set up an office in Albuquerque by BDM International, a consulting and technical services firm that had a sizable operation there and was a significant presence. BDM was considering a plan to bid on the contract to operate Sandia National Laboratories and was interested in having a technology commercialization capability. The CEO of BDM was an old friend of Steve Lazarus and, having followed the early work of ARCH, he suggested we consider an affiliation. That eventually led to ARCH and BDM establishing a joint-venture, called AB Ventures, with the goal of leveraging BDM's contacts at Sandia and Los Alamos National Laboratories and seeking opportunities to form new companies. BDM provided office space, technical due diligence in some cases, and initial contacts at the laboratories.

Martin Marietta (which later merged with Lockheed Corp. to form Lockheed Martin) won the contract to operate Sandia National Laboratories for the Department of Energy. Martin Marietta set up a company called Technology Ventures Corporation (or TVC), with a mission to help facilitate technology commercialization from Sandia National Laboratories. TVC was led by Sherman McCorkle and he invited ARCH and AB Ventures to office with TVC. This led to a productive working relationship we developed with TVC and that continues to this day.

During 1994, one of the groups we spent some time evaluating at Sandia National Labs (SNL) was the compound semiconductor group. Given Sandia's historic ties to AT&T, which had operated the laboratory since its founding, it was not surprising that the compound semiconductor research group had a number of very strong researchers from Bell Laboratories. Sandia and Bell Labs were pioneers in the research of novel compound semiconductor lasers, and Sandia's group had a significant research effort in vertical cavity surface emitting lasers. One of the leading scientists at SNL in this area was Dr. Paul Gourley. I met with Paul in early 1995 and began to dig into the technology further. At a subsequent meeting, Paul made it clear he did not have an interest in leaving Sandia or working on a start-up company, but he told me about two Sandia scientists he thought were interested and introduced me to them.

Semiconductor lasers are solid state devices and, as in electronics, solid state devices have a number of cost, size, speed, and performance advantages over gas or liquid operated lasers. The vertical cavity surface emitting laser is a specially designed and fabricated semiconductor laser. Semiconductor lasers were starting to emerge as important in applications like sensing, laser welding, and communications. The compelling thing about the VCSEL is that, compared with a traditional semiconductor laser, it is smaller in size, cheaper to manufacture, operates at faster speeds, couples more efficiently to optical fiber, and operates at lower powers. These attributes of smaller, faster, cheaper, lower power caught our attention.

I read everything I could find about the VCSEL and Sandia's work and talked with scientists in the field. I met with other Sandia scientists and got my partners involved in the analysis. We became convinced that Sandia's process could be commercially scalable, and that the attributes of the VCSEL could be exploited commercially.

It was pretty unclear at the outset. The VCSELs were small, fast, coupled efficiently to fiber, could be modulated at high speeds, and could maintain very stable wavelengths. Our speculation was that there were areas like sensing, scanning, and communications where these attributes could be exploited. However, there were no VCSELs on the market, so it was clear that the early process would have to be market-facing to find the lead applications. This was probably the first time we were developing a platform technology outside of life science.

Initially we spent time with the two gentlemen Paul Gourley introduced me to – Rob Bryan and Tom Brennan. Rob had left Sandia a few years earlier to work on a start-up in Boulder, Colorado, and I flew there a couple of times to meet. Tom was at Sandia and we spent a lot of time (including time when Rob was down from Boulder) discussing their ideas and goals and considering how to best get started. Keith, Bob, and Steve came out to Albuquerque and met with Rob and Tom.

Albuquerque was abundant at the time with contract research companies. This is probably not too surprising since it has the largest concentration of PhDs per capita in the U.S. and writing grants and doing research is a skill most PhDs possess. Starting a contract research company was a temptation for Rob and Tom because they were experienced in how to do that. On the other hand, they wanted to build something bigger than that and we were certainly not excited about a contract research company. We spent a lot of time discussing what a business plan for a new company might look like. Because none of us knew the right application to focus on initially, we all agreed that a component of the company should initially be contract research (government funded SBIR research grant) with a focus toward grants that would advance the commercial applications. We concluded a relatively small amount of initial equity capital money could be used to knock out key early milestones including securing a license to the technology, securing SBIR grants, identifying commercial applications, and finding the big hit opportunity

After six to nine months of discussion and the formulation of a basic business plan to get started, we formed MicroOptical Devices with Rob and Tom in August, 1995. ARCH's initial equity investment was $200,000, and included Keith and me joining the board and my spending a fair amount of time working with Rob and Tom directly to address early business milestones. While ARCH is a big believer in syndicating early, we did not try to find syndicate partners for the initial seed investment. Our belief was that we needed to get the company started, get patents licensed in from Sandia, and get an initial customer or partner to validate an early lead application. Rob and Tom set up their offices in cubicles right next to my office at TVC. Sherman McCorkle and his team were very helpful in the early days as we set out to put in place agreements with Sandia to use their facilities and to license the technology.

Key early risks were applications and commercial process development. Sandia had developed a process that appeared scalable, but had not demonstrated things like long lifetimes, repeatability, reliability, stability, uniformity, etc. We were able to reduce this risk initially by leveraging the infrastructure at Sandia to utilize their equipment, facilities, and people to make initial prototype devices and improve manufacturing processes. This allowed the company to focus on probing the market for the application areas that were commercially interesting.

Following the initial investment, we focused on answering the question of key markets and applications, and on securing a license to the intellectual property from Sandia. During this time, an early opportunity arose from contacts of Rob and Tom and researchers at Sandia. Symbol Technologies, a leading scanner company, was interested in developing a scanner on a ring and needed a number of the attributes of a VCSEL. They needed a red light source that was small, required very low power, could be modulated at high speeds, and could be integrated into a small ring-sized package. The VCSEL was an ideal fit, and MODE was the only company Symbol could find who could potentially supply them commercial devices. Symbol and MODE entered into a development partnership, where Symbol supplied $500,000 of NRE, and MODE agreed to supply devices and work with Symbol to design and make devices that met their specification. This commercial partnership with Symbol really provided the initial commercial and application framework for the company.

The big challenges that emerged after the Symbol relationship was in place were scale-up, repeatability, commercial reliability, etc. We had to raise the necessary capital to build a pilot fabrication facility to demonstrate commercial readiness. While MODE was able to make prototype devices at Sandia through a user facility arrangement, their equipment is set up for research, not for manufacturing. MODE needed to buy an epitaxial reactor and other process equipment and house it in a clean room environment. The company chose to purchase its epitaxial reactor from the same company that had supplied the reactor to Sandia, EMCORE. Rob and Tom knew the founder and senior management of EMCORE, and they went to work with them to design the reactor and negotiate price. While the reactor was being built over a six month period, the company leased a facility, designed and built-out a clean room, purchased used processing equipment, and hired a manufacturing head out of Intel. The epitaxial reactor from EMCORE, other process equipment, lease, and clean room build-out was completed for under $2.5 million. In early 1996, the company raised $6 million from a syndicate of venture capital firms, venture lease firms, and AMP (now part of Tyco). Since Rob had built a fab in his previous start-up in Boulder, he was able to work efficiently with local contractors, who themselves were experienced in fabs from work they had done at Intel, Sandia, and the University of New Mexico. Tom took the lead to work with EMCORE on the specifications for the epitaxial reactor, and both were involved in acquiring the other equipment and continuing discussions with customers about other application areas. During this period the two technical founders, Rob and Tom, worked extraordinarily well together. Following completion of the fab as the company began making commercial products, tensions between the two developed that ultimately led to a serious schism (proving the old maxim: "better to have co-workers as friends, than friends as co-workers").

Even with the initial customer, we did not believe we had found the big opportunity. We knew we had to find that. Rob and Tom took the lead in searching out other applications. In 1997, they began discussions with Fuji Xerox, and that ultimately led to a development partnership with them to develop an array of VCSELs for high speed printing applications.

We pursued other markets like sensing, for example. Rob identified a project with a major semiconductor equipment company to detect very low levels of moisture in a gas stream. Moisture is very bad for semiconductor processing and our VCSELS devices were well suited to provide wavelength stability, which could be exploited for very accurate detection capabilities. However, while technical progress on this application was not a problem, we concluded the market opportunity was not large enough to really warrant full scale effort.

Then the company got its lucky break as high speed data communications reached a level of gigabit speeds. At those speeds, most people believed copper would no longer be suitable, and MODE's devices were ideally suited for high speed gigabit Ethernet communications. They were small, cheap, high speed, coupled efficiently to optical fiber, and operated at low powers. In fact, today this is the big market for these devices – high speed datacom.

When we built the fab, we recruited an experienced fab manager out of Intel. When we focused on optical data communications devices, we recruited an experienced marketing executive from industry. In order to build out the fab we raised $6 million in capital and helped put together the syndicate to assemble that capital. One of the investors was AMP, which made connectors and was interested in applying its connector packaging expertise to make datacom transceivers for the gigabit Ethernet opportunity. AMP took a board observer role as part of their investment, and Narinder Kapany became an observer/advisor to the company. Narinder was running AMPs optical communications division, having sold his company to them a few years prior. Narinder was well known in the laser community, having made some of the early technical contributions to the laser field. In addition to Dr. Kapany, the company assembled a scientific advisory board that included some of the pioneers in the field of VCSELs and semiconductor lasers including Jack Jewell and Kevin Lear. Kevin Lear later joined the company as its CTO.

About 18 months after the Series B investment, the fab was complete and the company was selling devices, working with companies including AMP, Symbol, Fuji Xerox, Molex, and others. The tensions of building the company - keeping customers happy, solving manufacturing challenges, expanding the team, developing new customers – ultimately began to take a severely negative toll on the two founders, and their relationship began to unravel. Since they were jointly operating the company at this time, that tension was not easily compartmentalized. So Rob and Tom and the board agreed we should bring an executive chairman onto the board – someone with a lot of operating experience who could help build an organization to take the company to the next level. At the same time, the company began to make plans to raise a

Series C round of financing.

Bill Patton was added as executive chairman following a search. Bill was a very experienced operating executive, having run both large divisions of public companies as well as early-stage technology companies.

As all this was happening, the company was approached by both EMCORE and AMP with interest in acquisition. While MODE clearly had the beginnings of a promising supplier of datacom devices, the company also was at a point where it likely needed several key senior executive additions to build a big, stand-alone company. Building the company to the next level would likely create significant value in the company; whereas there was other acquisition activity in the marketplace as datacom suppliers concluded that VCSELs were a key part of the future of datacom. Ultimately, the board and founders believed it made sense to test the markets for the company to be acquired, and, agreed to be acquired by EMCORE.

In retrospect, we probably made the right decision to sell the company. The market for VCSEL-based transceivers took longer to develop, and the company was going to require important additions to its team in the form of experienced managers. On the other hand, the telecom boom in the late 1990s (that has now of course gone bust) might have provided a healthy exit opportunity for the company.

MODE was the first successful spin out from Sandia. To this day, it continues to be the most successful company to have come out of Sandia. Subsequent to the acquisition, EMCORE invested significant resources into the company, and today the EMCORE/MODE operation in Albuquerque employs several hundred people.

Dealing with a technology coming out of Sandia had pros and cons. On the one hand, MODE was able to leverage Sandia's sizable investment in compound semiconductor facilities and capabilities in some very important ways. MODE was able to reduce early market risks without having to first raise the capital to build a facility. By establishing user facility and work-for-other agreements with Sandia, MODE was able to move rapidly up the manufacturing learning curve once it built its own fab. At the time of MODE, there were no outsource providers of epitaxial growth capable of making a VCSEL. There are a number today.

On the other hand, dealing with Sandia on the licensing side was more difficult and took longer than almost any university licensing agreement we have worked on. It took about 18 months to ultimately secure an exclusive license from Sandia. Early on, Sandia was insistent on the idea of licensing the core patents to MODE, but also on retaining the ability to license them to other firms. After they finally became convinced of the flaw in this approach, they became insistent on the idea of licensing the IP to MODE on an exclusive basis, with the ability for them to also license the IP exclusively to one other firm. This was what they called a "co-exclusive" license. We finally got them to agree to limit the time frame in which they could issue a co-exclusive to any other company, and the time frame was short enough so we knew MODE could wind up with an exclusive license.

"FOCUSING ON A NEW SET OF IDEAS ALREADY INCUBATED IN A BUSINESS SETTING"

KEITH CRANDELL

On ARCH and NEON Software

George F. (Rick) Adam was a successful information technology executive who had most recently been a partner and Chief Administrative Officer at Goldman Sachs. Before that, he had worked with Steve Lazarus at Baxter Laboratories where he was Chief Information Officer and later head of the Information Systems business group. In the early 1990s, I met frequently with Rick to review the usefulness of various information technologies that ARCH was considering as investments. During one of these review sessions in Denver, Colorado, Rick described a new company he had started called NEON Software that he was seed funding with his own money. NEON intended to develop a new software technology for hospitals based on better middleware for integrating multiple applications. Health care was one of the more inefficient users of information technology and Rick believed it could benefit from better technology. Better application integration would also allow unprecedented transaction processing speeds. I had gotten to know Rick fairly well during our various review and consulting meetings and consequently, after a session on GPS technology, I suggested we talk more about the business plan for NEON and how ARCH could help.

Consideration of this investment was a new direction for ARCH. Until then, we had pretty much been purists about focusing only on leading edge science and technology from academic institutions and laboratories. But I was struck by the opportunity to engage with a highly qualified, experienced businessman who was focusing on a new set of ideas that had been incubated in a business setting. ARCH invested $500,000 in the first round of financing along side Rick Adam. The funds were basically used to recruit a team and define a business opportunity.

The CIO's at hospitals knew the NEON people were very smart. Initially, the hospitals would give newcomer NEON their toughest problems that tended to be one-offs rather than scalable customer projects. The sales cycle was long and there did not seem to be much opportunity to extend the product portion of the business to other hospitals because each hospital had a unique mixture of applications and a lot of legacy proprietary applications. Essentially, at the beginning NEON was operating as a high end job shop. The hospitals were also primarily running batches of data versus real time processing where NEON had its biggest advantages. Rick realized that it might be too early to push into the healthcare market. I was familiar with the trap of breakthrough technology coming too early to a particular market and I encouraged Rick to find a customer who needed the capability sooner.

ARCH was comfortable with this conclusion because we thought of the team and the technology as a platform that might eventually have many application areas. The key was to find the initial set of customers that would be willing to pay for a product as opposed to services. As a function of recruiting talent from Wall Street, Rick was able to secure contract funding to build a super efficient generation of a rules engine for Merrill Lynch that extended what had been prototyped thus far by NEON. The rules engine was to be used in the bank for processing transactions in a high-speed, twenty messages per second environment with guaranteed message delivery. NEON could make a case that it could integrate a series of applications and process these transactions in almost real time based on some NEON patented algorithms. In banking, time is money as well as competitive advantage. NEON went on to build the best performing middle ware software in financial services at that time. Once NEON had a major financial reference account, others wanted to follow. ARCH was also able to help NEON think about syndicating it's financings, get maximum credit for the progress it was making, and to recruit some excellent industry board members to advise the team.

NEON had a successful public offering in June, 1997, and went on to be one of the ten fastest growing software companies growing from zero to $180 million in revenue per year in five years. NEON eventually reentered the health care vertical through an acquisition where NEON products could be used to enhance existing system performance with established customers. Ultimately, NEON was acquired by Sybase.

ARCH EXPANDS

"OF COURSE IT'S HARD. IT'S SUPPOSED TO BE HARD. IF IT WASN'T HARD, EVERYONE WOULD DO IT. THE HARD IS WHAT MAKES IT GREAT."

- Tom Hanks in a *League of Their Own*

At some point in the 90's it was clear that ARCH needed to expand. It needed a critical mass of technology, managers, and capital to grow optimally. And it needed access to large research pools, traditionally at universities and national laboratories.

But ARCH had created a unique system that was built around a team of special individuals, schooled in technology and trained to explore the frontiers of science, much of it not fully formed or recognizable. Moreover, it had taken Steve Lazarus' 57th Street Irregulars years of trial and error to reach the level of excellence they had. From graduate students they had evolved into venture capitalists.

Bob Nelsen had already moved to Seattle. Clint Bybee was installed in Austin. Where would the next group of ARCH professionals come from? And would ARCH itself have to change as it took on new professionals?

Attorney Robin Painter talks about domain mastery. She is not overstating the case. For ARCH to be successful, each partner needs to be the master of the space. Each needs to be able to recognize the promise of potential, how to harness that promise, and how to transform it all into a real business. The process isn't all solo. The experience of the ARCH principals plays a key role in the overall development and shaping of the science and the eventual venture.

Venture capital firms have expanded, both in terms of capital and in terms of geography. But in most cases they've also had to revise their original mission. It helped ARCH that its next professionals – Scott Minick and Patrick Ennis were both technology veterans, already experienced in working with early-stage technology, familiar with management styles and structures and the capital markets. And well before they were formally established at ARCH, they were familiar with its principals and its style.

RAISING FUND II

ARCH Venture Fund I had been surprisingly successful. The $9 million fund had been invested in 12 companies: four had led to IPO's; four had been sold or merged; and four had failed. The ROI and cash on cash return had been excellent, and had realized Bob Halperin's hopes for ARCH's yield to the University of Chicago.

The University itself, in the form of ARCH Development Corp., had been the general partner of the Fund with Lazarus, Crandell, and Nelsen serving as employees of the general partner. But now the question was – what to do for an encore?

The ARCH board and the University administration, representing a tax exempt entity, concluded that it was probably not appropriate to have a profit making component inside the not for profit organization. They encouraged the three principals (shortly thereafter to be joined by Bybee) to create an ARCH entity in the private sector. This led to the establishment of ARCH Venture Partners.

The idea was that ARCH would continue a close and cordial relationship with the University, but no contractual right of first look was either requested or given. The strategy of Fund II was to take the technology transfer/funding model developed for Fund I and apply it to several other research universities and national laboratories. In order to be as "local" as possible, Crandell set up an office in New York City (at the invitation of Columbia), Nelsen moved back to Seattle and established a close working relationship with the University of Washington, and Bybee moved to Albuquerque (at the invitation of BDM Corporation) to focus on Sandia and Los Alamos laboratories. Later, he would relocate to Austin, thus returning to his native Texas. Lazarus and Crandell continued to be domiciled in Chicago.

The partners raised $31 million for Fund II with the major Fund I investors continuing to participate. Later, the Harvard Business School determined that this sequence of events was worthy of being taught in the entrepreneurial finance section and therefore created ARCH Venture Partners, case #N1-295-105. It is still being taught.

"ARCH IS VERY MUCH THE ENTREPRENEUR'S VENTURE ... IT'S THE OLD SCHOOL OF VENTURE CAPITAL"

SCOTT MINICK

From corporate science to entrepreneurial science and ARCH

A scientist, an executive and an entrepreneur, Scott Minick is a relative newcomer to ARCH. But he epitomizes the skills honed by the likes of Steve Lazarus, Keith Crandell, and Bob Nelsen in developing a system for transferring life science technologies into the marketplace. Not only does Minick understand the investment angle he also understands the issues entrepreneurs face and those inherent in the technologies. Here he talks about the experience that has brought him here and how he envisages the tech transfer process going forward.

I started as a scientist at the Salk Institute where I did my graduate work. At that time, there was a view in the life sciences that scientists who went into industry were basically second class citizens. That's a little of an overstatement, but it meant that if you couldn't get a job in a real academic research center, you went into industrial research as the runner-up prize. But something was happening in 1979. You couldn't quite put your finger on it, but there was a sense that something was starting to happen in commercially developing life sciences. Amgen and Chiron didn't even exist; Genentech was just a few people. But you could see things coming together where something like that was going to happen in a major way. And I realized, I know a lot about science, but I don't know anything about business. I made the decision to stop my scientific career right there even though the Salk was an incredible place. The person I was working for, Roger Guillemin, had just won the Nobel Prize. I stopped my studies in academic research and went to get an MBA. So I went to the 'other' business school in Chicago, Northwestern, with the express purpose of doing something in this convergence of life science and business.

While I was in business school, Genentech came on the radar screen and Amgen and Chiron got started. A number of other pioneering biotech companies were also getting started. You could see the reality starting to crystallize out of this solution. So I went into the pharmaceutical industry, initially for Eli Lilly and then for Baxter. At Baxter, I met Steve Lazarus. Steve gave me an offer to work directly for him and I thought working for Steve for a year is better than anything else I can do, period. He gave me the worst salary offer that I had coming out of business school and I took it with no hesitation because of the opportunity.

At the time, Steve was experimenting in Baxter. He has deep roots in this whole entrepreneurial thing. Baxter was a big corporation, but it was more entrepreneurial than most. Steve wanted to find ways to make it even more entrepreneurial, more like the pace of Silicon Valley. So he had set up this enterprise with support from Baxter's CEO to create start-up ventures within Baxter. The idea was to take away the bureaucracy and give some talented people some seed money and some running room and let them go. That's what Steve offered: "I want you to be a part of this start-up enterprise at Baxter." And I said, "Steve, that's a deal. But I want to be honest with you; I'm going to be gone in about 18 months because one of two things is going to happen: It'll be successful or it will fail." The history of start-ups inside big corporations is once they get to any mass they get folded into a big division. I said, "Steve, I have no interest in working for some big, low growth product division at Baxter. So, if it goes there, I'll leave. Alternatively, it'll fail." Baxter's culture was very much one strike and you're out. You might get more than one strike, but you didn't get more than two. So I said, "If this fails you're going to shoot me." Either outcome, I'll be gone in 18 months.

Steve said, "Great that's exactly the kind of person I want in this thing - It's a deal. "Steve was absolutely true to his word. He managed to keep the usual corporate bureaucracy off our backs. We started up this business quickly and it was very successful, but I didn't leave. Steve found something else very entrepreneurial for me, and then another. I ended up staying there 12 years, but never with an expectation for more than 24 months.

In 1986, Steve left Baxter to start ARCH at the University of Chicago. One of the commitments that Steve makes to people when he's their mentor is that it's not just for the time that you're working for him - it's a lifetime commitment. You will always have a call on his time any time you want help or advice. So you stay in touch with Steve. Even after he left Baxter, I stayed in close contact with him.

Steve brought Bob Nelsen into ARCH and Bob was the life science guy. I ended up spending a lot of time with Bob in the early days. Bob would look at these different technologies at Argonne or the University of Chicago and he wanted somebody as an outside sounding board to discuss whether something had commercial potential. So in one sense, I was a part of ARCH from the early days. I worked with Steve and Bob during the birthing of this thing. I always felt like I had a vested interested in the firm. I stayed at Baxter until about '92, and then I went and became the founder and CEO of a start-up biotech company, starting from a blank sheet of paper. I took that company through its IPO. Then I became CEO of another biotech, a turn-around situation that another Baxter alum-turned-VC, Pete McNerney, brought me into. We merged that into a public biotech company.

At that time I was talking to a few venture capital groups and I discussed them with Steve. I had decided to go into venture capital when I got a call from Liposome Technology (later called SEQUUS Pharmaceuticals). I realized that the one thing I hadn't done in biotech was to get a product through to FDA approval and get it launched. SEQUUS was an opportunity to do that, and it was just too good to pass up. So I put my plans for venture capital on hold and went to SEQUUS and we got two products through the FDA and EMEA and onto the market. These were products that saved people's lives. I helped build SEQUUS into a real vertically integrated pharmaceutical company, which was later merged into ALZA. Again, some venture funds approached me and I went to Steve to ask him for advice.

Steve said if you're going to join a venture fund you should join ARCH. I talked to Bob Nelsen. We talked about having been a CEO of venture-backed companies and the definite likes and dislikes about the way different firms work. ARCH is really very much an entrepreneur's venture capital firm. The guys there were entrepreneurial. They'd all gotten deeply involved in starting up companies. It's kind of the old school of venture capital. That approach was attractive to me, a situation where I could be the kind of venture investor that I would like to have as a CEO at a firm who invested in technology with the potential to have a major impact. So it was really a pretty easy decision to join ARCH. There are other firms that do that kind of thing too, but there aren't a lot of them. As funds have gotten bigger and invested in later and later stage, the mix of what funds do has changed. So, ARCH was uniquely attractive.

When I started, I told Bob I don't think I'm ready to just read business plans, listen to pitches, and sit in board meetings. I've been involved in running companies. I really enjoy helping to build these things and getting my hands in the soil. I still would like to spend part of my time doing that. That's a significant part of what I've done at ARCH - be the active chairman of ARCH portfolio companies at different points in time. And each one has had a specific objective. For example, I was chairman of Xcyte. They had a promising technology. They were in the clinic with indications of safety and efficacy. We needed to get that company to the next level. We needed to hit some clinical milestones and decide where this technology had its best chance of working. We wanted to get some corporate partnerships done. So, I came in there and worked with the management team to get those things accomplished. ARCH has allowed me to do an interesting hybrid of traditional venture investing: looking at business plans, meeting with teams, spending time in research laboratories to find innovative technologies for our companies, etc. And then I'd get involved pretty deeply through some period of time in helping companies achieve specific goals.

If you look at venture capital as an industry, it is investing later and later, particularly in life science. However, ARCH is still finding very promising technology that's still in a university and ready to come out or at a corporation where it is not being fully developed. We still do all that hard work of forming a company, licensing the technology, getting the IP and recruiting the team. Keith once described the process as making stone soup: you start with the stone and then you get all these other ingredients and you make something out of them. I think that's one of the unique things that ARCH does. We will go in very early and spend a lot of time at the University of California or Harvard or at other top schools, looking at the early stage science that has the potential to turn into a company. But you've got to find it, get it, complement it, build it, nurture it, and help guide it, often where there's no management in the beginning. I think that's what Arch does well and fairly uniquely.

SMALL GROUPS, ENTREPRENURIALLY MOTIVATED

Relative to the big pharmaceuticals, you can accomplish a lot with a small group of motivated, entrepreneurial people. You have the ability to collect a unique group of people who will take more risks and are willing to push the envelope a little harder, and even work harder. If you look at our companies, you'll see people in there routinely on Saturdays and Sundays and late at night more often than you would in a big company. They are willing to take appropriate risks in terms of what studies they do, what their clinical strategy is and so forth. You typically won't find that in a big company. I think we have the ability to put together the set of conditions that causes this to happen. That's not something only ARCH can do, but I think it's something we are very good at.

One of the things we do is challenge management. I don't mean we challenge management by saying, "do this or else," but "do you really need to do a 4,000 patient trial for that indication?" That's going to take us, $100, $200, $300 million and six years to do. Parallel to that, why not do a trial for this niche indication for an orphan drug where we only need 200 patients? Get into the market, get the approval, and do this while conducting this bigger study.

What we do is challenge company leadership and ask, "Are there other ways that we can build value faster in this company?" One of the things we do is look for non-equity sources and capital for these companies very early on. Where else can we get money to supplement the investment dollars coming in? What can we do to cut costs? Can we do studies or animal trials offshore? So I think it's the whole process of helping to encourage innovation and helping to bring other perspectives into a company.

There is a lot of accumulated experience in this firm. It is a stable partnership. All the founders are still here. Steve still comes to partners meetings and asks his very insightful, challenging questions. So the factors that would allow you to replicate your success - institutional knowledge residing in the key people - is certainly in place. We have every expectation to build this knowledge and experience over time.

At the same time, we also are pushing the envelope, continuing to innovate in what we do. In our latest fund, the University of California came in as a significant limited partner. They are interested in us helping them learn what else they can do to improve technology transfer. We've been going about systematically mapping the University of California, trying to understand what technology is where, who the key scientists are, and who has technologies that can be commercialized. This has been a very productive relationship.

EDUCATING SCIENTISTS ABOUT COMMERCIALIZING

One thing we do is to help educate the scientists about commercializing technology and to explain what venture capital is. We are working with the deans of some schools in trying to set up new models of funding and innovation, up to the point where they're ready for venture capital. Because venture capital is happening later and later, we have to find new ways to bridge the gaps. Projects that would have been venture funded five years ago won't be funded today and they are usually too far along to get grant funding. So, we've been working with a number of university people on developing new models to try to address that gap.

The success of technology transfer totally depends on the university. And even within the university it varies by department and by school. Some departments still see us as evil and say, you're going to corrupt us. Then there are other departments that see commercialization of academic research as an important extension of their mission. They argue that it's good for the academic community to have this commercial interface.

UNIVERSITY FRIENDLY

We are very university friendly at ARCH. If you're a professor and you've got a technology, we're going to be very collaborative with you and get your perspective on how you want to do this. What role do you want to play in it?

That's not to say that it's still your technology and you get to use this as a substitute for grant money, because that doesn't work. So you have to find the right balance. I think one of the things ARCH does very, very well is to help a faculty member get to play a role in the company where they're comfortable and productive. So, it balances the company's interest and their interest. And it's not one size fits all. It's not a formula. As the chairman of the start-up, you could devote three hours a week to the company. If you want to take a year off and do your sabbatical with the company, you can do that. Finding that sweet spot for a scientific founder is a skill that ARCH has developed through trial and error. We've found the range of productive ways to work, and we've also come to understand what the unproductive ones are.

At the end of the day all we can do is present people options. We never try to force it down their throats. We don't go to the tech transfer office and say, that professor's uncooperative, but we want to sneak his technology out of here. That's not the way to build your reputation in universities. Frankly, there are too many good opportunities where people want to work with us. If you don't want to that's okay, we'll go to places where we're accepted ... there are many of them.

"I DIDN'T WANT TO BE A RESEARCH SCIENTIST MY WHOLE LIFE"

PATRICK ENNIS

On his evolution from scholar to corporate technologist to ARCH

Patrick Ennis earned his undergraduate degree in 1985 at William & Mary in physics and math with a minor in classical civilizations. He then went on to graduate school at Yale and Wharton to obtain a Ph.D. in nuclear physics and an MBA. After stints as an engineer and manager at Bell Labs, in the spring of '98 he found himself at Lucent running a group of 50 people. Seizing an opportunity, he left Lucent and joined ARCH in the summer of 1998.

THE ROAD TO ARCH

In many ways, time spent working in academia and at national labs is very appropriate preparation for a career in the venture capital industry. Most of my time was not spent dreaming of esoteric theories. Instead, much of my time was spent in activities that represented transferable skills to industry: teaching, publishing articles, planning experimental schedules, coordinating projects, traveling internationally to perform research and deliver lectures. Of course, a great deal of time was spent in the laboratory, but it was often on applied science in areas useful for future start-ups: building computer hardware, writing software, building semiconductor detectors, building equipment, machining, plumbing, soldering, etc. I was fortunate enough to have support from my home institution and the U.S. Department of Energy to travel widely, performing experiments at many universities and national labs around the world. These included U.S. National Laboratories (Oak Ridge, Argonne and Brookhaven) and British and Canadian nuclear facilities (Daresbury and Chalk River). This encompassed the period from 1984-1991.

What was interesting about the mid and late 1980's was that few institutions thought about commercializing their work. In fact, at Yale, it was viewed as a bad thing. It worked against you if you developed something practical - you were viewed as a lesser scientist. The conventional wisdom was that great scientists have great thoughts and great thoughts are above something as pedestrian as a real-world application. If for some reason you did invent something practical, it was viewed as compounding the error by patenting it. The faculty couldn't be bothered to sully their hands with a patent. This mindset was wrong on so many levels. Human civilization has progressed nicely throughout the millennia partly due to the virtuous cycle of research, experimentation, and commercialization. The words have changed, but the activities remain the same. Somehow, in the mid 1980's, schools like Yale lost their way and forgot that basic research shouldn't exist in a societal vacuum.

The good news is times have changed for the better. I love it now when I visit university labs. Scientists, engineers and professors are all aware of the good they can do for the world by developing practical applications for their technology. "Products" and "Start-up" and "Patents" are no longer dirty words. They want to do something good for society. ARCH has been a big part of this, first at the University of Chicago and Argonne, and very quickly at other top institutions throughout the country.

I suppose I should be thankful for the elitist attitude of the Nuclear Physics community in the 1980s – it made me realize that I didn't want to stay in academia much longer. Admittedly, my time in academia was enjoyable and productive; I co-authored 15 papers and some are still heavily referenced. But I felt that I didn't have much to add beyond those papers and I didn't want to be the type of professor who spends the rest of his life redoing their thesis over and over again, with occasional expansion around the edges. I was more interested in people, business, practical applications and all the other challenges that are present in the real world. Perhaps that meant I wasn't smart or creative – but after 7+ years in venture capital, I can honestly say that splitting the atom was easy compared with the multitude of challenges one faces when building a business.

I was fortunate in 1992 to join AT&T Bell Labs in New Jersey. They had a program at the time to hire basic Physicists and turn them into productive engineers. The work was very interesting and challenging and I learned many new areas. Soon I began the slow transition into business and leadership roles. The standard progression was roughly: engineering, software development management, project management, product marketing, sales and general management. It was a busy several years but we achieved a lot as a business, culminating in the 1997 Lucent spin-off.

At that time, I was finishing up my MBA while I was working fulltime. The optical networking market was booming and Lucent was doing great. I had been promoted and was helping sell billions of dollars of product to customers around the world. At the age of 34, I had a lot of responsibility in an organization that was dominated by men and women in their 50's. But something was very wrong. It was a combination of factors including the bureaucracy, the sheer size of the organization and the relative speed with which Lucent moved versus its competitors. On the personal side, I didn't want to be one of the folks I saw at the cafeteria at Lucent that were getting old before their time, buying a house with a big New Jersey lawn and 2.4 kids. That's fine for many people, but it wasn't what I was after. The problem was what did I want? I was ignorant and unsure – I didn't know what I wanted.

New Jersey was far removed from entrepreneurial centers both geographically and culturally. I literally didn't know what venture capital was. So I was talking to someone at Wharton who was a banker at JP Morgan. He said, "You know, you should consider looking into the venture capital industry, because it sounds like you are interested in something that is fast moving and entrepreneurial, you love technology, you love business, you love people and you love bridging the gap." I responded by saying, "Thank you. What's venture capital?" Seems hard to believe by today's standards but in 1997, in the depths of a multinational with hundreds of thousands of employees, I didn't even recognize the term.

THE KAUFFMAN FELLOWS PROGRAM

He explained what VC was and I did some searching on the web, and I quickly concluded that it would be impossible to get a job because there really wasn't a "VC Industry" per se. It was very small and clubby – it wasn't like applying for a job at Goldman or Mckinsey where they hired a big fresh class every year. So I forgot about it and went back to building and selling telecommunication networks. But then I found out about something called the Kauffman Fellows program, which was then in its third year. Unbeknownst to me at the time, ARCH founder Steve Lazarus was one of the key people involved in designing and starting the Kauffman program. The program wanted to attract non-traditional people into the VC industry and they had a wonderful process that only involved one application, as opposed to sending letters to all 600 VC firms in the country. I applied and interviewed with the program and made it to the finalist event, which was in Kansas City in January 1998.

I took some vacation time from Lucent (I had months and months of unused time) and spent more than three days at the event. Two of the first people I met were Steve Lazarus and Bob Nelsen who were representing ARCH and I was very impressed by everything about them. They were knowledgeable, engaging, funny, experienced in business and technology and just genuinely nice guys. Then the formal presentation section started where all the VC firms talk about who they are and what they do. Out of all of them, ARCH was the most impressive. I thought, these guys get it; venture capital is about generating returns through breakthroughs. It's about speaking the language of science, and helping translate that into business. It's about being a jack-of-all-trades. It's not about just being a Harvard MBA and hitting the table and yelling at the CEO for not delivering the revenue numbers. It's about doing a little bit of everything. One of the phrases they used that day was a good early stage VC needs to be "VP of whatever the heck needs to get done that day" at their portfolio companies. It's a role we all continue to serve in the early stages of every start-up.

I did my background research, talked with the other VC firms, spent the evenings on the phone with friends and colleagues who were familiar with the VC industry, and we collectively concluded that ARCH was the best venture firm. These were the boom years and I was lucky enough to have offers from other firms, and I was thrilled and honored to accept ARCH's invitation to join them as a Kauffman fellow.

I came to ARCH in July of 1998 and moved to Seattle. At the beginning, I checked my ego at the door and realized I was entering a new industry of which I knew nothing about. I basically spent the first few months following Bob, Clint, Keith, and Steve around. My first week, I went to several board meetings. This is an apprenticeship business. I tried to keep my mouth shut and my eyes and ears open. It truly was like drinking from a fire hose and I had several great mentors to accelerate the VC learning process. I think many people fail in this business because they do not spend the time upfront to learn the basics, and then to gradually chime in where they can add value. Before you know it, you are contributing in various ways and working 24/7. But those first several months and first few years are key to one's transition from industry to venture capital. As I had some deep technical and industry knowledge in some areas, I would use that as a hook for being more active in these board meetings, even though I wasn't a board member. I would have dinners and lunches with the companies.

So what differentiates ARCH? It gets back to how I viewed everyone else who I saw presenting at the Kauffman program. First and foremost, we are money managers. Our limited partners entrust their assets to us. Thus we have to wake up every morning knowing that the goal is to increase the size of those assets. Of course, the art is the way in which early stage venture capitalists make money. It involves being a jack-of-all-trades and especially having a passion for technology. Naturally, you must have a passion for business too, but that alone isn't sufficient. Plenty of humans have a passion for business but far fewer have a passion for technology. But that still isn't sufficient; beyond that one has to have an ability to identify useful research or embryonic developments and see how it can be commercialized in the near future. This has to be balanced with an ability to not become overly enamored of technology for technology's sake, and that is where maturity and business experience comes into play.

I've found from listening to many other venture capitalists at the Kauffman event that they just as easily could have been a partner at McKinsey, a partner at Goldman, a corporate executive, or a politician. But they didn't exude passion about technology transfer, they didn't spend time with researchers developing business plans, and they didn't pull equations out of notebooks and turn them into products that customers will buy. That was the difference with ARCH. It was obvious that Steve and Bob understood the end to end venture capital process, had a passion for it, and had years of successful experience. Many of the other folks that presented at the Kauffman event said all the right words, but they weren't born to be venture capitalists.

VENTURE CAPITALIST

One of the beauties of early stage venture capital is that it is a highly leveraged model: one great scientist can come up with fundamental breakthroughs that can keep 100 engineers busy, who can then keep 500 business people busy. Thus, it is critical to pick that great scientist or small group of scientists. Large businesses can be created from that one person, and large profits and returns can result.

As an example, Carver Mead has helped co-found more than 20 companies, including Impinj. Carver also has an almost infinite network of relationships throughout the world in the semiconductor industry. Many of the leaders in the industry came through Carver's lab at Caltech during the last 40 years. It is like an extended family and the leverage comes from building a close relationship with Carver and then earnestly getting to know everyone else in the family. You can spend a lot of time in academia talking to a whole bunch of professors who are never going to have the brilliance and creativity of Carver and his extended family. As a venture capitalist, it is key to make sure one spends time appreciating a field that allows one to correctly identify the thought leaders and, more importantly, to have the credibility and integrity to be accepted into the circle.

Many lab discoveries look really exciting and unique, but before you invest you have to think carefully about the eventual products and markets. Of course, if a researcher figures out how to cure cancer, or how to make a battery last 1000 hours instead of 10 hours, then one doesn't need to spend a lot of time on a market study since those products will obviously sell. Clear breakthroughs like those make for easy investment decisions. Unfortunately, most lab discoveries are not so clear-cut; either they point to some sort of incremental improvement, or they show promise of a breakthrough, but not a confirmation. That is where the hard work begins. We do a lot of market research to figure out the need. Often this is inconclusive because customers frequently don't know what they will need in the future, especially if it is an innovative product or capability that they haven't pondered in the past. If one is comfortable with the future market need, then one necessarily focuses on engineering and development. How do we take a lab prototype or a research result and turn it into something that can be sold profitably in volume? Graveyards are littered with start-ups that had a really great prototype, but were never able to scale it up in a cost effective manner. This may sound like a boring part of a VC's job, and people don't write about it much, but it's a key part of the path to success.

We stay in touch with different technology areas. We try to be aware, at least with a high level summary view, of what's going on in many different areas of science and engineering. We keep an interdisciplinary focus and an eye on the convergence of technologies and markets. This requires a lot of traveling, reading, and talking to experts all over the world, and it pays dividends when forming companies and building relationships with key founders and business executives.

We also keep a database of all of our contacts with the Fortune 500. It's amazing that with our small team at ARCH, our collective relationships with the Fortune 500 are quite extensive. We can get to almost all personally, and get call backs in a timely fashion. This is a huge value addition to our portfolio companies. Many investors ignore big companies since they only invest in small start-ups. But the big companies are key because they are often incredibly important customers and partners with our start-ups.

THE NEW UNIVERSITY ENVIRONMENT

Some universities today have acknowledged that there isn't enough angel funding and seed stage investment money. Also, many university projects are just not ready to attract investment capital; they are still too "researchy" and the time horizons are too long. Some universities are trying to bridge that gap with their own funds – to provide money to projects that are beyond the basic research stage, but still too embryonic to attract further development funding. As an example, the University of Washington has started a program where they take a small portion of their ongoing licensing income (approximately $500,000 per year) and they call it the 'Technology Growth Fund.' This gets distributed in $50,000 dollops to professors and researchers to help them hit a technical milestone and develop a business plan. They give out ten of these a year, using a review committee consisting of local venture capitalists and entrepreneurs. They definitely wouldn't have done that in the old days – the money would've been recycled into the overall university budget. This program is important since many professors sometimes over-estimate the extent to which they've developed their technology. They often feel, "Hey, I've done this, let's build a company," and they really haven't done enough, maybe they've built one lab prototype, or maybe just an idea on a paper. Funds like this help bridge that gap and get it a little bit closer to where VCs will look at it.

DON'T OVERSPECIALIZE

There is a lot of over-specialization in today's investment world. As a seed stage venture capitalist, one needs to have a broad view and understanding. A development in a laboratory is, by its nature, novel and it may not fit neatly into a pre-defined technology or market category. If you take a generalist's viewpoint by letting the technology develop before large investment dollars are committed, and before a particular product direction is taken, you will be rewarded with out-size returns. Virtually all successful start-ups wind up executing a business plan very different from the original concept. Thus the key is to stay nimble and fleet of foot. Great management teams and entrepreneurs need to be flexible enough to take breakthrough technology and match it up correctly with the appropriate products and markets.

MINING THE CORPORATION

From *Done Deals*

After focusing on university and laboratory technology primarily, we started to see opportunities in technologies that had been developed by corporations but were not being pursued by those corporations. In Fund Three, which is a $107 million fund, we dealt with several companies that are spin-offs of technology from company research and development locations. The techniques are quite similar to doing university research. We still take pure technology, act as entrepreneur or general manager—until one can be recruited in—and then nurture and support that concentration of technology That appears to be a portfolio-expanding idea, getting away from just purely doing universities and laboratories, and having a different set of opportunities that balance the deal flow.

We tried to come to grips with the question of specialization versus generalization. It was being argued in venture capital circles that technology was becoming so sophisticated and so granular that you had to restrict yourself to life science or information technology, for example, or sometimes a subset of information technology. Because we were casting our net so broadly at a university or in an industry, we felt that that specialization would be a mistake for us. What we decided was that the general partners should become reasonably knowledgeable in one or more technological areas. Then we would hire a group of very, very sharp consultants—PhD-level academics or practitioners who understood the subsets of technology very, very well—and then pair the consultants and the partners together while working the deals. We felt that this was a successful approach to the generalization versus specialization problem.

In Fund Two, a $31 million fund, we recognized that we were sub-optimizing our capability for return by only raising the fund levels that were traditionally associated with seed and early-stage investing. We would do the start-up investment in the fund, the seed investment. We would invest substantially in the first round, but when the second, third, and fourth rounds were required, we would take an increasingly smaller position, and turn the control investment position over to a larger fund like Venrock. Essentially, that meant that we were doing the heavy lifting, and then inviting the larger fund in after a great deal of the risk had been washed out of the project. Although the price was somewhat higher, it wasn't all that much higher. So giving Venrock—who were great investing partners—that kind of a position was ceding to them much of the value of the deal. We determined when raising our third and subsequent funds that we would raise enough money to allow us to invest proportionately through all rounds to liquidity. We have 25 investments in both Fund Three and Fund Four, and these larger funds have enabled us not only to remain true to our seed and early-stage investment approach, but also to maintain a position that allows us to have somewhere in the vicinity of a 20 percent ownership by the time a deal goes to liquidity, either through an IPO or through a sale to a larger entity.

Our biggest success to date has been New Era of Networks Inc. (NEON), a company for which we help to bring the technology and the entrepreneurs together. Rick Adam founded NEON, an Internet infrastructure company. Even though he had come out of the financial services industry, he thought the great need was in health care. That turned out to be a mistake. Health care was not mature enough or ready to buy. But because Rick knew the financial services marketplace, he found very quickly that there was a demand for the product, shifted resources almost on a dime, and started to penetrate the financial services market. That propelled NEON's great success. It's either knowing where your market demand driver will be when you go in with your product, or having the background and the knowledge to sense where it's going to come from. If you don't go there first, you go there second. So Rick had a track record, deep market experience, and experience in having supervised some people before, having done a lot of hiring and some firing. That's helpful, because you're going to have to fire some people in these small companies. You can't afford to hesitate and wait until they really do damage. If you've got a vice president of marketing or sales who is not penetrating with your product, you cannot afford to stay with that person very long. The general manager has to be able to make that change. We've learned some other lessons. We're going more toward formal executive searches, where the executive search companies have exhaustive records on people.

Modern techniques of interviewing, a lot of reference checking, and exhaustive due diligence can go a long way toward making ideas bear fruit.

REFINING THE MODEL

The idea that only a venture capital fund, and a specialized one at that, can successfully execute technology transfers is not totally accurate. Many individuals, call them angels, have successfully done one-offs. When James Smith McDonnell, MIT graduate and founder of an aircraft manufacturing company that failed as a result of the Crash of 1929, approached Laurance Rockefeller with an idea for a company that would be developed around jet engines – a still undeveloped idea – Rockefeller willingly financed it. He was intrigued by science and its implications for defense. He also shared with McDonnell an interest in space objects and aliens.

Although Rockefeller may have later also helped shape the fortunes of the McDonnell Aircraft Corporation as a naval officer overseeing the production of fighter planes, his major contribution was his capital and his corporate network.

How do you convert one-offs into a pattern of systematic development? And how do you establish a ready source of raw material for your needs?

At its inception ARCH was helped by the presence of a national lab such as Argonne and the academic environment provided by the University of Chicago. But Argonne, funded by the Department of Energy, was limited in what it could offer in the way of raw material. And it took connections with the research and academic establishments in Texas, New Mexico and California to create a deep enough pool to draw from. The connections went deeper – into the research bases in Washington, in Massachusetts. Now there was a system.

But for the system to work there had to be recognition that it would add value to its participants – the research establishments, the researchers, and the underlying economy. Would it attract more research dollars? Would it attract more venture capital? More important, would it entice more researchers and scientists?

Underlying it all, there has to be a desire to make it work – from the perspective of the scientists and the science administrators. University of Washington's Ed Lazowska and Arizona State's Michael Crow discuss the elements of a technology transfer system and its significance for their institutions. Entrepreneur and venture capitalist Leighton Read explains how the ARCH model evolved over time and reached Silicon Valley.

"THE GOAL OF TECHNOLOGY TRANSFER IS MAXIMIZING THE IMPACT OF FUNDAMENTAL RESEARCH"

ED LAZOWSKA

On innovation and how universities can best facilitate successful transfer

Ed Lazowska has been at the forefront of computing and communications for more than 30 years. He currently holds the Bill & Melinda Gates Chair in Computer Science and Engineering at the University of Washington in Seattle. Professor Lazowska and his students have made numerous fundamental contributions through the years that led to innovations in computers, semiconductors, and the Internet.

Among his many honors include membership in the National Academy of Engineering and the American Academy of Arts & Sciences. In 2003, President Bush named Ed as co-chair of the President's Information Technology Advisory Committee.

Ed Lazowska has seen the good, the bad, and the ugly in technology transfer and commercialization throughout his career.

When one talks about university technology transfer, the most important issue is: what's the goal? To me, the goal is maximizing the impact of fundamental research. People in universities need to be looking far into the future, because no one else is. The University of Washington has a top-ten computer science department and our faculty is not thinking about products. They're thinking about fundamental research ten or more years out. Perhaps paradoxically, fundamental research is almost always the best progenitor of innovative products and businesses. And that's one of the reasons why we must continue to support pure research. Since industry typically does not conduct pure research, the role of universities and government (at the state and federal levels) in funding such research is critical.

Upon quick reflection, one might conclude that the best way to get innovative products is to fund product development. While that is a necessary step, it misses the research breakthroughs that occur years before any product is ever dreamed of. Think of pure research as the creative and practical foundation upon which new businesses rest. Virtually all of the things we take for granted in the modern world would not exist if it weren't for the strong societal support of basic research. But it is difficult in today's sound bite world to concisely trace the lineage of every day items like the Ipod or Lipitor to the foundational basic research performed in computing and biology decades ago. Yet the lineage exists, and given enough time, it can be accurately described as a complex series of causes and effects.

MOST COMPANIES DON'T INVEST IN FUNDAMENTAL RESEARCH.

There are many studies explaining why companies don't invest more in fundamental research. The answer is relatively simple: in general, it isn't appropriate for a company to perform much fundamental research due to investment timelines. This makes it all the more important that, as a country, we keep our university research enterprise healthy. Of course, most technology companies have large R&D budgets, but they are typically entirely focused on engineering and support for existing products. There are very few exceptions. I don't mean to demean the technical challenges of producing the next version of an existing product. A lot of incredible clever work goes into it, but it isn't laying the groundwork for future breakthroughs.

Microsoft is one of the exceptions that invest significant resources in world class research. It has arguably the world's strongest computing research organization of approximately 700 people with a ballpark budget of $300M a year. That's a lot of people and a lot of money for a company to devote to basic research. To put it in context, Microsoft's entire R&D budget is several billion dollars a year, involving tens of thousands of people. Most of that is focused on development and supporting existing or near term products. When most companies report their R&D budget, usually zero percent is true research. For a very few (such as Microsoft, Intel and IBM), only a single digit percentage is focused on true research. The rest of the computing industry such as Dell, Oracle, Cisco and everyone else do not invest in anything beyond one or two product cycles. That's in fact an enormous compliment to Microsoft relative to the rest of the industry. They're putting $300 million a year into fundamental research in computer science and the rest of the industry is doing very little.

BASIC RESEARCH INTO PRODUCTS

Funds such as ARCH are out there trolling for ideas and talking to people, and seeing what sounds interesting. That's incredibly important. It helps professors to be more attuned to what research might result in a commercial innovation. But we don't want professors too attuned - otherwise that will limit the potential of their research.

Let's use Lee Hood as an example. Lee is one of the most important figures in science and is currently the founder and head of the Seattle-based Institute for Systems Biology. Among other things, he invented the gene sequencer and his work has catalyzed the entire biotech revolution. He has founded and worked with many successful commercial companies. But Lee Hood is not sitting in his office trying to figure out what the next company is going to be – he never has. His labs have always worked on long-term basic research problems and his innovations were developed along the way as tools to help solve his problems. These tools happened to have amazing and profitable real world uses.

Today, his long-term research interests involve predictive, preventive, and personalized medicine through systems biology. For the previous 15 years it was the genome, and there were a set of technologies he needed in order to pull that off. He invented those technologies, but the goal wasn't to invent those technologies and create companies, the goal was to solve the scientific problem.

What's interesting about ARCH to us at the University of Washington is that they always seem to "get it." In addition to being VCs and business people, they are also geeks and scientists – whatever word you want to use - they're highly technical people. More than other venture capitalists, they're willing to invest in innovative technology, even if the product potential isn't clear. This model leads to the most exciting products and the best rewards.

Netbot is a good example. I was the department chair from 1993-2001, a period when we transferred many technologies, and Netbot was the first one we did with ARCH. At the time, the professors behind Netbot weren't thinking about building something practical; let alone forming a company, they just had ideas. ARCH was the fund that was willing to invest in these ideas and bring them along and get in there and roll up their sleeves and figure out how to turn it into a product. It became a very successful company.

The co-founder, Prof. Oren Etzioni had this incredible idea in the shower one day regarding software robots on the Internet. He was engaged in a 10 to 15-year program of research on artificial intelligence for robot control and decision-making under uncertainty. He wasn't planning on doing a company. Oren's initial insight was in the area of virtual robots and it opened up an enormous set of possibilities. They weren't focused on Internet search or shopping specifically. They set about seeing if there was someone who might be interested in licensing some of their software. The tech transfer office at the time got wind of this and said "no," it isn't commercially interesting. Fortunately, we knew ARCH and they were walking the halls and helped us with the commercial applications.

Impinj is a company co-founded by Chris Diorio, a faculty member of ours, and Carver Mead who is one of the most important figures in the development of the semiconductor, electronics, computing and telecom industries. Chris' PhD thesis work resulted in a transistor that exhibited plasticity and tunable behavior that allowed analog circuitry in a standard digital CMOS process. Chris figured out how to make multi-transistor circuits and he devised algorithms to exploit it and thought about a wide range of hypothetical applications. But there was no clear notion of how practical this was going to be and no idea what the market might be.

Impinj started working with ARCH and Madrona and examined many potential products and markets. Somehow, in the folds of time, they migrated towards RFID, which turns out to be a really interesting market. But again, it's totally different from what they thought they would be doing initially. RFID is a very narrow use of the technology that this company has. The self-tuning analog silicon has an incredible variety of applications. And while they are making a success out of RFID, it exploits just a tiny sliver of what they are able to do, which bodes well for growth and future products. This is a hallmark of successful companies formed on breakthrough research; the initial research is very broad and powerful. Initial products need to narrow down the technology, and then if successful, additional products are developed in the future using the same core technology. This represents great leverage off of the original basic research investment, and it's why the return on investment for government support of university research and technology transfer activities is very high.

Successful spinouts help the University in many ways. Professors learn a skill in entrepreneurship and forge ties with industry and other people in the venture community. They then can serve as a model for other students and faculty. They bring all this back into the university and it becomes a virtuous cycle. The best students worldwide want to study at universities that give them an exposure to entrepreneurship and the opportunity to see their basic research discoveries percolate into the world.

ORGANIZATIONAL CHALLENGES

The point of university tech transfers is to maximize the impact of research. There are many ways to do this: graduating students, publishing papers of influence and commercializing the research. Universities in general tend to view tech transfer offices as profit centers. In my view, that's not the optimal role, because the tech transfer offices often focus on smaller short-term returns and often miss the big picture. I think the tech transfer office should be more or less a breakeven operation for the university. Its goal should be to maximize the impact of the university's innovation by getting it into use. Sometimes that might entail licensing terms that do not initially bring a lot of cash to the university, but in the long run it can increase the impact of innovation which will eventually bring far more money back into the university. Attempts to maximize revenue in the short term can wind up reducing impact by restricting the scope of a license.

Nevertheless, there are two sides to this story. Imagine if you're the person at the University of Illinois who let Marc Andreesen and Netscape out the door (Netscape was founded without using the original University of Illinois technology). Although Netscape eventually paid $3 million to the University to settle the dispute, that is a pittance compared to what the University would have realized through a license (such as Stanford did with Google). Imagine the constipating effect stories like this have on tech transfer operations; nobody wants to be the guy who lets the next Netscape slip away. Tech transfer groups then create a chilling climate for the type of lenient terms that maximizes impact. So I think it's really important to have a notion of why we're in the business of tech transfer. Why we're in the business of being in the universities. We're in the business of universities to have research impact and tech transfer is part of that.

During the time I was chair at the University Of Washington we had a revenue distribution that was out of step with other major universities. It took us 6 years to get it fixed. The majority of all revenue was maintained in the provost's office. Very little went to deans and departments. So there were no incentives for the department chairs to encourage or facilitate tech transfer. When I was chair, I encouraged tech transfer because it was important and the right thing to do. But it was a thankless job because it entailed a lot of work with no extra resources or reward. When a start-up is formed, often a faculty member takes a leave of absence, and the chair is the person who has to ensure all the classes are taught. The chair has to mediate the disputes regarding the start-up between the founding professors and their graduate students. But the provost keeps all of the money! So that choice about how funds were distributed wound up creating a funny alignment of incentives in which many chairs didn't facilitate tech transfers. It just created headaches for them and they weren't given rewards to offset those headaches.

Let me try and recount some of the challenges of venture capitalists coming on campus and working in transfer technology. A challenge always is protecting graduate student interests. That's because you have an inevitable conflict of interest situation. You've got a faculty member who's advising the student at the university, and a faculty member who's founding a company using some of the students' technology, and who may be working for the company. You have to oversee that in a way that protects the students' interests and also protects the faculty member from false accusations of exploiting and taking advantage of the student. So that's difficult, and while there isn't always a clear path through it, good upfront procedures and communication can help navigate the thicket.

The better venture funds make it clear to faculty that they don't want them to take the CEO role. Founding faculty can add much more value as the key technical lead of the company. Learning on the job is required, but not as CEO. Professional management can greatly increase the chance of success. It is very easy to confuse maximizing the size of the pie and maximizing the percentage of the pie that's yours. The leverage is maximizing the size of the pie. Bringing in professional management early on will reduce the size of everyone's piece, but as a result the pie will grow much larger and everyone will be better off. But founders often say that because bringing in professional management costs money, wouldn't it be better to wait to hire a CEO. With the money we save, we can operate for an additional six months before we need to raise another round of money. Often this turns out to be just enough extra time enough to drive off a cliff, where if you had adult supervision for that period, it would have cost you a little money, but you'd actually still have a company.

THE GOOD VC

Faculty members often don't realize that technology is just a tiny fraction of a successful company. The majority of the work involves business, marketing, finance, recruiting management, etc. That's where a good VC comes into play, especially ARCH who can understand both sides of the equation, the raw technology and the business aspects. Also helpful is having faculty that has gone through the start-up process in the past, to provide role models for new faculty and students. Having a significant number of venture funds around is key. ARCH was one of the first who worked with many professors and researchers, and they are people we can trust. That means we know we're going to get good advice from them and they're not going to try to take anybody to the cleaners. They'll be candid with us, and we can be candid with them. And that's made a huge difference.

Many universities are successful at transferring technology without the world's greatest tech transfer office, but a good provost's office is essential. It's the provost's office that can decide whether or not a faculty has a conflict of interest or not and they set the tone for what the rewards system is. As a professor, are you rewarded for patents in addition to publications? Is entrepreneurship valued? Are there policies to back that up? What is the incentive system for faculty? Income is one incentive, as is the ability to make an impact and see the fruits of your labors diffuse out into the world. Being an entrepreneurial faculty member can also make you a better professor. Going out and doing companies gives you additional dimensions that you bring back and enrich your teaching and your research.

Often, more important than formal process is the serendipity factor. When Bill Gates and Paul Allen were high school students they were horsing around and figuring out computers by using an old terminal that happened to be connected to computers at the University of Washington. It's not in our official mission statement to let brainy high school kids sneak in and use our equipment but it's part of what happened and it changed the world, and of course Bill and Paul have been forever grateful!

"UNIVERSITIES ARE TRYING TO BE AS INVENTIVE AS POSSIBLE"

MICHAEL CROW

Arizona State University President Michael Crow discusses the need for technology transfer

If there's someone who understands the ins and outs of the technology transfer process, it's Michael Crow. Currently president of Arizona State University, he has been involved with technology transfer since the 1980s when I first met him at Iowa State University. There, in Ames, this dedicated missionary of science and technology tried to create a whole new avenue of development for Iowa State, a predominantly agriculture-related university. Crow's next stop was as deputy provost of Columbia University, in New York City, which had already had some success with technology transfer. At Columbia he worked on systematizing the entire process of technology commercialization, taking it from the one-off to a system. As president of ASU he is responsible for leading one of the nation's largest public universities, but advancing technology transfer remains one of his major objectives.

Universities and colleges assumed their present institutional form almost a thousand years ago, and their predecessors span the preceding millennium. This is an ancient institutional form that has undergone only minor organizational modifications during the past century, and in this context, technology transfer is, in a sense, a whole new thing. Technology transfer is a mechanism developed and enlisted by universities - and, I think, driven in large part by the unprecedented changes in science and technology of the past fifty years - to position themselves three steps rather than five steps away from the market. Universities still do not overlap the market to any degree, but they are two steps closer. And to achieve this proximity, however removed, the university has had to build some kind of mechanism.

Basically, several forces have been pushing technology transfer.

One factor is the government, which provides much of the overall research funding. The government encourages universities to advance technology transfer. For one thing, it is perceived to be important for the national economic competitiveness agenda. Whether or not it is, that is a different story. I think a second driver is that the general stock of knowledge has become so big and so broad. With tens of thousands of journals and hundreds of thousands if not millions of articles, it has become much more difficult to sort out those things that have "technological immediacy," if you will. And so the overwhelming expansion of the stock of knowledge drives what I call "technology nuggets" to the surface. And with technology transfer, universities have a mechanism to deal with those technology nuggets. And I think a third factor is the funding profiles of universities. There is the assessment that institutions can make some money off this stuff to put back into their core enterprise, and that is certainly important.

The returns are not always real in the short run, and they are real in only a handful of places, but I think that technology transfer has potential as a modest source of income for universities over the long term. And that is notwithstanding the bureaucratic infighting that might take place over it. The article in *Fortune*, which you may have read, does take a serious attack at the whole model. The author is in effect saying, I thought all this stuff was supposed to be free. That person, of course, is thinking about the stock of knowledge. But that is not the case when it comes to technology nuggets.

That author is thinking about the fact that taxpayers are paying for research and expect something in return. So, in a sense, why do universities have to be paid again? And that is actually the corporate model. Taxpayers *do* want something more definitive back from their investments than just a larger stock of knowledge.

Another motivating force is that universities are highly competitive with one another. Over time that competition is one of the driving forces of excellence among American universities. Each is always looking for more ways to be more and more competitive. And so MIT and Columbia and Harvard—as well as ASU and other schools across the nation—want to demonstrate that they too add to the stock of knowledge. Yes, we produce great students, but you know what? We have also developed the drug that cured glaucoma. We also developed the corn variety that created a new amino acid profile for lysine production or starch production, or whatever it happens to be.

THE DRIVERS OF TECHNOLOGY TRANSFER

Each of these institutions wants to be on that list. We did this, we did that, and we made these contributions. And so competitiveness is a huge driver. It was a driver at Columbia, and it is a driver here at ASU. We gain political support based not only on what we do in term of our core mission—teaching, research, and public service—but also for our capacity to be an inventor that offers return on investment. Another driver is the notion that centers for innovative activity are places where economic development occurs. And while the data on that is complicated, universities are trying to be as inventive as possible. Pittsburgh is an example of a place that has tried this as their central strategy.

There are certain key elements that make the process of transfer efficient. One is the ability of an institution to hire experts, both in the form of lawyers and technology specialists, who have the capacity to translate between what the university is doing and what the market wants. Wherever the staff cannot do this, the institution does not succeed. It fails totally because almost all university inventions are not "pulled" by the market, and they are not driven by some market strategy or some company. They are basically random. They are derived from non-market-oriented problem solving. And so the key is the translational energy that goes into translating between university discovery and market application. And the more sophisticated the staff is in performing that function, the more successful the unit.

LATENCY REDUCTION

Somebody has to have the vision to say, let's do it, and here is what we need. The dots may not be connectable because they may not even be visible. It is almost always the case that university research may not be visible, because, again, the market is not demanding the product. The product is derivative of another set of forces. So it has what I call a high level of "latency," and that latency has to be reduced through the efforts of a technology transfer shop or through the efforts of an ARCH Venture Partners-type group. These are the people that bring a particular expertise—you could even call it "latency reduction." They take something that has little potential, and they find out how to plug it in. To most people it may seem to have no potential at all because it is not derived based on its potential.

If you consider the process at universities, even when they get the right people to translate, there are always other forces that contribute or detract. There are the normal academic forces, among these the inventors themselves. Faculty members are very intelligent and capable and many of them believe that their intelligence and capabilities translate across all areas when, of course, this is not the case. And that presents problems. You are dealing with really smart inventors who think they can basically advance companies into commercialization without much effort. And anybody involved in the process realizes that the effort is immense, but the skill set is very different from the process of discovery. The translatability between the two is low.

Some universities are willing to pay the cost of what it takes to actually engage in technology commercialization, at least in the early stages. They are willing to be protective of their intellectual property. They are willing to litigate because it is a highly complicated and litigious arena, with lots of disputes that have to be resolved by the courts. If you think that the courts are a threat to the overall enterprise, or the university is unwilling to engage in that arena, then you have a problem. Universities are often not prepared for the business aspects of being involved in technology commercialization.

Sometimes the example of other successful entrepreneurial activity encourages universities to take something from a raw early stage to a more mature commercial stage. Another factor is the proximity of large corporations and technology institutions. These factors force the university to assume a different working modality in this particular space. Once the business mechanisms are put in place, they become the way in which technologies are commercialized, and those universities that understand this do well, and those that do not understand it do poorly.

No university has more than ten percent of its research agenda funded by industry—ten percent at most. There might be one or two at twelve percent or so, but most are between seven, eight, or nine percent. Given the small percentage of the overall research volume, to become a corporate research lab would mean that corporations could say, I want you to solve these problems, I want you to solve them only for us, and you cannot write about the solutions to these problems to anybody else. There are very few universities that would sign up for that - almost none. And so this notion that there is a corporatization process underway is a fallacy. What we have instead is a boundary spanning process underway. Technology transfer organizations are trying to cross the boundary between the non-market organization - the university - and the market organization: either the start-up company or the corporation.

THINKING ENTREPRENEURIALLY

The universities that have succeeded with technology commercialization— Columbia, Stanford, California, MIT, and a few others—all have a unifying set of matching characteristics, and this is comprised of an ability to think and act entrepreneurially as an institution. These institutions value technology transfer as a core element of their mission, and they have built the capacity to span the boundary that I talk about with a highly professionalized group of experts that have the capacity to accomplish this. The University of Chicago, to consider a counterexample, does not think of itself as an entrepreneurial institution. They do not see technology transfer and that part of the knowledge discovery and distribution process as a core element of their mission in quite the same way as other universities. And they probably go up and down in this context in terms of the kind of people that they bring in on the process.

How does an organization like ARCH Venture Partners fit into all of this? Even when a new technology is brought out of a university, it is still far from the market. The university needs an entity like ARCH that understands from beginning to end the special steps that have to be taken for there to be any hope whatsoever of taking some of these innovations forward. They are not the only group working in this arena, but they are highly unusual because most venture firms would have no connection at all to these kinds of early stage enterprises, particularly those that have come out with so many unknown factors.

THE GAP BETWEEN MARKET AND ACADEMIA

What makes ARCH work is an understanding of all the factors I have been discussing, and an understanding of the gap between the market and the university. An understanding of the peculiar characteristics and sensitivities of the academic inventor, and an understanding of the need for very careful nurturing at the $500,000 or even $200,000 investment level which is highly unusual. It requires the ability to very carefully select which of these technologies have some possibility of linking with another broader technology stream. It also requires an awareness and acceptance of the complexity of the university.

Universities are very unusual places, and those involved in this process can sometimes be hard to work with in many ways. Universities are very flat organizations and have characteristics that make it difficult for businesses to connect. So if a counterpart to ARCH Venture Partners has the capacity and the tolerance to work in that arena, they can do well. If they are not designed that way, and most of them are not - if they are not designed to take the raw nugget, as opposed to the process goal - they will fail every time. ARCH designed itself to succeed in this arena.

ARCH has succeeded in financial terms, and they have succeeded on many of the projects they have taken on. I think they have succeeded because they are in a niche role, and they are playing this particular niche and playing it well. If everyone were playing this niche, I do not know whether that would make it easier or harder for them. I think they have succeeded because of the commitment of the founders of ARCH -

Steven Lazarus and Keith Crandell and their colleagues - to stay focused in this particular way. In the case of Crandell, he grew up inside Argonne. And I think that it was their willingness basically to differentiate. What these guys founded was not just another venture firm, they founded a completely different approach. You come in, you take the company over yourself, and you operate it for a while.

They have been doing things differently in more recent years. But their heritage has been in a very different kind of venture role. They have come in, they have understood these companies, and they have made small investments historically. They have advanced ideas that are, in a sense, tiny. They are willing to take a tiny idea. The outcome of that idea may not in the end comprise the company. It may be a piece of what becomes part of another company. So basically they see the potential outcome. They are sending lots of things across the bridge, if you will - some times small things. They have de-risked them a little bit. And they know that many of them will not make it. But because of the way technology is evolving - the speed and pace of change - they are getting some things to stick.

ARCH alone is not enough. And what I did not know is whether or not there was a threshold. If you had one hundred firms working in this space, whether or not that would be enough. We confront this problem at ASU. We do not have anybody like this working with us locally, on a more intimate basis, to help us advance the kinds of things that we think have a lot of potential, not just to be licensed to a company, but actually to help start a company.

ARCH went national. In certain environments they are finding more feedstock than in Chicago. If you look at a list of all their portfolio companies, you will see they are coming in based on technology from all over. The probability that there is going to be a fit between something that they are looking at and some market development opportunity is really low. So you need a lot of throughput.

Steve and Keith talk about the idea that they are really looking at a global technology environment, and the notion of roll-ups. It's the idea that you could have someone in South Korea, or someone in India working on something in parallel. And that bringing it all together in terms of so much happening that you have got to "nuggetize."

At ASU we have built this entity called Arizona Technology Enterprises (AzTE) during the past few years. The first thing we look for is the people that can bring the skill set necessary. So we are actually constructing not an ARCH, but the vehicle that might be attachable to an ARCH. That is one vehicle out of the institution, and one vehicle into the market.

ARCH IN ARIZONA

From the lessons we have learned thus far, we are going to try to do it better than ARCH Development Corporation. So we have created Arizona Technology Enterprises. Now we are looking for partnerships and alignments with others, to build the ARCH equivalency. I think we have done some deals with ARCH, and they are looking at technologies that are here, and so forth. But that is done in their mode. We need things more ostensibly local, and so we are looking at a range of models that take some of what ARCH has to offer. The most important thing that ARCH offers is its ability to transact decision making and do deals around technologies that are at what I call "below stage zero." Below-stage-zero investment opportunities have technological potential but indeterminable market potential.

You basically have to be willing to operate off intuition on that indeterminable market potential, and have the capacity to do so because of an understanding that some of the things coming down the pike out of academic institutions are potentially highly valuable. And ARCH has proven that to be the case. So what we are looking to do is to build partnerships to work with ARCH-like ventures.

There are some universities that are entrepreneurial - the best examples are MIT and Stanford. There are some competing directly against entrepreneurial universities like California. There are what I would call immature universities, like ASU, with institutional cultures that are not yet rigid. And so at ASU we can look at what is going on and say, "Okay, let's take this, and let's do this, and let's build some of that, and let's do that," and we do not encounter institutional or faculty resistance. And we are instilling this "culture of academic enterprise" at the very core of the institution.

We do not have access to a national laboratory as ARCH did. But we are making enormous progress without one. Would it be helpful to have a national laboratory nearby? Of course, it would because it puts more random technology nuggets onto the field. And so it would be valuable if somebody could gather those things together and connect them and leverage them in certain ways, but we do not have that. What we have are highly entrepreneurial people in our AzTE unit working with very good inventions from our faculty. And we are finding that there is a way to get those to move ahead.

At Iowa State it was hard to convince people because it is a more traditional school. And it was running against the culture of the institution. And so people responded, "What's this all about?" The question was always "Why? This is not something we're supposed to be doing." And if that mindset is already built into the organizational culture, it is tough to alter. But now - years later - places like Iowa State, while they may not have been wildly successful, are certainly giving it a significant effort.

Columbia, by contrast, is a very tough and scrappy institution, sitting inside the center of entrepreneurial energy, in terms of ideas and finance. The board at Columbia, and a few of the senior officers, including myself, felt that we could put together the business acumen and the legal support to advance our intellectual property. We knew we had great scientists and great ideas. What we needed to do was to link those with other people. So Columbia was really driven by this competitiveness thing. I said, "Let's beat Harvard, let's beat MIT, let's beat Stanford, let's make some money, and let's use our great inventions to express the power of the institution."

"THE STORIES ABOUT ARCH AREN'T ABOUT THE SYSTEMS, THEY'RE ABOUT THE PEOPLE"

LEIGHTON READ M.D.

Entrepreneur and venture capitalist

The founder of Aviron, a biotechnology company that ARCH helped put together, J. Leighton Read is now a general partner at Alloy Ventures. A scientist, an entrepreneur and a venture capitalist, Read co-founded Affymax NV, under the direction of Dr. Alejandro Zaffaroni. Searching for something more entrepreneurial, he then went to launch Aviron, a biopharmaceutical company focused on vaccines for infectious disease, where he served as Chairman and CEO until 1999 and its director until it was acquired by MedImmune.

ARCH had an interesting set up and a system given the way it was formed, but the stories about ARCH aren't about the systems, they're about the people. It's about Steve and Bob and the team they assembled, and not particularly about Argonne, Chicago, and their birth with the trend features of tech transfer and finance. What has happened with ARCH is about the people.

ARCH in many ways exemplifies the transitions in the thinking of universities and venture capitalists over time from a very brand new immature industry and relationships to a very mature industry and relationship, where most of the players have learned a great deal. But there's now an interesting disconnect. It used to be that neither the entrepreneurs nor the investors knew what they were doing at the beginning of this industry, and now there's a whole cadre of investors, all the way through to the public market, that are very smart about looking at technology and analyzing risk and there's a whole management pool.

But there is also a continuous new stream of young investigators who don't have any of that background. So we've got this sense that there's a gap or a big funding gap, and there's a big problem in translation, which

I attribute to the fact that we have a constant turnover - thank god - a wonderful replenishment of the pool, of young entrepreneurs with no background or experience in what it takes to turn things into products. Twenty years ago that's where the investors were too. Now we've got a whole group of investors that have seen the movie many, many times before, and therefore their investment criteria are a lot more stringent. So there's a perceived gap that results from the differences in understanding what's commercially ready and what's not. And ARCH has lived through that. Then there's another theme that I'm not so much an expert on, but have watched through my career, which is that universities have gone through this period that I think Niels Reimer at Stanford first described as politically incorrect and very suspect for faculty to cooperate with commercial ventures. Tech transfer offices were very, very strict. Then they went through a period of realizing this is a really good thing to do, and then the investors and the entrepreneurs were taking advantage of the universities and cutting deals that were unfavorable to the universities and unfair. Over time, universities have found a more balanced medium, because of the people at ARCH and their efforts. I think they helped institutions avoid some of the excesses of being too strict or too easy.

Is technology transfer about process? I think I disagree with the thesis that there's a process here. All you can do is increase the odds. Each deal is still very unique. You can try and fit these deals into a pigeonhole, but it's a professor's relationship with his university, more than the technology itself, and the pathway that technology is going to take to market. If you can convince me there's a pattern and a system there, I'd be happy to learn about it, because I just don't see it. I think every deal is unique. All you can do is create a system to improve the probabilities, but there's just really is no way to systematize this, in my view.

This is an industry that grows up. After five or ten years, people start to figure out things that work and things that don't work - that's for sure. We have seen a professionalization of venture capital. In the past it was just well organized angels, but now it's really a profession.

A lot of the process is also geographic. Los Angeles has a number of technology rich higher education institutions, and a number of biotech companies that, for example, are high tech based. But those institutions, in relation to their research funds versus the Bay Area are totally different. The geographic concentration of start ups and venture capital is really a key part of your story there. It's not just the institutions, its geography. All of the institutions in the Bay Area have spawned lots of companies. But other than Amgen, I can't think of an important biotech company between San Jose and La Jolla.

It's really geographic. So there's some kind of network effect going on involving investors, the innovators and the discoverers, and their university institutions that represent them, and I think this is really important and it's overlooked. A big, big part of Intel, Gordon Moore probably would argue, is the venture capital, the thing that made the Silicon Valley possible. In fact, if people could leave Fairchild under California's lax non-compete laws, and go start their own companies and then leave Intel and start generation after generation of companies … I've funded a company that's a third generation spin out, and Alex Zaffaroni is extremely proud of the dozens of companies that have been started by people that had some relationship with Alza. That's a culture that may not be allowed to flourish elsewhere.

ARCH's success is interesting, because Chicago is not a great locale for entrepreneurial activity. It's not one of the great loci of start up innovation.

I was stuck with ARCH, and I'm much the better for it. After I left Affymax, my goal was to start my next company, as opposed to Dr. Zaffaroni's next company. I left Affymax just six months before it went public, after we had recruited John Dyckman and a great team to run it, and I was ready to go do my first company, as an entrepreneur. So I went back to the family partnership that I had helped Alex organize before Affymax and they loaned me some money. I was then in a position to start a company and I wanted to do it with first class venture capital. I was incubating a number of ideas with folks at IVP, Sam Colella, and Jim Strand. Through a series of conversations with some of the great infectious disease doctors, including Joshua Lederberg, from Affymax, and met Peter Palese at Mount Sinai Hospital, who introduced me to Bernard Roizman at the University of Chicago, and a third founder. We saw the opportunity to take technology from Mount Sinai and the University of Chicago as a basis of a company that would pursue live attenuated virus vaccines for important indications.

My public health background has persuaded me that ultimately one could make a very strong cost effectiveness case for new vaccines, and I knew enough about virology and infectious disease to know that live vaccines had a spectacular track record, they were just out of favor in the rush to follow peptide and vaccines that Chiron had started with their successful hepatitis vaccine. So it seemed like a good bet to me. These were terrific scientists, the third was from the University of Alabama. In organizing the company I was interested in, IVP was interested in taking the lead, and we needed the technology from Roizman's lab, along with Palese's at Mount Sinai. ARCH was the gatekeeper in Chicago. They said, "Well, we think this company makes sense, we like the syndicate, but we're not going to license the technology to this new company unless ARCH gets to invest." We actually pushed them back into a smaller position than they would have been happy with, because I didn't know them, and IVP and I were fighting over how to divide things up. I only had about ten percent of what IVP did.

And so we gave an investment to Steve, with whom I had primary relationship. And as part of the deal, ARCH had an observer right at the Board meeting, and so as we made progress with that company, we did a Series B, which was led by Accel Ventures, and Paul Klingenstein came on the Board a year later. Throughout those early years, Steve Lazarus would come to the Board meetings, and I found him to be a terrific advisor and contributor. And ARCH would stay in touch. Steve had had a lot of experience, and he was not in Silicon Valley here, he offered different perspectives, his involvement as a Director of Amgen provided a lot of big company experience that I really hadn't been exposed to - different from my experience with Alex and his background. Steve was also just a great source of common sense.

Not being a Valley person helped. He dressed differently than those other guys. He had that dark suit and a good tie, and none of us were wearing ties then in the Valley, even though it was the '90s. Steve is a cosmopolitan and that was a good thing for us. Also, ARCH was supportive at every financing. There really wasn't any question about whether ARCH was going to do their pro rata. I'm almost positive, that when we needed their help in the IPO, our IPO was not a financing event, and ARCH was also helpful there.

We started with technology from Chicago and that was absolutely academic research. There were no products. The first year was setting up our labs and picking out our strategies for how we were going to take the tools that Roizman and Palese had and build from scratch viruses that had the right properties of being attenuated and weak, and then safe, to produce a good immune response to influenza. RSV was the Mount Sinai lab technology, and Roizman technology was herpes and cytomegalovirus. There was a third case that was a different type of vaccine that had been created in Roizman's lab but it was licensed from ARCH.

All of our work was done at Aviron, in Mountain View , or at several different locations here on the peninsula in the Bay Area. None of it was done in the labs, none of it was done under contract. We took the ideas, maybe some biological materials to help us get started from both groups, but we were building viruses from scratch, using design principles, tools and genetic engineering techniques which were covered by the respective patents. And that was how we began. It was a very naive business plan, looking back from the perspective of 2005, because the time horizon for vaccines from beginning to end is at the extreme unfavorable end from an investment time horizon.

What allowed this company to be very successful? The credibility that we established by tackling these tough live attenuated vaccine challenges at a point when another vaccine that had been the subject of NIH research for 20 years of clinical trials, and it was already a 30 year old idea. Wyeth hadn't merged. American Home hadn't merged with Lederle, might have had a small vaccine business, and they had been in the CRADA with NIH, and they had a license from the University of Michigan for a technology that was 30 years old to make a flu vaccine that was a live weakened form of a flu vaccine. It was the kind of vaccine we were trying to build using genetic engineering in our labs. But it had already been built using old fashioned techniques that are involved in basically propagating the virus under progressively cooler temperatures, starting at body temperature down to the temperature in your nose, and a fellow at the University of Michigan named John Maassab had invented this vaccine.

In any case, Wyeth had dropped their interest in this program, and we knew a lot about it because it was basically the competitor to the vaccine we were building with genetic engineering. The old fashioned version, right? But I look at the data, and this thing had been in 20 clinical trials and it was just like our product, only five or ten years in the future. So we made a tremendous effort to bring it into the company, and take over its development. We were successful in getting the NIH and Michigan to sign up, over their initial skepticism about a start-up, because we had shown a real commitment and had built a real expertise in dealing with live viruses, in particular flu. Even though bringing in this program and the vast amounts of money it was going to consume was a threat to the science that Roizman at Chicago and Palese at Mount Sinai had, you wanted to see it advanced in a company. They also realized that it was a very important commercial opportunity for this still venture-funded company. So we brought it in, and it became the feature story for our Series C financing in '95, and the basis of our IPO in '96.

It did take resources away from the other programs, but it also provided resources for it, because I don't believe the company could have been funded if we hadn't continued. So some of Roizman's work continued as a result of this, as did several programs related to Palese's technology. In 1998, when the first bird flu epidemic came along, we built a version using Palese's technology modeled on the Maassab vaccine that was a live attenuated vaccine, and really combined the two - the old and the new technology - we built a bird flu vaccine that had very good results in chickens and ferrets.

The hurdle was the very long road of taking vaccines from scratch and funding their development all the way through to success, the enormous regulatory barriers, both on the clinical side but even more than we realized on the manufacturing side for vaccines. And then the opportunity to license in something that was much farther down the road and that could be financed, and that wouldn't have been financed if it was a dengue fever vaccine. It was a vaccine that people could understand, and it was in a period in which the public health authorities and physicians in general were increasingly aware that flu vaccination was a good idea. So we had the market, we had marketing, and we had demand at our back as we began the heavy lifting.

We didn't have to work very hard to do that, because the public health sector was doing that for us. Well, we did a lot of things. When we would have meetings for investors in September or October, we'd have a nurse there giving free flu shots. We had people talking about pandemic influenza to help people understand what was at stake. This was in '98 and '99, long before you were focused on bird flu.

Hurdles and challenges? Some of it is not serendipity. You're still out looking for this NIH Michigan type of thing, the Wyeth kind of thing, and things like that happen, but you can't write into the business plan that serendipity will happen.

Another company might not have been able to do that because the founders might have said, "No, no, no, we founded this company to work on my idea." These founders, and I know that Steve was supportive of this, and our other investors were very perceptive in saying, "Look, this is much closer to market, and that's what this is about, that's why we put the capital into the company to build valuable products, not to pursue any one particular academic dream." And it didn't snuff out any of those dreams, it just meant that they took second place.

The lesson from the benefits I had from ARCH is that you want a syndicate of investors that are diverse, that represent different points of view. You want people with the same business model, so they're going to be on the same page as you when it's time to make key decisions about bridge loans, about exits, and on dilution. You want people with the same business model, and that's a problem with angel investors and corporate investors, although they bring other advantages.

When I'm putting a syndicate together today, I want to see investors with a different perspective. So having ARCH in a deal in which we have two other local investors is great. While I was running a public company at Aviron, one of the big challenges there was finding the right CEO because I never intended to run it long term. I didn't have much contact with ARCH, I almost never talked to those guys, because we weren't really doing any business. After I joined Alloy Ventures and started investing, I started hearing from Bob Nelsen, and we started looking at deals together. He showed me some of his and vice versa, and we ended up co-investing in a raw technology start up, called Cambrios

Technologies - a wonderful company.

Bob called me because there were a bunch of interesting fits there. The core technology at Cambrios has a lot to do with two of the core technologies at Affymax using the genetic diversity of viruses to find peptides and then semiconductor tools. So I've really enjoyed getting re-acquainted with Bob and Steve and their colleague, Clint Bybee, who is on the Board of Cambrios. And what I like about that Board at Cambrios is that it represents a diversity of people. We're the only classic Silicon Valley venture firm in the deal – there's Harris & Harris, and Intel, and then ARCH.

EXTREME VENTURE CAPITAL

It took some time to recognize the uniqueness of ARCH, what it was doing and what it had accomplished. What was so complex about technology transfer? What made the passage of research from a laboratory to the market so difficult and arduous? And what do you call this style of investing?

Fortune Magazine has called ARCH's approach Extreme Venture Capital. Three of the discoverers currently working with ARCH - Carver Mead, Angela Belcher, and Mark Roth – demonstrate what this approach means. Bob Nelsen tells the story of building the long term relationship with Mark Roth that led to the founding of Ikaria.

Extreme Venture Capital - ARCH Venture Partners unearths ideas for start-ups where most VCs don't care to tread: the ivory tower

David Stipp, *FORTUNE* Magazine, October 26, 1998

The Lamont-Doherty Earth Observatory is only 18 miles north of Wall Street, but it runs on an entirely different clock. At the abbey-like research center overlooking the Hudson River, events that unfold in less than a century barely register—Lamont's cloistered scientists ponder things like the movements of continents and the genesis of ice ages.

Yet when the contrarians at ARCH Venture Partners heard about Lamont, they were eager to explore it for seeds of new companies. They soon found one: a scheme to take a navigational device for nuclear submarines and transform it into a divining rod for oil. Bell Geospace, a company ARCH formed in 1994 to pursue the idea, stumbled at first--not surprising, given that it was trying to commercialize an ultrasecret military technology glimpsed in The Hunt for Red October, Tom Clancy's 1984 thriller about a defecting

Soviet submarine. But now Bell is starting to take off--in September, Texaco awarded it a contract to probe 4,500 square miles in the Gulf of Mexico.

Chalk up another improbable hit for ARCH, a Chicago venture firm that specializes in ferreting out hidden treasure in the nation's ivory towers. Kleiner Perkins and other venture capitalist giants occasionally dip into academia. But "ARCH is the only good example of a firm I know of whose institutional format is incubating companies from academic labs," says Larry Bock, a venture capitalist in San Diego whose firm, CW Group, has worked with ARCH in funding early-stage companies.

"We've found most of our projects by walking the halls at universities," says Steven Lazarus, one of ARCH's four managing directors. The list of schools ARCH explores includes more than a dozen off the venture industry's beaten track--the universities of Michigan, Washington, and Chicago, for instance, and even City College of New York. ARCH also walks halls at federal laboratories, another venue seldom visited by VCs.

Most venture capitalists regard such places as byzantine backwaters populated by fractious eggheads. "We just haven't found [the places ARCH goes] all that fruitful," acknowledges John Mumford of Crosspoint Venture Partners, a Woodside, Calif., firm known as a leading seed investor. "Entrepreneurial people typically aren't in those institutions, and you need entrepreneurs to start and run companies."

There are two prominent exceptions: Stanford University and the Massachusetts Institute of Technology, which have long traditions of spinning off businesses with venture money. Not surprisingly, about half of the nation's $13 billion of venture investments last year went to California and Massachusetts companies--northern California firms alone pulled in 28% of the total, according to Venture Economics Information Services, a Newark, N.J., company that tracks the VC business.

ARCH's hinterland hunting has turned up one of its industry's most diverse investment portfolios. "The venture business tends to be narrowly focused," says Josh Lerner, a Harvard Business School professor who wrote a 1993 monograph on ARCH. "For a long time, more than 80% of its disbursements have been in just two fields, information technology and health care. ARCH has been more willing to look outside the box." Its startups include companies involved in electronics repair, oil exploration, lasers, and materials science (for a selection, see table).

ARCH's focus on seed investing also runs counter to an

industry trend. Since the mid-1980s, the average size of U.S. venture funds has more than doubled, reaching $76 million last year, thanks to inflows from pension-fund managers and other institutional investors seeking a piece of the next Microsoft before it goes public. As a result, VCs have increasingly invested at later corporate stages than they used to; only about a quarter of venture disbursements last year, or $3.1 billion, went to early-stage companies, says Venture Economics. The reason: It's a lot easier to administer a $100 million fund disbursed as, say, $4 million chunks in established companies ramping up to go public than as $200,000 seed investments. Venture firms typically derive much of their compensation from fees geared to the total capital they manage--so why bother breaking it into teeny bites for corporate newborns?

"The idea of VCs rolling up their shirtsleeves and starting companies out of a garage is really a myth," says Jesse Reyes, Venture Economics' research chief. There are still a lot of venture capitalists who do early-stage investing, but even those "tend to wait until there's actually a product shipping." While the Internet craze has bumped up seed funding over the past few years, he adds, "It's not a bad joke to say that many VCs have become investment bankers in sheep's clothing."

All the more reason to invest where other VCs ain't, says Lazarus. A surfeit of money is now chasing high-tech wonderkids in Silicon Valley and around Boston. Their best ideas often spark auctionlike bidding among rival VC firms. In the offbeat places ARCH looks, commercially promising ideas are harder to find. But making seed investments in them is cheaper, potentially yielding higher returns.

It remains to be seen whether this logic will play out as Lazarus hopes. Since 1993, ARCH has handily raised two sizable venture funds, mostly from institutions such as State Farm Mutual Automobile Insurance Co. and John Deere Pension Trust, and is now disbursing the $107 million in its second kitty. Most of the payoffs are at least several years away.

Still, ARCH is getting a reputation for prizing valuable nuggets from ivied walls. The University of Washington, for instance, "has proved to be a Comstock lode," says Lazarus. ARCH's first bet there paid off in just a few months. In 1996 it led seed investing in NetBot, a company that sprang from research at the school on software "agents" to aid online shoppers. Less than a year later, Internet search company Excite bought NetBot for $35 million in stock, giving ARCH a $9.9 million return on a $1.3 million investment.

With its wide purview, ARCH has proved adept at cobbling together startups that buy patent rights from different institutions' labs, none of which may have enough intellectual property to go it alone. For instance, Caliper Technologies, a Palo Alto company that ARCH co-founded in 1995, has rolled together patents from Oak Ridge National Laboratory, the University of Pennsylvania, Harvard, Princeton, and other schools to develop technology for fast, automated chemical analysis with miniature "lab on a chip" devices.

ARCH's main claim to fame may be its ability to deal with university bureaucracy, a rapport traceable to its academic roots. Worried about U.S. competitiveness and frustrated by a dearth of commercial spinoffs from federally funded research, Congress in 1980 passed two bills to promote technology transfer from universities and national labs. But problems persisted--for instance, an ambitious plan for a $100 million tech-transfer fund at the University of California was killed by faculty critics.

In 1986 officials at the University of Chicago and Argonne National Laboratory thought they saw a way to break the tech-transfer logjam and commercialize their researchers' work. They set up a nonprofit company called ARCH Development Corp. and chose Lazarus, a former Baxter International executive, to head it. The company had a shoestring budget and two employees--Lazarus and a secretary. To boost his credibility with professors, the university named him an associate dean at its business school and gave him an office there.

Other schools had mounted similar efforts, but most focused on licensing professors' patents to established companies. Lazarus was more ambitious: He wanted to spawn companies based on such patents, since licensed inventions often wither on the shelf at big companies--the not-invented-here syndrome. But he would need a lot of help, especially with the never-ending chore of sorting through the academic haystack to find golden needles worthy of funding.

Imitating fellow academics, Lazarus brought student power to bear. "In the first year, I got 20 MBA students working for me free," he says. "They were sentinels walking the halls looking for seed ideas. They looked and spoke like post-docs, and scientists felt more comfortable talking with them than with gray-haired guys in suits." Most had worked at corporations, he adds, and were aiming "to transmute themselves from worker bees into general managers of their own enterprises." Three of Lazarus' most eager understudies, Keith Crandell, Robert T. Nelsen, and Clinton Bybee, stayed on as ARCH partners after getting their MBAs.

With $9 million cobbled together from investors with ties to the university and from the university's endowment fund, ARCH invested in a dozen startups. The results were mediocre. Says Crandell: "Two years into our first fund, we had eight or nine companies on the verge of running out of money. It was hard to get out of bed in the morning." Five went under or were sold at a loss to ARCH's investors. The fund's cumulative return was 14%--ho-hum by VC standards at the time. Says Lazarus: "We made mistakes we won't make again," mainly misjudging market potential and underestimating the amount of money some startups needed.

Still, ARCH had developed a formula it felt basically worked. Importantly, it skirted a land mine that blew up similar efforts to bridge business and academia--professors' resistance to enterprises they regard as diverting university research to corporate ends. Part of the trick, says Lazarus, is keeping a high profile: "We disclose what we're doing to the entire faculty." That doesn't prevent academic purists from dismissing ARCH's staffers as meddling minions of Mammon, but it prevents imbroglios about covert conflicts of interest, such as professors' quietly using their university labs to do R&D for a company they have on the side. While its startups engage professors as consultants, ARCH avoids leaning on them too much--it generally seeks business veterans to do most of the work.

ARCH also stresses that it doesn't hinder academic publishing. That's usually not an issue, says Lazarus, thanks to the firm's sentinels--they tend to pick up on important discoveries very early, enabling ARCH to orchestrate patent filings before beans are spilled in scientific journals. With their varied interests, ARCH's scouts also help maintain the unusual diversity of its portfolio, letting the firm spread its risks in a way that more specialized venture funds can't.

Inspired by inquiries from other universities hoping to emulate ARCH, Lazarus and crew in 1993 reformulated the firm's operations to seek deals at far-flung schools and national labs. They raised $30 million, then set out for new places. One was Columbia University, whose vice provost, Michael Crow, had recently been asked to invigorate the school's technology-transfer program. Facing the usual bureaucratic inertia, Crow knew just what to do, he says, "I called the guys at ARCH."

One of its hall walkers, William Doyle, was soon installed at

Columbia's business school as an adjunct professor. On Crow's advice, Doyle dropped in at one of the university's little-known satellites, Lamont-Doherty, the earth-science center north of Manhattan. What followed was a classic instance of ARCH's calculated serendipity.

Doyle soon found himself talking with researchers Roger N. Anderson and Robin Bell about the U.S. Navy's classified technology for helping submarines run silent and deep. As Tom Clancy fans know, subs' navigational tasks are complicated by the need to traverse the murky depths with minimal use of sonar--its pings might reveal their positions to the enemy. In the 1970s the Navy launched a top-secret program to tackle the problem with the help of a technology called gravity gradiometry.

The basic idea wasn't new--in fact, it's mentioned as a historical curiosity in geology textbooks, says Bell, who recently wrote about it in Scientific American. In the 1890s a Hungarian physicist invented a device that could detect tiny variations in gravity's tug. His gradiometer--essentially a metal beam, with weights at both ends, suspended by a wire--was so sensitive that it could register the gravitational force exerted by a person standing near it.

Geologists after World War I put the invention to work finding massive underground deposits of salt often associated with oil--gradiometers can detect them because salt is less dense than rock and therefore exerts an infinitesimally gentler tug. But using the finicky instruments required removing swaths of trees and other confounding gravity sources all around, and painstakingly protecting the instruments from wind or temperature changes. By the 1930s, the oil industry had switched to less precise but far easier ways to get a window on the subterranean world.

Fast-forward 50 years: After expending more than $200 million on development, engineers at Textron's Bell Aerospace unit achieved their goal: a compact, computerized gradiometer that could be used in ships or even aircraft. Technically known as a full-tensor gradiometer, it measures how gravity varies in three dimensions, revealing much more about objects of scrutiny than did earlier gradiometers. Despite showing the way for the Soviet sub in Clancy's novel, though, the technology was never deployed in nonfiction subs--the U.S. version was still only in test mode at the end of the Cold War. "The Navy was using it to build navigational maps of the sea floor," says Anderson, "but they kept seeing things they didn't understand. We were consulting with them, and they would say things like, 'This crazy gravity machine says there's a mountain, and the sonar shows there's nothing there.'"

That was actually good news to the Lamont researchers; it suggested the device was registering masses under the sea floor--just what geologists want to do. Shortly before the man from ARCH showed up, the scientists at Lamont had learned something else. "For a long time I'd wanted to use the technology for research, but the guys at Bell Aerospace always shoved me away," says Bell, who had tried a relatively primitive gradiometer to study Antarctic geology. "Then one day, one of them asked if I knew of any applications." Hint, hint: With defense funding on the wane, funding for the gradiometer had been cut, and the Textron unit was desperately trying to emerge from the dark side. With ARCH's help, the scientists showed a way: Their new company, Bell Geospace, would license the machine for use in the oil patch.

There was a hitch: The technology was still classified. "Looking at that, 99 out of 100 VCs would have taken a pass" on investing in it, says Crow, the Columbia vice provost. Plowing ahead, ARCH added a potent player: John Brett, a retired Singer Co. executive and former Defense Department official with top-secret clearance. He made such a strong case to the Navy that it leased one of its research ships to Bell in order to test whether gradiometry could register signs of oil in the Gulf of Mexico. The ship came complete with a Navy crew authorized to operate the gear. Funded by $75,000 in seed money from ARCH, plus $25,000 from Brett, the test went well--among other things, it revealed a geological formation missed by an oil company's survey with seismic instruments, which delineate underground objects by bouncing sound waves off them. Anderson, who frequently consults with oil companies, soon lined up several to buy gradiometry data.

A series of snags nearly scuttled the startup. Though the Navy soon declassified the technology, Bell Geospace nearly ran out of money waiting to license it--Textron wanted more than the startup could pay. After finally working out a deal in 1996, Bell hired a management team and raised money to develop a version of the technology geared for oil exploration. All told, "we've raised $25 million in four rounds," says Brett, now Bell's chairman. "The fact that ARCH stuck with us was important. It made other investors feel secure enough to stay too."

So far ARCH has invested about $6.9 million in Bell, including $3.4 million in the latest round, completed in July. The firm's participation in Bell's later rounds shows a common pattern: As seed firms raise bigger sums, they move away from pure seed investing. Explains Crandell: "If we put $280,000 into a company as a seed investor, we might get $2 million out at the IPO. That's a very good return. But if we put in $2 million in a follow-on round, we might get $8 million"--less impressive in percentage terms but more lucrative in total dollars.

Is ARCH destined to become another investment banker in sheep's clothing? No way, says Lazarus. "We are an oxymoron, a $100-million-plus seed fund," he insisted in a recent speech. While ARCH is doing more follow-on investing in companies it has helped start, he adds that it isn't shifting to an investment-banker-like strategy of funding lots of companies it has not helped form. ARCH's partners still spend most of their time working on startups. They're extending their horizons to places that even they find surprising. Recently ARCH invested in ImproveNet, a Redwood City, Calif., startup that helps consumers find home-improvement contractors via the Web. ARCH discovered the fledgling right in Silicon Valley--it was hatched at Stanford, of all places.

"A REAL VENTURE IS SOMETHIING WHERE YOU HAVE NO IDEA WHAT THE PRODUCT WILL BE AND YOU HAVE NO IDEA WHAT THE PATH IS"

CARVER MEAD

Carver Mead is one of technology's pure avant-gardes. A sixth generation Californian and the Gordon & Betty Moore Professor of Engineering & Applied Science at the California Institute of Technology, he is a true pioneer and innovator who thrives in the culture and freedom of America's entrepreneurial society. Carver is the father of modern semiconductor design and his work and key insights in microelectronics have laid the foundation for entire industries. Every computer chip in the world is designed using concepts Carver and his collaborators articulated and espoused beginning in the 1960s. Today, virtually all aspects of our economy are heavy users of semiconductor chips – and there are chips in everything, including examples as diverse as computers, hearing aids, automobiles, cows, and cardboard shipping boxes.

Carver foresaw the technical and business implications of rapidly developing chip technology years before anyone else. At a time when integrated circuits contained a handful of transistors, Carver envisioned a day when hundreds of millions of transistors would be on a chip the size of a grain of rice. Carver's predictions came true, but more importantly; he worked tirelessly to ensure that society would have the tools to design these chips in a useful and cost-effective manner. Without his tools, modern chip design would be impossible. Carver Mead worked closely with Gordon Moore (co-founder of Intel) and Carver himself coined the phrase "Moore's Law".

Mead is a realist when it comes to true innovation. Those who really invest in innovation – in the unknown – are few and far between these days, he contends. More important, the transfer of innovation into the marketplace requires a community of workers, the collaboration of scientists, engineers, business people and financiers. And the path is full of trial and error. Mead has himself founded and invested in over 20 companies, including Impinj, an ARCH portfolio company. Here, he talks about innovation, the fragility of innovation, and what "the truth" really is.

THE REALLY INNOVATIVE VENTURE

A real venture is something where you have no idea what the product will be and you have no idea what the path is to the product. However, you do have something: a kernel of a possibility. Some may call it a technical or a scientific base, but there is no good word for it. This kernel may be a mixture of things that are written down, things that have been proven, hypotheses yet to be proven, or simply a set of experiences that people may have. These kernels typically come out of university research labs. There are exceptions (corporate labs, national labs, garages, etc.), but the majority of real breakthroughs have historically come from universities. There's something special about the environment: a mix of freedom combined with pressure to achieve. A diverse group of researchers from all around the world, the energy and optimism of young students and the battle scars of experienced professors - such a culture is very difficult to duplicate in anything but a university setting.

Out of this culture comes wonderful things: new stuff. The best universities are really good at it and this is one of the great strengths of America. Entrepreneurial innovation begins when someone thinks, "There must be a way to turn this new stuff into something valuable." In this context "valuable" means something that could solve some problem somewhere out in the world. In the old days, that was what a venture was: raw, risky and with all the challenges and rewards yet to come.

All successful ventures wind up being successful at something different than what was initially intended. The first "business plan" is always wrong. What's more important is to be flexible and to react to market, technical, and customer changes as they occur, and to be creative with the technology in order to keep up with the changes. It is a myth that things proceed linearly, and that is why today the vast majority of venture capitalists do not "do venture." Their appetite for risk and ambiguity does not match up with the realities of market and technical change.

Good VCs don't waste time with spreadsheets and shiny-shoed MBAs. Yet today the industry has been overtaken by a very bureaucratic process, what they call "due diligence." That assumes that everything's figured out already, but if it were figured out, it wouldn't be venture capital. So the modern people called venture capitalists are not venture capitalists all. They're what we would have called mezzanine investors in the old days. "Early stage" to them means that once a company has figured out what it's going to do with no risk then they'll be happy to invest.

The risk and all the creative stuff happens before you have it figured out. What I like about ARCH, is that they understand that scientists and entrepreneurs aren't going to have it all figured out in the beginning. The ARCH guys know they need to be part of that process and to help figure it out. Good venture capital isn't solely about providing money, it's about adding value and rolling up sleeves and understanding that there are going to be ups and downs.

Much of the early stage investing role in the world has been taken over by people like me who do what's called "angel investing." I don't like the word because I think a lot are devils. But the people who have been through it before know what's involved and they're willing to invest money early to get a substantial equity stake. It isn't one of these things that you could sell to most venture capitalists because those guys want it all spelled out.

ARCH invests in companies as early as I like to invest, although I invested in Impinj many months before ARCH did. At that time, we talked to ARCH a great deal and we figured out a lot of stuff in the meantime. So I look to them as an innovative fund who invests side by side with individuals and are happy to build relationships before an investment.

The MBAs and their "due diligence" are actually incredibly vulnerable to failure and bad investments, because a start-up can spell out the future in a most convincing way during due diligence and subsequently, it could still fail in a spectacular way. And all of the VC due diligence wasn't worth a dime because it had nothing to do with the fundamentals beneath it.

FIRST MOVER ADVANTAGE?

When you look at entrepreneurship, there is an inherent survivor bias – people only talk about the successful ones and they forget the failed efforts. The first failures often were the ones that had the original ideas, understood the concept, figured out that there was a practical use for it, did all of the hard work, and perhaps they just screwed up on some practical detail.

It takes a very keen intellect to figure out how a failed effort actually had it mostly right, except for a few critical details. I'm not taking anything away from entrepreneurs that become successful based on the ideas of prior start-ups. But an incredibly important contribution would be to study the prior efforts that failed. They often pioneered the way, and then later start-ups came along and became the big hit and got all the credit for it. A result that occurs when, in fact, someone else plowed most of the ground for that start-up.

Thus, the first mover advantage may not be much of an advantage. The first mover is very apt to fumble the opportunity because there are so many unknowns. Of course, the second mover also fumbles, and then it's the third or fourth mover that becomes a success. There are almost always two or three precursors to any successful company.

INTERCONNECTIONS

I've always been irritated when people ask me whether I am an engineer or a scientist, because to me, the answer depends on what hour it is. If you're trying to create something new, first you have to attain deep understanding. The world would say that step is science, and then, when you're using that understanding to build things, they would say that is engineering. They'd be wrong. Science and engineering are so inextricably intertwined that it is neither possible nor useful to make the distinction.

There's no way of creating anything practical without also understanding basic principles. Likewise there's no way of understanding deep principles without crafting an experiment to test hypotheses. We do ourselves a disservice by labeling folks scientists, engineers, theorists or experimentalists. At the best start-ups, a person may fill the role of entrepreneur, marketer, scientist and engineer all in one day.

Of course, if you left it solely to the scientists to figure things out, they'd never make progress because they don't have access to the latest findings in the real world. I learned this in an interesting way. I was a wet behind the ears, new assistant professor at Caltech, and this guy walks into my office, barges in unannounced and says, "Hi, I'm Gordon Moore. What are you doing?" He must have heard about me because he asked me about my research and the classes I was teaching.

He said, "Would you like some transistors to use in your lab?" In those days, I was using what was available from the Caltech stock room, a CK722 Raytheon transistor which was a gigantic device of limited usefulness. Gordon reached into his briefcase and he pulled out a bulging manila envelope. He opened up and out poured dozens of new, small transistors: 2N760s, 2N697s, etc. I had never seen so many transistors in my entire life. It was like going to heaven. So that's when I started my lifelong policy of always letting my students pick their own projects. I would supply any components that they needed, like the transistors. If the project worked, then they could keep them; otherwise they had to give the components back.

This incentive approximately doubled the project success rate because people like to work with and keep the latest equipment. They want to take it home to Mom or something, I don't know, but it just worked well. It was true in 1955 and it is true today. Entrepreneurs I know today insist on the latest electronic gadget. It may seem unnecessary but it's an important part of maintaining enthusiasm and stoking the fires of creativity.

Innovation and progress only occurs at the intersection of disciplines. Yet most universities are still organized around historical areas. I don't know anybody who's ever made a major contribution and has done it within the boundaries of one particular discipline. The disciplines were formed long ago, before anyone knew what future innovation would be. So how could you expect those to be guides for you? Well, they aren't. They are useless. Fortunately, academia has begun to adapt, and campuses are no longer littered solely with buildings for traditional areas such as physics, chemistry, biology etc. Now there are "biochemistry" buildings and "biophysics" and "computational biology." It's not enough, but it's a start.

EXAMPLES: DEC, MICROSOFT, INTEL

When General Doriot provided initial funding for DEC, they started to make these little logic modules. It later turned into a computer company (and one of the most successful and influential computer companies of all time). People forget that they became successful because of a paper company in Canada that had several plants that were all a little different. Some smart guy at DEC figured out they could make a little programmable thing – a computer - out of their existing logic modules and then program it to accommodate the differences in each paper plant. Call it serendipity, but it was about being clever and creative and not being religious about previous plans or technologies. They spotted a possibility and they followed it and kept following it which is, to me, typical of a really good start-up.

General Doriot said that after DEC became successful, a lot of people came to him and said, "When you find the next DEC, we want to invest with you." As if you could tell the winner from the beginning with any certainty. They wanted guaranteed huge rewards with no risk; an accurate time machine with which to see the future.

Most people know Intel is a successful company. I was badge number five at Intel, so I know what happened there. I had a great relationship with the founders: Gordon Moore, Bob Noyce, and Andy Grove. I love those guys and they've done fabulous things and two-thirds of my students for several generations went into Intel and did fabulous things there. But at the beginning, they had no idea which areas they would eventually go into – both technical and business. That's the way all great start-ups are. In the beginning, they decided they were going to make a high volume semi-conductor part, memories in particular. So they built a bipolar scratch pad and sold a few to people who wanted to experiment.

And then they built a thing called the 1101 and they sold a few of them. Bob Noyce was walking the halls wondering if they'd done the wrong thing, and then we hit the downturn in 1969 which caused Bob to pace the halls even more. One day I came in and talked to Gordon and he said things were going great.

One of their early customers was a computer company that was buying similar parts from National Semiconductor. But they were having quality problems and delivery problems. So the computer company wanted a second source and came to Intel and said, could you make this part for us? Intel agreed, and it wasn't glamorous and it wasn't brilliant, but it was business. Intel redesigned the part and made it cheaper, faster and more reliable. So they basically replaced National as being the primary supplier of this high volume product. That was their first profitable experience. But none of the history books about Intel tell that story because it wasn't sexy. But we needed business and it was business. It didn't matter that it wasn't in the initial business plan, especially since there never was an initial business plan! To get started, Intel second-sourced a National Semiconductor product - Second mover advantage!

Microsoft was the same way. Bill had personally written a Basic compiler to get initial business, but it didn't lead to the big break. That came along with the IBM PC opportunity and he went and found DOS which was originally developed at another company. He wasn't religious about it - even though he didn't write it - he aggressively purchased the rights to DOS to solve a customer's problem and create a huge business opportunity for Microsoft.

All great start-ups begin with a unique technology and a vague idea of some future product and market. But they never know at the beginning what direction it will take. A great team is fleet of foot, serendipitous and never gets wedded to any particular direction. It was true at Intel, true at DEC, Microsoft, and every other great start-up

HISTORY'S WHITEWASH

What actually happens with start-ups is always rewritten to look like it was all planned out in the beginning. None of us ever have it together in the start-up. We're fumbling in the dark and doing our best. And every once in a while, we get a few breaks and we're able to make it happen.

Any linear tale-telling of constant progress and accurate initial plans is pure nonsense. It is fable. I wish people would be honest about what really happened. I've been there dozens of times. I've been on the ones that fail and I've been on the ones that succeed. I've been on the ones that neither fail nor succeed; these are the living dead and they are the worst.

History is written the way the start-ups want to be remembered instead of what really happened. It's horrible because then the next generation of entrepreneurs come along and they think, "Oh my God, those guys were so much smarter than I am, how could I ever do a start-up?" And I tell them no, they weren't any smarter than you are, they're just the same. So the real damage from rewriting and sanitizing history is that it makes the past seem so much more intimidating to the next generation of entrepreneurs. As a community, we all need to do our best to let start-ups know that it's okay to flail around in the beginning.

"LOOKING AT THE INTERFACES BETWEEN CHEMISTRY AND BIOLOGY DIFFERENTLY"

ANGELA BELCHER

The recipient of the Macarthur Fellowship, better known as the Genius Grant, Angela Belcher is an unusual materials chemist with expertise in the fields of biomaterials, bio-molecular materials, organic-inorganic interfaces and solid state chemistry. An expert on abalone and black pearls, the focus of Angela Belcher's research is understanding and using the process by which Nature makes materials in order to design novel hybrid organic-inorganic electronic and magnetic materials on new length scales. Her research is incredibly interdisciplinary in nature and brings together inorganic chemistry, materials chemistry, biochemistry, molecular biology and electrical engineering.

It was at the University of Texas at Austin that Clint Bybee first began to work with Belcher on the project that evolved into Cambrios. Now that she is at MIT, she continues to be involved with Cambrios and ARCH.

I have a very varied background. My undergraduate degree is in biology. It is actually in creative studies, which means you design your own major; there are no required courses in my undergraduate curriculum. You can take any course you want and mix it any other way. I went to school at the University of California, Santa Barbara. It is a small college within the University. There are about a hundred students within the College and it was really the basis for how I see the world now because I feel you can mix anything together, try and see how it fits together and how you can improve on it. That is very much the basis of how I see the world, how I work in the lab and how I do the fundamental research that has gone into the company.

After my degree in creative studies, I went on to get a degree in something that I didn't know much about – solid state chemistry. I wanted to look at the interfaces between chemistry and biology in a different way. I stayed at the University of California not because I didn't want to move and it was a beautiful place to live, but because it's one of the early institutions to do truly interdisciplinary work in a way that was exactly what I wanted to do. I pursued research on how abalones grow shells. Even though living organisms have been able to self-replicate it wasn't until 500 million years ago that organisms began to make shells. Over a short period of geological time of about 50 million years, the organisms learned to make materials and it was actually fairly rapid development. In 50 million years time they were in the ocean. When the ocean conditions changed and it got pretty toxic, they had to learn to deal with increase in calcium. They dealt with that by growing structures. So these organisms learned how to make materials better than we can turn around and make them. They are relatively inexpensive and non-toxic. It was fascinating to me that they could make materials in a relatively short period of time. But they were very limited in the kind of materials they can work with. They work with calcium, they work with phosphate, they work with iron, and they work with silica. And why is that? Organisms involved with the ocean have to be able to work with their environment. As a graduate student looking at the periodic table, I was saying, "Wow, what about the rest of the periodic table?" Could organisms use those materials if they had the opportunity? And that's where my research comes in today. Can you encourage an organism to work with materials they normally wouldn't work with?

It's almost like seeding the pearl. Pearls were my hobby and I consulted in the pearl business, but I have been interested in pearls since high school. I did my PhD research on pearls, on black pearls

I am interested in interfaces, interested in real materials interfaces within the interfaces of science. I haven't watched Sesame Street for a very long time, but I probably will now. I remember they had "what things go together?" The idea was to take objects that normally wouldn't go together. Can you make them fit together? Can you encourage them to fit together and can you make them better? I get most excited by putting together these two things that people would normally not associate and make it work. And that's a huge space to work in. In some of the research we are doing right now, we're using viruses to synthesize batteries. There are two things you wouldn't think of putting together, a virus and a battery, but can you genetically evolve it to make a material.

Over time, the organisms have developed a DNA sequence, a genetic code that codes for a protein. The protein's job is to make this material and to make it the same every single time. This organism will spawn millions and millions of offspring and pass on to its offspring the genetic information that allows them it to replicate this shell again perfectly. It allows those offspring to give rise to millions and millions of offspring to replicate that perfectly every single time. So, if you could do the same thing, can you pass on genetic information to allow organisms to replicate batteries? To replicate solar cells, to replicate transistors and electronic components in a way that is always the same? Or, could you do this through natural evolution to make it better? I think that kind of goes to who I am and how I like to learn something that's new. I have no problem admitting I know nothing, and starting from there I think is a great place to start. Absolutely nothing, then you have nothing to lose and act as a sponge to absorb as much as possible. I am not intimidated going into new fields such as batteries. I know nothing about batteries, but can we make improvements on it? I know nothing about solar cells, but what can I learn and can I make improvements on them?

Let's go back to the calcium which is in the ocean. The calcium is dissolved in the ocean. In order to make the shells, we have to take the ions and make them into a solid and show what happens to these proteins that have amino acids. These organisms learn to grab the calcium through a special chemical interaction and start to plate it to make a solid structure. When they do that, it allows them to take the corresponding ions out of solution, start to layer them and build them up forming an inorganic solid. Our bones have the same amino acids that have the same functional groups. Chemically and crystal-wise, calcium and phosphate in our bodies make bones very specific. And these organisms evolved to make this over 50 million years.

If I knew the sequence of amino acids, I could make it synthetically and I could add those to solution and precipitate them out on a very small scale, but I can't do it and form a really complex structure. So, what the organism does is it give you the basic building blocks to allow you to do that. It gives you hierarchical arrangement; it gives you spatial and temporal control to build a large complex organism. That's the difference between why you could do this relatively quickly and why it could take millions of years to evolve. It's the complexity of it all. I could just go in and get the amino acid sequence, spend a couple of thousand dollars precipitate out relatively small pieces of calcium carbonate. The thing that is fascinating to me is that it is a protein. Proteins are actually encoded by DNA sequences. Proteins aren't transferred from parent to child, DNA is. What the abalone did, what we did when I mineralized, is to pass on the genetic information.

So passing on proteins would be a slow process and passing on DNA gives you the ability to build all the codes we need to live. That's what I want to do with electronic materials - let's create the building blocks, let's pass on all the genetic information so that organism can make the building blocks on its own. Once it has the genetic information, it can make it over and over again, and keep passing it on. I am going to have only one offspring, but abalone is going to have millions. We mostly work with viruses that infect bacteria. For every one virus that infects bacteria, it makes a million copies of itself and it does this in our period of time. That's the power of passing on genetic information instead of passing on protein sequences. What does the organism do? If you want to set about how you make a totally new material, a material never made before with computer modeling and simulation you could take what we know about diatoms that make silica, you could take what we know about all the marine organisms and all the organisms that make material and you could think about how you put together the right sequences of amino acids together to build those.

The point that I took was a relatively unpopular one at the time for a chemist. People actually told me I was crazy. A reviewer of my first grant proposal said I was insane. Our idea was you can do that, but why don't we throw the idea of a billion possibilities at once at a material and let the material select the winner. In a way, that's not very scientific – it's trial and error and a billion experiments. So that's what we do - we do a billion possibilities in time. We were the first people to do it for materials. We were the first people to say. Let's take a material that doesn't grow something, and let's see if we can force it to grow something. It's called the combinatorial approach and let's use the power of genetics to improve it - that was the big idea.

I came up with the idea just before I took my first faculty position at the University of Texas at Austin and I started my lab based on that when I moved to Texas. It was risky and I put all my eggs in one basket and said this is what we are going to try. And I wrote grant proposals. I got one review that said this is incredible. Another review said she is insane and then, within the year we published our first paper on this idea in *Nature* and now I have an incredible funding record.

I started out very interested in just the fundamental science. After my PhD work on how abalones grow shells, I wanted to try growing synthetic shells with other technologically important materials. I wanted to know what the limits were for what biology can work with. Obviously there are certain chemical bonds that are easier to make, covalent bonds, ionic bonds, hydrogen bonds but what were the limitations? I am so very interested in the fundamental science of that my dream is a DNA code for the synthesis of anything you want. You want to grow a battery – here is the DNA sequence that codes for the ability to grow that battery. Most of that work is done through unicellular organisms, a bunch of DNA that infects other organisms. Why use organisms like that instead of abalone? This is easy enough for someone who has little experience to pick up. It also happens rapidly, easy to work with, and it replicates quickly and inexpensively.

Now we are getting much more applications oriented. Part of it is being at MIT, this is a place to make things happen. Part of it is that my funding at the research level is very "department of defense," which has also become very applications oriented and is much less interested in fundamental research.

We have three DARPA grants. You have milestones and the milestones are very sharp and very rapid. We have to produce things. It's a tough way to train students because PhD students are four or five years, DARPA funding is now in one year and 18-month cycles. Meet all your milestones, otherwise you'll get cut completely and we are pretty good at meeting our milestones.

I was a first year faculty member when I set up my labs and got this idea to publish the light bulb paper - this is the idea: genetically controlled materials. I had no commercial applications in mind at all, but I was trying to do extreme research, set up a lab and get tenure. When I first presented this idea and I got past the insane aspect of things, we were very excited. When our first paper came out I was flooded with calls from companies and I would have 30 calls per day, can I come fund your lab, are you interested in starting a business, and I hadn't thought about any of these things because I was thinking about how to put the lab together and how to get tenure. It was completely overwhelming. I didn't know what venture capital was. I was a first year faculty member so I hadn't made any money and was still in debt, didn't know anything about companies or economics but from the excitement of it I realized that this was something important and I should probably protect myself; get patents written. I was smart enough not to take money from companies in exchange for IP or allow people from companies to come into the lab. I needed to figure this one out so I pushed everyone off. I started meeting with the people from the venture community. There were people I liked and trusted, but I didn't know what the big names were. I met Clint Bybee and another venture fund several times, but I really liked Clint because he was really smart and he was interested in the technology. He thought there was something there - a platform there to start a company. It didn't matter that we hadn't defined the boundaries of the technology or the company. Now I realize that was extremely unusual because I was walking into it pretty much blind. I realized this was possibly a disruptive technology further down the line. I knew I didn't want to license out the intellectual property so that it got shelved and was never used. I was interested in fundamental technologies, but I also wanted to do something that was important so I liked the idea of starting a company based on that. Clint was definitely the most open-minded person who felt there was something big here and didn't want to know what the first product was going to be. He wanted to understand what would have the most impact. The fact that he had an engineering degree and was incredibly smart helped. He understood the small aspects of it and was open to the big picture.

Scalability is huge; if you can make one battery or one transistor can you make 100,000 or many more? And whenever you go from a lab process to a commercial process there's a scale issue and the scale issues for different kinds of processing are very, very different. For polymer processing, scaling issues are huge. Regarding the biology in this case, the scalability should be preserved because the DNA is conserved. In terms of the product, will one nano-wire be of as high a quality as a million nano-wires? The answer is yes. But the hard part about that is the scalability isn't in the quality. The scalability in learning how to scale organisms is hard. If you think about scalability in any kind of nano structure materials, I'm not sure with the Nanotech's and how they're doing that, obviously they're scaling that if you can get them at Macy's. But the challenging issue is exploiting your organism and getting it to turn over - working out the conditions to get it to turn over and over again to get a very large quantity. Again, Budweiser has done it with the yeast and it definitely seems like a possibility, but there's a learning curve in there. I'm not worried about scaling the products; I'm more worried about scaling the organism to scale the product.

What if I have a defect in the gene that also gets multiplied? You can check for defects in the gene very easily. Our organisms are very stable in that we've never seen any reverting, only when they've kicked out the entire gene. You have to learn the rule of how to design something so that is stable. By DNA sequencing we test things as we go along and by DNA sequencing we take samples and sequence the DNA and make sure it's the same sequence.

Still, the skills that are required to run a lab are different from the skills required to run a company. I don't think I have the personality to run a company. So there's a couple of ways at looking at it - this is a conversation that Clint Bybee and I have had quite a bit. A lot of the details of what the company is interested in and the details of what the lab is interested in are very different. What the company is interested in is how to solve a very specific problem. I'm interested in developing tool kits to make major changes in how things are made and I don't really care as much in terms of what we make, but I want to develop the tool kits so that you can go in, create change, manipulate and make this other stuff.

Cambrios is working with its partners who will say, well we're making a display, but we're having trouble making this component of the display with these dimensions. Can your technology help? So Cambrios will come to me - can you help solve this really specific problem? I'll say yes, and so we have these sequences over here and these sequences will be good for this and this will be a good start. So quite often we are customizing a solution.

For me, that is not an intellectually interesting problem at all. In the lab I want to choose problems that I'm not sure can be solved. Those are always the problems that are the most fun to work on. But that's a practical problem and it's one that's needed to make a product and a problem that's important to make money. I'm interested in that aspect of it. It's the perfect relationship for me, because we can do something that can help improve a product in a short period of time, and then I can also be interested in problems that change the world. A lot of times we'll have a company come in and say if we give you $500,000, if we give you this money, can you help with this problem? I'm not interested in this problem. Its not an issue of money, its an issue of whether it's fun, is it intellectually interesting, can I convince my students to work on it, is it something that keeps you up at night because you're so excited about working on it? But moving somebody from point A to point B - I'm not interested in that type of work. I'm not saying Cambrios isn't interested in moving things from point A to point B, but they have to look at things in terms of here's the problems that we can help solve in the next three months, here's the problems that we can help solve in the year. They're interested in whether they own the intellectual property for the tool kit that could go off in probably 20 or 30 different directions, but they're having to choose the right directions right now to get their foot into the technology marketplace to make a difference. In the end, they want to hold this product up and say that this product is better than it was before, it's cheaper, it's faster, yet they don't necessarily want to say it was made using biology. They don't necessarily want you to see the biology component to it, but I do.

PUTTING INORGANIC MATERIALS INTO ORGANIC STUFF

There is a fear of putting inorganic material into organic stuff, but I don't experience it in a major way. I give about 75 lectures a year, and occasionally I come across people that have that aspect to them, but it's not the community that I come across a lot. I think it's more the way that I sell my research by giving it a lifelike component that it'll be able to do things like self-assembler and self-correct. Those are aspects that help us sell the research. We also sell it in an environmentally friendly aspect because organisms don't actually add a lot of toxins into their environment. They use what they have in their environment and when they're gone they leave it back, but they don't actually add a lot of toxins to their environment. So we evolve our organisms to work with the least toxic pressure as possible. I went to a very large company to talk about this idea at one point and tried to sell it as an environmentally friendly approach. And this company said, we're not interested in environmentally friendly unless it's environmentally friendly and cheaper, so I think that companies would like to have it as a public image but ultimately, if it's not cheaper and faster and doesn't solve the problem, they're completely not interested in it.

KEEPING THE WORLD IN BALANCE WITH WHAT YOU WANT IN YOUR LIFE

Why do so many people have such a hard time, what does it take to arrive at this well demarcated view of the world?

Getting to do exploration of science is why I get up in the morning and getting to solve real problems to be able to make technology better in a shorter time period is the best of both worlds. It may seem like there is a smooth transition between the lab and the company, but it was tough setting it up and I don't think of myself as someone who has a big ego in this, you have to have some ego to be in this business, but I had to let go of a lot in terms of what I thought was interesting and important. I was thinking this is my technology, I know what's best, and I don't think that's true. I think I know what's best to run my lab, I actually rely on really smart people to know what's best to run my lab, but I don't know what's best to run a company that makes money. So you hire people, VP of technology and CEOs, who know better and the relationship is absolutely critical in terms of my passing on technology and ideas and then receiving those ideas that can actually be used in technology to make money. That's been a huge learning thing, I don't always know best and all I can do is help facilitate what they come up with that they think is important. I was trying to push batteries for a long time, and they weren't interested in batteries. I thought batteries were important and intellectually interesting and I thought they were important for the good of the country and important to the department of defense. Now they actually think batteries are important, and just having that open working relationship, and realizing that I founded the company is important, but the company is a lot bigger than me.

WHAT IS THE VENTURE CAPITALIST'S IDEAL ROLE IN THE TECHNOLOGY TRANSFER PROCESS?

I think of that as a partnership, a partnership between Clint and myself and my other partner Evelyn, and UT was a catalyst. I cashed in my retirement fund to pay for some of the first fees that we needed for the patents. UT wouldn't give up the patent, and so there's no way I could have even if I had the ability to know what it took for tech transfer. I definitely didn't have the money to do it.

Clint is a friend of mine and he has taught me a lot and guided me through this whole process, so there would definitely be no company without him. I may not have partnered with anybody else. I might have said it's just not important enough to me; I may just wait and do this later in life. It was a complete partnership and I should know more, but he taught me all the aspects of how to protect the IP and how to get the patents. He taught me how to start a company, how to go out and talk to potential partners, and how to talk to other VC people to bring in as partners and start the company. Clint would ask, do you like this person and I would say yes or no. If I didn't like them and he liked them, he would try to introduce me to other people within that venture firm or tell me what he thought their strengths and weaknesses were and why he thought they'd be viable. So we spent a lot of time together in the first couple of years of starting the company.

LOOKING AT THE FUTURE

My position probably won't change - Cambrios was my first company. There will be more companies based on other ideas. Not all of the ideas that are coming out of my lab are linked to that technology so there will definitely be a second company and probably even a third company. Right now, all I can tell you is that there will be a second company because I think that it's the perfect relationship in developing a new technology and trying to create an impact in the market place. We haven't done that yet, but I can't wait for our first product and its going to be the best of both worlds. I also love not knowing about fields and I feel like I've learned a little about setting up a company. I'd like to take that experience and do it again. It's very stimulating intellectually in a different way.

Clint has mentored me a lot and he mentored me through all the steps of the first series of funding. He's one of the reasons I came here because he spent a lot of time with me. I think it will be very difficult as I develop more companies. But compartmentalizing that and keeping that going is a lifestyle that I really like because it's intellectually interesting on many different levels.

BUSINESS VS. SCIENTIFIC VS. ACADEMIC

There's this aspect of the process that was really hard to learn, but I think I'm getting better at it. There are legal and moral aspects of it. What I get paid for is educating students. And I will never let my companies or any company I have compromise the integrity of the research or the integrity of the students. When students get PhDs their primary job is to publish original research. The students are my primary responsibility. I will take from my students' research when approaching problems and, when approaching a problem, I'll say here's the best way to do it, or this didn't work for us, but I won't let the two interact. It would be really convenient to let that happen, but that compromises the integrity of the research and the integrity of the student.

I've never accepted one penny to do research for a company on a specific problem, because I wanted the students to be able to publish. One of the things about being at MIT is that the students are very smart. Convincing an MIT student to do anything you want them to do is very difficult. I get hundreds of applications for four or five spots in my lab every year so I get the best students, and what I do is I give them boundaries or ideas and then let them loose. They don't need to be directed on a day to day basis. I say we are interested in these particular areas using biology and then I let them go. That's not compatible with the company. What they find out in their research is that all the ideas will be passed on through communication with the company, but then employees of the company and my second PhD student who actually works at the company can pick those up and try to work them into specific ideas.

"STOPPING THE BODY METABOLISM TO SAVE IT"

MARK ROTH

In "Buying Time in Suspended Animation," an article from Scientific American's June 2005 issue, the authors Mark Roth and Todd Nystul write,

> Recent studies in our laboratory at the Fred Hutchinson Cancer Research Center in Seattle and by other researchers have shown that hibernation-like states can be induced on demand in animals that do not naturally hibernate. Moreover, such animals seem to be protected from the usual effects of blood loss, such as oxygen deprivation, while they are in a suspended state. These results raise the exciting possibility that suspended animation may be feasible in humans as well…

But before you enter a realm of fantasy, also read about the implications:

> Inadequate oxygen is a major cause of tissue damage and death in explanted donor organs and in peoples experiencing blood loss or obstruction. Restoring oxygen supply to these tissues is not always immediately possible. Blocking all available oxygen, however, can induce a variety of animals to enter protective suspended animation and might do the same for human injury victims or tissues.

> Hydrogen sulfide, a chemical produced naturally by our bodies, blocks cells from using oxygen and triggers suspended animation in mice. It may be a natural regulator of cellular energy production that could be employed to induce a protective suspended state in humans.

Mark Roth is the quintessential scientist, a visionary who has been able to make connections between the past, the present and the future, in a fashion that is too abstruse for most people to follow. And he himself will tell you that the connections are not easy to make. Indeed, most connections are unique mixes of knowledge and intuition. To try and quantify their scope and dimensions at the initial stages is almost impossible.

It is this "almost impossible" that ARCH has been able to tap into. In Roth's case, Bob Nelsen persisted in staying with Roth and his work until an identifiable pattern emerged. And it was Nelsen who provided some of the business templates that Roth's company, Ikaria, has adopted.

Here, Roth discusses his research and its role in a unique business venture. He shares with us how concepts emerge, how they baffle us and what it takes to transform seminal ideas into concrete applications.

A BUSINESS - SEEING THE FUTURE

The idea for Ikaria began several years ago when we were studying the changes in metabolism that occur when nematodes are exposed to very low oxygen concentrations. We found that the animals stopped all of their life processes that could be seen by light microscopy—and yet the animals could be reanimated the next day without harm. This led to the idea that this technology could, in principle, be used to buy time for people who are suffering from poor perfusion of their tissues during trauma. This, of course, is quite a big leap since initially we were only working in nematodes and fish. Around this time, December 2000, I met Bob Nelsen. We sat and talked about possibilities for this work and I remember thinking that this guy is either crazy or he has incredible vision. He immediately said, "I can see it now. This stuff will be in every ambulance." His enthusiasm was infectious. Bob put me in touch with Richard Ulevitch, who at that time was working with a group that Bob thought might be able to assist in financing a venture around this idea. Along with another associate of Bob's, Pat Gray, we thought we'd form a small company that would do chemical screening in fish to find drugs that would mimic oxygen deprivation and allow us to move into mammals. At about this time the tech transfer office at the Hutch, introduced me to a person with a great deal of experience in biotech start-ups. He said we should hold off, that it would be better to wait until we had more evidence we could slow or stop the metabolism of a whole mammal without damage before starting a company. As it turned out, we didn't have to think about this too long because 9/11 happened and starting biotech companies wasn't on anyone's agenda for a while.

Over the next couple of years we kept looking for ways to slow or stop the metabolism of mammals in the lab, but without much success. I remained in touch with Bob but we were basically in a holding pattern. Then one day I thought I'd hit upon the compound that would do it, and that drug was hydrogen sulfide. The first few experiments were disasters because it is hard to maintain a constant atmosphere around an animal. Once we overcame this problem the next issue was determining whether this constant atmosphere of hydrogen sulfide would actually lower metabolism. The question was how to test that in real time? I went to Mark Groudine who was then chairman of the Division of Basic Sciences at the Hutchinson Center (he had also played a role in putting Bob and I in touch originally) and asked him if I might get some center funds to purchase telemetry equipment that would allow us to monitor the metabolism and body temperature of animals as they are exposed to the drug. Without his help at this critical time we would have either been set back years or never done the critical experiment that showed that we could reduce the core temperature of mammals in a way that is seen in reptiles.

Once we knew that we could drop the rate of oxygen consumption in a mouse by 10-fold without harm, we knew we had something special. Also, the knowledge that hydrogen sulfide is naturally produced in our cells gave us the feeling that this drug might be involved in the mechanism by which our cells control the rate of oxygen consumption. It led us to explore the work of many other physiologists that had been attempting to hibernate non-hibernating animals as a means of protection. The basic idea is that, while hibernating, an animal is using much less oxygen and as a result is much less sensitive to damage from low oxygen or poor perfusion. Throughout this period I had strong support from the Fred Hutchinson, particularly from senior administrator Peggy Means and a new director of the tech transfer office at the Hutchinson Center, Spencer Lemmons. Spencer had experience in starting companies and really moved the process forward. In September 2004 I got back in touch with Bob and said I think it is time to get going. Bob didn't miss a hitch. He called Kevin Tomaselli, someone I'd met earlier when we were starting the fish screening company that never got off the ground.

When Bob told me about Kevin he said, "You'll love Kevin, he is a jack of all trades. You guys will be great." Bob was right. Kevin and I got along from the start. After signing on as the first employee of Ikaria (although we didn't have a name then) he set about showing me the ropes, everything from how to make presentations to how to think about a business plan. Together we set off on the adventure of selling the idea of Ikaria. In a few short months we met many people who would later help finance the company and serve on the board. During this time we benefited tremendously from Bob and the ARCH team who worked tirelessly behind the scenes to make sure we got the chance to meet great people and that we were prepared when we got there. By April of 2005 we signed the papers and have been off and running ever since. I am very enthused with all of the help we've gotten from the other investors: Bryan Roberts from Venrock, Andy Schwab from 5AM, and from members of the board who have made the whole start-up process so straightforward.

One of the first real challenges during our first six months was looking for a CEO. Bob along with Bryan and Board Chair Vaughn Kalian worked for several months. I met with excellent candidates as they came through during the summer of 2005. Then Flemming Ornskov came to visit. He was nothing like the others; for one thing, he already knew the science. Being a physician, the first thing he said was, "This idea is very important for medicine. It could change the way we treat critically injured patients and I want to be a part of it." I felt that this would be a great chance for Ikaria to get superb business leadership but did not allow myself to think that someone as qualified as Flemming would want to pursue something that was so rough and undeveloped. We are now six months past Flemming's start date and what a transformation it has been!

Many challenges lie ahead for Ikaria, but with the leadership and commitment of so many talented people and the preparatory work we've done thus far, I think we're ready to tackle them.

"I ALWAYS TELL PEOPLE THAT THIS IS THE MOST EXCITING THING WE HAVE SEEN IN OUR LIVES"

BOB NELSEN

IKARIA

The question is how do you find a guy like Mark Roth who runs a 2/30 marathon, who is a pioneer in molecular biology, and who will ultimately win the Nobel Prize and change healthcare?

The way I find a guy like Mark Roth is I go ask Lee Hartwell, director of the Fred Hutchison Cancer Center and a Nobel Prize winner himself, "Who is the smartest guy at the Hutch?" He'll give you a list of two or three folks and then he'll say, "There's this guy, Mark Roth, who is quite innovative and quite out there in his thinking , go talk to him."

I think the ARCH difference is that most people would not keep an open mind when they sat down with somebody who said I am working on suspended animation. They would never take the meeting and probably just walk away. Our lesson over and over again is don't listen to the dogma, don't listen to the industry. It's almost safer to do the opposite of what the industry is doing. The pharmaceutical industry, especially, is extremely bad at innovation. They spend billions of dollars a year and don't get much out of it and then have to go back to biotech for new ideas. Too many investors, too early in the game call up their pharma and ask if this is a good thing and they're wrong.

We are looking for potential, we are not looking for the killer application and we are willing to bet on the innovative scientist. Mark Roth is one of the most interesting and innovative people I've met who can go from a hundred thousand feet, talking of concepts that will boggle your mind, to the extreme practicality of how to finance the company, and "What's the burn rate?" That's an extremely rare capability.

We sat down with Mark who said he was working on suspended animation. "I have been able to suspend a zebra fish and my goal is to suspend a human." And you can hear the sound of VCs fleeing and that's what really happened. No one was willing to engage except me and Richard Ulevich, a scientist at Scripps. So Mark told me a story about being able to take a zebra fish and turn it off and turn it back on. It was still alive and I was quite amazed, suspicious, and excited. The whole idea was a bit crazy, but it could work. So we once again started the Tom Sawyer fence process which was to show it to a couple of folks to see if we had any believers. Ultimately, we found Kevin Tomaselli and Pat Gray. Kevin was one of the founders of IDUN Pharmaceuticals who we had backed, and Pat was one of the persons who had cloned hepatitis B and was one of the early guys in Genentech and ICOS and an ARCH venture partner at the time. They all thought it might be interesting to explore the formation of a company based on the zebra fish work.

We worked on it for six months and we ultimately decided that we didn't have a clear commercializable agent to suspend the zebra fish that had enough data to go into a streamlined discovery path. And while zebra fish were interesting, they weren't mammals. So the mutual decision among Mark, Pat, Kevin and I was that we should wait for more data.

Some period of time passed, probably eighteen months, where Mark was working in his lab on the technology and we kept in touch thinking ultimately there would be a company here - a fairly typical thing for ARCH. We tend to start working on something two or three years before it actually happens.

Once again I got a call from Mark, similar to the Graeme Bell call, saying "I got it." I said "It being mammalian data?" and Mark said yes, and I said "Holy Shit." That was the exciting moment. It's hard to underestimate the potential of this technology. We think of DNA and antibiotics as comparables in terms of its potential impact. We decided to explore starting a company with Mark and the Hutch. The Hutch was innovative enough to want to get involved. They had just hired a guy named Spencer Lemons to head up tech transfer and they had the support of Lee Hartwell and Peggy Means to give Mark support and some money, even fronting the money for attorney fees and the incorporation.

We decided to explore what it would look like, what the impact would be, whether there was a commercial aspect to the idea of suspended animation. Ultimately, what we found was that some of the potential here could change critical care as we know it and save countless lives and probably make a multi-billion dollar company. We created the company in coordination with Mark and the Hutch, to recruit a board, develop the nest, the technology and people for a CEO to land in. We were working in coordination with another VC firm that ultimately pulled out because it thought everything was too early. That was a bit of a setback, but we were true believers in the technology and we still decided to recruit both the Board and the people. We called up Kevin Tomaselli again and he had the vision and he was a believer who decided that if we could pull this thing together and get some money he would join as chief technology officer and co-founder.

What is interesting and differentiates Ikaria - as exciting an idea you can imagine – is the idea that you can turn off people and buy them time when they are having a stroke, a heart attack, are hit by a car, shot in Iraq or under cardiac bypass surgery. And being able to buy them the time they need is the ultimate proof of our ability to save people.

The interesting thing about Ikaria was that it had an agent that could do this and had the practical aspect and the commercial aspect along with the big idea - something totally unprecedented. It wasn't a conventional single-target, mechanism-based pharmaceutical paradigm, it was more like anesthesia or critical care where you are affecting a lot of different systems. So we decided to recruit a board of directors first and then the CEO to do a bit of the Tom Sawyer fence and nest building.

From the very beginning we knew Ikaria was a special company and we believed it was almost unprecedented. I always tell people that this is the most exciting thing we have seen in our lives, and I'll bet people $20 that this is the most exciting thing they have seen in their careers as well. I haven't lost a bet yet.

So the first guy to whom we showed this to get him on the board was Ben Shapiro who used to run all the research at Merck. At a restaurant in Boston, I told him there was a crazy idea that he really needed to look at. Vaughn Kailian was there as well and he was the founder of COR Therapeutics and then the vice chairman of Millennium. They both said, "We have too many boards, we are offered board seats on multi-billion dollar companies every day, we are not interested in some crazy new start-up." So first Ben met Mark and, after the first meeting, he said he would do it. Then Vaughn fell into the same trap and agreed. I ran into Bill Gantz who was the former President and COO of Baxter and the founder of Pathogenesis at a JP Morgan conference in San Francisco and told him about this and he said the same time thing, "Just going off the Gillette board." But I told him, "Just meet Mark." And after one meeting and a couple of phone calls, he also said it's the most amazing thing I've seen and it's got this strange mix of practicality and vision. So we began to build this group and then added David Shaw from Venrock courtesy of Bryan Roberts, a Venrock partner I work a lot with, and to whom I introduced the deal. Richard Yulevich had introduced us to Andy Schwab and John Diekman at 5AM Partners. Both Venrock and 5AM got it and although it was early they appreciated it and they understood that I was serious about making it a real company. They were excited about the science. So we decided to create a syndicate of ARCH,

Venrock, 5AM, Aravis, and the Washington Research Foundation.

The next step was obviously developing a plan and Kevin Tomaselli and Lynn Zydowsky (introduced by 5AM), the VCs, and the Board created this straw-man and funded it for over $11 million in a tranched financing which would trigger when we got a CEO. So we had some walking around money and we began the CEO search. Through relationships that Vaughn and I had, we were able to convince one of the best search guys in the biotech business to take on a search, a deal he would normally not take. We saw a bunch of candidates and every single one wanted to run the company and these were all fairly big fish. Then we were introduced to Flemming Ornskov, an MD with a big pharma background. I met him at an Italian restaurant in New York over some good pasta and within five minutes it was clear that he got it. He understood that Ikaria was going to change the world, that it was not a conventional pharma paradigm and although he was out of conventional pharma he had the ability to think out of the box. So Vaughn cut the deal with Flemming and Flemming took the risk which most people in pharma wouldn't do.

We knew we had the right guy when on the first day in Seattle he managed to cut the hotel rates down from $300 a night to $140 and we all smiled and said that this was an entrepreneur who wants to make something big.

The real Ikaria chapter is yet to be written. There is plenty of technical risk to go around. We can't always tell when things won't work or won't scale. So we are trying to mitigate that risk. We are currently ahead of plan, planning to go into the commercial markets via the regulatory process. And we get at least a call or maybe two a week from VCs wanting to get in on the deal.

The goal articulated by Flemming is to build the largest critical care company in the world, nothing short of changing critical care as we know it. We are not thinking of hundreds of millions, we are thinking of billions. I really think we have the ability to save millions of people and change healthcare as we know it.

EPILOGUE

"THE UNITED STATES CONTINUES TO POSSESS THE WORLD'S BEST PROCESS FOR BRINGING SCIENTIFIC DISCOVERY AND TECHNOLOGICAL INNOVATION INTO THE MARKETPLACE"

STEVE LAZARUS

The founder of ARCH cautions that cumulative efforts of the anti-development community may be approaching a tipping point

Sixty years have past since Vannevar Bush presented his report entitled *Science: The Endless Frontier* to President Harry Truman. His prophetic words are as cogent today as they were in 1945. The United States remains the world leader in research, although strong and energetic competition is emerging in many quarters of the globe. The United States continues to possess the world's best process for bringing scientific discovery and technological innovation into the market place, but this process is not very well understood and is vulnerable to the unintended consequences of policies designed to achieve unrelated ends.

The small start-up businesses that carry discoveries into the market place are susceptible to an unrestrained plaintiff's bar, a militant regulatory community, and the neglect of a careless legislature. These businesses most often begin as experiments conducted by gamblers. They are high risk and must attract not only unusually smart and competent people but people who are comfortable with a far higher level of risk than is typically encountered.

We call these people entrepreneurs. With rare exceptions great scientific and technological discoveries do not come with entrepreneurs attached. Entrepreneurs like the opportunity to build new things, to succeed using one's own skills, and to create wealth. They must be attracted into a start-up.

Start-ups rarely have much discretionary cash. For almost thirty years the incentive that intrigued the entrepreneur was the stock option. There was no way of costing these instruments at the start-up stage. They represented a piece of a hoped-for success, the ownership of part of a dream, but by no stretch of the imagination could they be considered hard assets. The Federal Accounting Standards Board (FASB) determined that they represented a violation of accounting orthodoxy and, after a multi-year campaign to gain approval, imposed a requirement that options be assigned an arbitrary value and be considered a cost of operation.

As if this was not sufficiently discouraging, the Orwellian sounding American Jobs Creation Act added section 409A to the tax code. This requires consideration of options as deferred income and threatens an ex post facto 20% tax if the strike price is less than the fair market value. A conservative company thus feels it must obtain an expensive third party fairness opinion each time options are issued. Smart start-ups may gamble but they don't take imprudent risk.

The Sarbanes-Oxley law was rushed into existence by a Congress outraged by the excesses of a number of corporate executives managing large public companies. Section 404 of the law requires a certification by the senior management of a company that management systems are complete, comprehensive, thorough and accurate. False or inaccurate certifications carry the potential of severe personal punishment. Small start-up companies were, at least initially, exempt. But there was a catch.

Audit partnerships, having observed the destruction of Arthur Andersen incident to the Enron debacle, had no particular desire to set forth standards of thoroughness and accuracy. Auditors formed themselves into an array of committees which endlessly debated appropriate policies for individual situations of particular companies. Audit costs quickly doubled. Many large audit partnerships simply discharged small companies from their practice. A brand new class of consultants emerged offering expensive help in preparing the 404 certification.

The entire financing structure of a start-up increased. A greater number of expensive overhead personnel had to be hired earlier. Full

Sarbanes-Oxley compliance became a pre-requisite for Initial Public Offerings and M&A transactions, thus making the two classical sources of start-up capital more difficult to achieve. High quality entrepreneurial managers had less incentive to move to risky start-ups or else it cost a great deal more than before to get them.

This growing amount of collateral damage was brought to the attention of the corporate governance community which acknowledged the problem and said they would correct it later. We're still waiting. Meanwhile, big government played havoc with the start-up industry. Limitations on H1-B visas, limitations on SBIRs, intrusive FOIA requirements, and other issues arose. As Charles Dickens said, "Every man for himself said the elephant as he danced among the chickens."

The start-up community will survive each of these new difficulties but of greater consequence is the re-emergence of an old question about the idea of financial gain for scientists who perform research using public funds. The argument is not that it is unethical or immoral, but that it is "inappropriate," and this charge is made by critics who believe that discoveries somehow leap off the laboratory bench and transform themselves into things of economic value. All the old complaints – an interest in commerce corrupts the pure environment of the academy, anything discovered utilizing public funds ought not to be commercialized exclusively, certainly scientists ought not to enjoy any financial benefits from their discoveries – are taken out, dusted off, and voiced again.

These arguments deny the lessons of history, ignore the function of incentives, and aggressively fail to understand the necessary role of capital and fair ownership in bringing innovation to market.

The tendency of innovation to come through the technology transfer process remains powerful, but if the cumulative efforts of the anti-development community reach a tipping point and private equity becomes discouraged by a rising cost of capital and a growing concern about ultimate returns, the burgeoning international competition will surely begin to catch up and overtake. In the March 13, 2006 issue of *The Wall Street Journal*, Chinese Premier Wen Jiabao is quoted as saying "… the central government will increase spending on science and technology by nearly 20% this year. 'China has entered a stage in its history where it must increase its reliance on scientific and technological advances and innovation to drive social and economic development.'"

Despite its 100 year record of world dominance in innovation driven world economic leadership, there is no categorical imperative that says the United States will always lead. Just as China, India, and others are waking to the enormous potential of permitting and encouraging as many individuals as possible to be entrepreneurs, the United States is beginning to create an environment of sclerotic regulation, adversarial response to growth agents, and challenges to the very ideas of risk, financial incentives, and ownership.

We have met the enemy and it is us.

Index